Does China Matter?
A Reassessment

Gerald Segal, a world specialist on Asia, was a prolific writer, including on China's role in world politics. Before he died in 1999 the journal *Foreign Affairs* published his provocative and significant article 'Does China Matter?'.

Expanding on Segal's theme, this volume gathers together ten leading writers on China to reassess his argument. This book opens with a discussion of Dr Segal's contribution to scholarship on Asia, and also reprints the 1999 article. The authors then address the question 'does China matter?' by examining both the global and Asian dimensions of China's presence in the military, political, economic and cultural fields.

These essays provide an extension and critique of Segal's work, and represent an authoritative evaluation of China's current policies and future prospects. The question 'does China matter?' remains central to world politics. This book sets out a detailed case for exactly how, why and to whom it matters.

Barry Buzan is Professor of International Relations at the London School of Economics and Political Science. **Rosemary Foot** is Professor of International Relations and the John Swire Senior Research Fellow in the International Relations of East Asia at St Antony's College, the University of Oxford.

The New International Relations
Edited by Barry Buzan, *London School of Economics* and
Richard Little, *University of Bristol*

The field of international relations has changed dramatically in recent years. This new series will cover the major issues that have emerged and reflect the latest academic thinking in this particular dynamic area.

Does China Matter?
A Reassessment

Essays in memory of Gerald Segal

Edited by
Barry Buzan and
Rosemary Foot

Routledge
Taylor & Francis Group

LONDON AND NEW YORK

First published 2004
by Routledge
2 Park Square, Milton Park, Abingdon, Oxon, OX14 4RN

Simultaneously published in the USA and Canada
by Routledge
270 Madison Ave, New York, NY, 10016

Reprinted 2005

Routledge is an imprint of the Taylor & Francis Group

Typeset in Sabon by
Florence Production Ltd, Stoodleigh, Devon
Printed and bound in Great Britain by
The Cromwell Press, Trowbridge, Wiltshire

British Library Cataloguing in Publication Data
A catalogue record for this book is available from
the British Library

Library of Congress Cataloging in Publication Data
Does China matter?: a reassessment: essays in memory of
   Gerald Segal
   Edited by Barry Buzan and Rosemary Foot.
      p. cm.
   Includes bibliographical references and index.
   1. China – Foreign relations – 1976–.   2. China – Economic
   policy – 1976–2000.   3. China – Politics and government –
   1976–.   4. Segal, Gerald, 1953–1999.   I. Title: Essays in
   memory of Gerald Segal.   II. Segal, Gerald, 1953–1999.
   III. Buzan, Barry.   IV. Foot, Rosemary, 1948– .
   DS779.27.D64 2004
   951.05–dc22   2003018856

ISBN 0–415–30411–3 (hbk)
ISBN 0–415–30412–1 (pbk)

To Rachel Segal

Contents

Contributors

Shaun Breslin is Professor of Politics and International Studies at the University of Warwick. He is author of *China in the 1980s: Centre–Province Relations in a Reforming Socialist State* (1996) and *Mao* (1998). He has recently co-authored two volumes on regional theory and practice: *New Regionalisms in the Global Political Economy: Theories and Cases* (2002) and *Microregionalism and World Order* (2002).

Barry Buzan, FBA, is Professor of International Relations at the London School of Economics. His recent books include: *Anticipating the Future* (1998, with Gerald Segal); *International Systems in World History: Remaking the Study of International Relations* (2000, with Richard Little); *Regions and Powers: the Structure of International Security* (2003, with Ole Wæver); and *From International to World Society? English School Theory and the Social Structure of Globalisation* (2004).

Rosemary Foot, FBA, is Professor of International Relations and John Swire Senior Research Fellow in the International Relations of East Asia at St Antony's College, Oxford. Her publications include *Rights Beyond Borders: the Global Community and the Struggle over Human Rights in China* (2000); *Human Rights and Counterterrorism in America's Asia Policy* (Adelphi Paper, 2003); (co-edited with Andrew Hurrell and John Lewis Gaddis) *Order and Justice in International Relations* (2003); (co-edited with S. Neil MacFarlane and Michael Mastanduno) *US Hegemony and International Organizations* (2003).

Lawrence Freedman has been Professor of War Studies at King's College since 1982, and is currently head of the School of Social Science and Public Policy. His most recent works include *Kennedy's Wars: Berlin, Cuba, Laos and Vietnam*; a third edition of *Evolution of Nuclear Strategy*; and the forthcoming two-volume official history of the Falklands Campaign.

Bates Gill holds the Freeman Chair in China Studies at the Center for Strategic and International Studies (CSIS) in Washington, DC. A specialist in East Asian foreign policy, politics and security, particularly with regard to China, he is the author of the forthcoming volume entitled: *Contrasting Visions: United States, China and World Order* (Brookings Institution Press).

David S. G. Goodman is Professor of International Studies and Director of the Institute for International Studies, University of Technology, Sydney. Recent publications include *Social and Political Change in Revolutionary China* (2000), and (with Werner Draguhn) *China's Communist Revolutions: Fifty Years of the People's Republic of China* (2002). He and Gerald Segal wrote and edited seven books together, from *The China Challenge: Adjustment and Reform* (1986) to *Towards Recovery in Pacific Asia* (2000).

Stuart Harris, FASS, Professor in the Department of International Relations at the Research School of Pacific and Asian Studies, Australian National University, has written extensively on economic, political and strategic issues, particularly on the countries of Northeast Asia. His most recent volume (2001, with Greg Austin) is *Japan and Greater China: Political Economy and Military Power in the Asian Century.*

Samuel S. Kim is Adjunct Professor of Political Science and Senior Research Scholar at the Weatherhead East Asian Institute, Columbia University. His recent publications include: *China and The World* (ed., 1998); *East Asia and Globalization* (ed., 2000); *North Korea and Northeast Asia* (2002, with Tai Hwan Lee); *Korea's Democratization* (ed., 2003); and *The International Relations of Northeast Asia* (ed., 2003).

Jean-Pierre Lehmann is Professor of International Political Economy at IMD (International Institute for Management Development) in Lausanne, Switzerland. He is Founding Director of the Evian Group, a coalition for liberal global governance, based on a network of business, government and opinion leaders from both developed and developing countries. Under Jean-Pierre Lehmann's leadership, the Evian Group is actively involved in working on trade and development projects, and recently founded the Open World Initiative, which is an extensive network and movement of young people, the next generation of leaders, engaged in analysing reform in global, national and corporate governance in order to establish an open world economy, human development and sustainable growth.

Michael B. Yahuda is Emeritus Professor of International Relations at the London School of Economics. His recent books include: *Hong Kong: China's Challenge* (1996) and *The International Relations of the Asia-Pacific, 1945–1995* (1996).

Foreword

This book aims to follow up Gerry Segal's article 'Does China Matter?' (*Foreign Affairs*, 78: 5, 1999: 24–36). The article made a significant splash, and was Gerry's last major published work before he died. Had he lived, it is certain that he would have followed it up with a book on the same theme. Nobody can write the book that Gerry would have written, but the question of the title remains central to world politics, and the article gives clear guidance on what the main themes should be. Michael B. Yahuda opens the proceedings with an assessment of Gerry's life and work, and that is followed by a reprint of Gerry's 1999 article. Chapters 3–10 make a more systematic distinction between the Asian and the global forums than Gerry did, and also separate out the core themes of economy, military, politics and culture. Each of these eight chapters subjects Gerry's arguments to a full and up-to-date empirical investigation, on the basis of which their validity is either supported or questioned. They ask how well his points have stood up over the intervening years, and attempt to project their likely durability. Aside from these general guidelines, each author has been free to give the subject their own interpretation. A major purpose of the book is to pay testament to Gerry's life and career by completing his last project. Another, entirely in keeping with Gerry's critical spirit, is to assess whether his arguments have endured, and to give them more detailed examination than was possible in a short article.

We would like to thank Edwina Moreton for giving her blessing to this project, and for helping with some of the background research. *Foreign Affairs* earned our gratitude by allowing us to reprint Gerry's article free of charge. All royalties will go to the IISS's Gerald Segal Research Fellowship Appeal. We thank Routledge, who published many of Gerry's books, for entering into the spirit of the project, and for donating the indexing. We dedicate this book to Gerry's daughter Rachel.

Series editor's preface

Does China matter? When Gerry Segal posed this question at the end of the twentieth century, he considered it more than likely that his audience would regard the question, in the first instance, as a foolish one, because China was being so widely heralded as one of the superpowers of the next century. Moreover, because China is one of the few ancient civilizations that has managed to survive to the present day, for many people it seems almost self-evident that China must always have played an important role in world politics. So when such a significant scholar as Segal asked if China matters, then it might be concluded that he was adopting a rhetorical stance. Of course, China matters! But, from Segal's perspective, the question was neither rhetorical nor foolish; on the contrary, once his audience had read what he had to say, then he hoped that the question would be seen as deliberately provocative. It was primarily a didactic question, designed to get policy-makers and the general public to rethink what Segal considered conventional but erroneous wisdom.

By the same token, however, Segal did not intend to suggest that China does not matter. If this were the answer to the question that he was asking, then it would have required him to stand much of his previous writing on its head. After all, only a decade earlier he was promoting the view that China was 'a rising power'. The problem for Segal was that this message had been taken too much to heart, and it was now being assumed that China had already reached a position of unassailable dominance in international society. As a consequence, decision-makers were intent on devising policies that rested on a false premise. Whatever might happen in the future, Segal was quite clear that China had not yet achieved great-power status, and he was equally sure that it was extremely unwise to be formulating policies on the basis of the assumption that this status has already been achieved. It follows that it is essential to engage in constant reality checks to minimize the inevitable gap that exists between reality and the image of reality that decision-makers adhere to. Segal asked whether China matters, therefore, to encourage decision-makers and others to engage in a more rigorous form of reality checking. His check suggested that an inflated image of China's economic and military status prevailed in the West.

This book draws together some of the most significant scholars in the field to re-evaluate Gerry Segal's assessment of China and to see how well his judgements have stood the test of time. It is tragic, of course, that Gerry is unable to participate in this venture. Without doubt, his views would have been modified to take account of some of the momentous events that have occurred since his death. But it is unlikely that the main thrust of his argument would have changed. None of the contributors to this book accept his line of argument uncritically, and some depart very substantially from his position. However, there is no doubt that Gerry would have been extremely dissatisfied with the editors of this book if they had failed to bring together a heterogeneous group of scholars who could develop vigorous and independent lines of argument to answer the central question that he posed. In any event, there is not going to be a definitive answer to this question in the near future – if ever. It is, after all, not the fundamental questions about international relations that change – only the answers.

Richard Little

Abbreviations

ABM	Anti-Ballistic Missile
ACFTA	ASEAN–China Free Trade Area
ADB	Asian Development Bank
APEC	Asia-Pacific Economic Cooperation
APT	ASEAN Plus Three
ARF	ASEAN Regional Forum
ASEAN	Association of Southeast Asian Nations
ASEM	Asia–Europe Meeting
CAEC	Council for Asia–Europe Co-operation
CCP	Chinese Communist Party
CME	Commodity Manufacturing Enterprises
CMI	Chiang Mai Initiative
COSTIND	Commission on Science, Technology and Industry for National Defence
CSCAP	Council on Security Cooperation in the Asia Pacific
CSIS	Center for Strategic and International Studies
CTBT	Comprehensive Test Ban Treaty
ECSCAP	European Council for Security Cooperation in Asia-Pacific
EU	European Union
FDI	Foreign Direct Investment
FII	Foreign Indirect Investment
GAD	General Armaments Department
GDP	Gross Domestic Product
GNP	Gross National Product
G-1	Group of One
G-7	Group of Seven
G-8	Group of Eight
ICBM	Intercontinental Ballistic Missile
ICC	International Criminal Court
IEA	International Energy Agency
IGO	Intergovernmental Organization
IISS	International Institute for Strategic Studies

IMF	International Monetary Fund
INGO	International Nongovernmental Organization
ITICs	International Trade and Investment Corporations
JSDF	Japanese Self-Defence Force
MINUGUA	United Nations Human Rights Verification Mission in Guatemala
MONUC	United Nations Peacekeeping Mission
NATO	North Atlantic Treaty Organization
NCO	Non-Commissioned Officer
NIC	Newly Industrialized Country
NIE	Newly Industrialized Economy
NMD	National Missile Defense
NPL	Non-Performing Loan
NPT	Nuclear Nonproliferation Treaty
OECD	Organization for Economic Cooperation and Development
OEM	Original Equipment Manufacturer
PAP	People's Armed Police
PLA	People's Liberation Army
PLAAF	People's Liberation Army Air Force
PLAN	People's Liberation Army Navy
PNG	Papua-New Guinea
PPP	Purchasing Power Parity
PRC	People's Republic of China
P-5	Permanent Five (on the UN Security Council)
QDR	Quadrennial Defense Review
RDT&E	Research, Development, Testing and Evaluation
RIIA	Royal Institute of International Affairs
SEZ	Special Economic Zones
SOE	State-owned Enterprise
SSBN	Missile-launching submarine
TMD	Theater Missile Defenses
UNFICYP	UN Peacekeeping Force in Cyprus
UNPKO	UN Peacekeeping Operations
UNPREDEP	United Nations Preventive Deployment Force
UNSC	UN Security Council
UNTAG	UN Transitional Assistance Group
UNTSO	United Nations Truce Supervision Organization
WTO	World Trade Organization

1   Gerald Segal's contribution

Michael B. Yahuda

Gerald Segal's last important writing, 'Does China Matter?' was an article which brought together much of his recent thinking about China for the key journal read by the American foreign-policy elite (Segal, 1999). The article typified Segal's mature writings, combining innovative scholarship with a policy orientation in which the concern was with the implications for the immediate future, rather than with analysis of how we had reached the present position. Written in his customary crisp and snappy style, the article was illustrative of the particular approach to international politics that he had developed as a mature scholar and commentator. Although Segal was not interested in theory as such, he had a distinctive mode of analysis. He combined a tough-minded appreciation of the realities of power with a belief in the liberalizing effects of market economics allied to governmental transparency and accountability. Above all, Segal delighted in challenging the conventional wisdom of the day. As he once said, it was 'not always wise'. This article was intended as a kind of wake-up call for many in Washington and elsewhere. In Segal's view the persistent exaggeration of the significance of China was damaging, as it prevented the development of sustained coherent policies commensurate with the security and commercial interests of the West. Moreover, that exaggeration also made it difficult for people in China to come to terms with their own problems and address the substantive reforms that were needed if China was to reach its true potential. However, the article should be seen as more than just a polemic and more than an argument addressed to policy-makers. It should be seen as a significant mile stone in Segal's long-standing attempt to persuade the China-watching community and the broader circle of Asian and International Relations specialists to think more critically and realistically about the rise of China and the implications of that rise for academics, opinion leaders and policy-makers.

Other chapters in this volume will review aspects of Segal's article in detail. My purpose is to discuss briefly Segal's approach to the analysis of international relations, Asian and particularly Chinese politics and foreign relations.

Gerald Segal's approach

Gerald Segal's career, tragically cut short by cancer at the age of 46, essentially spanned the two decades of the 1980s and 1990s. During those twenty years, books, chapters, articles and commentaries flowed from him at a prodigious rate. Segal authored or co-authored 13 books, was a contributing editor or co-editor to 17 more, published over 130 articles in scholarly journals and wrote newspaper commentaries and op-ed pieces that are too numerous to count.

Despite having developed the reputation as one of the West's leading interpreters of Chinese politics and foreign relations, Gerry Segal never saw himself as a China specialist. He regarded himself more as a generalist who took an interest in China. He never studied the Chinese language, nor took time out to immerse himself in Chinese culture. A Canadian by birth, he graduated from the Hebrew University in 1975 at the age of 23, where his major was international politics and his minor was in Asian politics. His mentor, one of the world's leading authorities on the Chinese military, Ellis Joffe, remained an important influence and became a close colleague and a warm friend. Gerry then went on to the London School of Economics to carry out a research degree under my supervision. He was awarded his Ph.D. in 1979 for a dissertation on the emergence of the 'Great Power Triangle'. The thesis gave evidence of many of Segal's qualities that this most prolific of authors and commentators was soon to bring before an ever-widening readership. These qualities included an independent cast of mind that delighted in challenging established views with reasoned argument, deploying wit and a wonderful facility with words. They also included a concern with a generalist approach in seeking to explain how international politics worked, rather than a more country-centred point of departure in which politics was explained with reference to the particularities of culture.

Given his initial interest in the modalities of strategic relations between the great powers, his earlier writings may be seen to fall squarely within the tradition of power politics. He was particularly interested in exploring how these affected relations between China and the Soviet Union. His Ph.D. thesis argued that the tripolarity, or the 'Great Power Triangle' emerged in the early 1960s after China broke away from the Soviet Union, rather than in the early 1970s with the Kissinger and Nixon visits to China. Based on what might be seen as a neo-realist structuralist approach, Segal sought to show how the dynamics of triangular power politics shaped developments in Indo-China – from the lack of direct American military intervention in Laos to its initially slow and then massive intervention in Vietnam. Within this framework he was able to delineate China's changing policies with greater skill and success than would have been possible had he followed the more conventional sinological route (Segal, 1982b).

Thus, far from his lack of traditional sinological skills being a draw-back, Segal turned this to positive advantage. This gave him greater confidence in writing on China itself. By treating China as 'just another country', Segal was not beguiled by claims from China or from other China specialists in the West that the country should be treated *sui generis*. Not for him claims that China should be dealt with on its own terms, that is in the self-serving terms advanced by its leaders or by those close to them.

Contrary to what was thought by some in China, especially in official circles, Segal was not motivated by hostility or by concerns to belittle the country or its people. As noted above, his first major work showed that China had become a major international player in great-power relations – a whole decade before the accepted view then and now conventionally allows. Similarly, his next book, on China's experience of defending itself, pays tribute to the readiness of China's leaders often to resort to force to overcome adversity, despite apparent inferiority in weapons capability (Segal, 1985b). But, more to the point, Segal's analysis of each of China's wars, beginning with Korea in 1950 and concluding with the incursion into Vietnam in 1979, is based on conventional means of assessing military engagements, rather than on China-centred explanations of the special characteristics of Chinese ways of warfare. Accordingly, Segal was able to dispense praise and criticism according to clear criteria. Segal also wrote, with his mentor, Ellis Joffe, on the changing roles of the military in Chinese politics (Joffe and Segal, 1978). Meanwhile he continued to publish on other matters of abiding interest to him, such as strategic questions, Soviet foreign policy and Sino-Soviet relations (Baylis *et al.*, 1983; Segal, 1983).

For most of the 1980s, Segal taught successively at the Universities of Wales (Aberystwyth), Leicester and Bristol respectively. He then moved to major British 'think tanks', which he found more congenial. He joined the Royal Institute of International Affairs (RIIA, Chatham House) in 1988, before becoming a Senior Fellow for Asian Studies at the International Institute for Strategic Studies (IISS) in 1991, and its Director of Studies in 1997. By the middle of the 1980s, Segal was recognized in Chinese academic circles as someone with a distinctive 'voice' of great interest. Although they may not necessarily have agreed with much of what he wrote, as realists themselves they had no difficulty in understanding the thrust of his arguments and of according him considerable respect. His lack of sinological skills and interests did not pass unnoticed, but they did not prove a barrier to communication. He visited China several times in the 1980s, but gave me the impression that at this stage he did not gain much of intellectual value in his exchanges with Chinese academics. However, he found the visits worthwhile for gaining an impression of the prevailing 'atmosphere' or climate of opinion. His Chinese interlocutors found his views of great interest, even if provocative at times. In fact, both sides found it easier to exchange views in the UK, rather than in China, where the Chinese found themselves more constrained from speaking openly about what were for them sensitive issues. The Chinese interest in Segal substantially increased after he left universities in the late 1980s to find his *métier* in the research institutes.

By this stage in his intellectual development, Segal had begun to place emphasis less on seeking to analyse how a particular point was reached in foreign or domestic affairs than on what were the implications for the future. In other words, his analysis began to take on a more forward-looking dimension. This came easily to a scholar who was also interested in the policy implications of his analysis. This had the result of placing him at the forefront of those who identified new trends at an early stage. As a close student of Sino-Soviet relations (before the collapse of the Soviet Union in 1991), Segal was early in detecting the thaw in relations between the two in the early 1980s. Interestingly, he was the first to point out that, contrary to Chinese claims, it was they who had taken the initiative (Segal, 1985a).

Segal was also to the fore in attempting to come to terms with the international significance of the process of reform in the communist world that was occurring in that decade, especially after the advent of Gorbachev. He convened several meetings and conferences at the RIIA (where he was then based) to focus on the implications for foreign policy and foreign policy-making (Segal, 1992). Although as far as China was concerned, this could have been construed as essentially a domestic issue calling for particular sinological skills, Segal was able to bring his more broad-based interests into play through considering the Chinese case in a cross-communist comparative framework (Segal, 1990a). It was consideration of the character and the implications of reform communism that may be said to have broadened Segal's approach beyond the conventional bounds of strategic studies and power politics to take more account of what would now be called good governance, or even neo-liberalism. That is to say that he saw the potentiality of reform communism to lead to a more transparent rules-based order that would allow those countries to be better integrated into the international community by following the market, becoming more pluralistic and eventually democratic. He placed much emphasis on the reform of the foreign policy process itself, and on the need for the West to balance policies of engagement with sufficient toughness to deter back-sliding or undue aggressiveness.

By now Segal was beginning to cast his net more widely in geographical terms. As the Cold War receded in the late 1980s, the Asia Pacific had become more important in world affairs, to a great extent because of its rapid and sustained economic growth. At the time much was made of the region's consensual form of collective decision-making as a major contributor to its astounding economic development. Segal challenged much of that. While giving due weight to the significance of its economic growth, Segal argued nevertheless that it did not make sense to think of it as a separate region and still less as a separate community. In his book, *Rethinking the Pacific* (Segal, 1990b) he claimed that the new developments in the Pacific area were best understood in the context of global trends in ideology, security and economic affairs.

The end of the Cold War also brought out new dimensions in Segal's approach to China. Freed of the kind of calculus associated with the strategic triangle, or with that of a comparative communist perspective, he was able to consider what provided a sound basis for thinking about China's future, especially in the light of Tiananmen and the way in which the Chinese communist regime gradually recovered from that blow to its legitimacy. His approach was affected by at least three sets of questions: first, what were the implications of a China that was driven less by a communist vision and more by a nineteenth-century kind of nationalism replete with an irredentist agenda? Second, were there possible fissiparous implications for the Chinese state that arose from the process of economic and administrative reforms? Finally, in what ways could the outside world and the West in particular prevent China from using force in pursuit of its irredentist agenda and promote its integration into international society? These of course were not questions that endeared Segal to the Chinese authorities. His Adelphi Paper on the possible disintegration of China (Segal, 1994) proved to be a breaking point. Apparently, the analysis was interpreted as advocacy, and it was even misconstrued as advising Western governments to contribute to the break-up of China. Thereafter Segal was denied access to China until shortly before his death.

As the decade of the 1990s unfolded, Segal further sharpened his own approach to international affairs, as a result of thinking through the question as to what facilitated the integration of countries into the globalized international society in the coming twenty-first century. He saw this as entailing the opening of economies to outside influences, embracing pluralistic democracy and surrendering key aspects of sovereign control of their economic, social and foreign policies. This also led to the development of small, professional armed forces, and to an aversion to the use of military force. These pluralistic countries that were tolerant of diversity within and that appreciated the significance of debate and criticism necessarily tolerated differences with similar countries and sought resolution to problems by peaceful means (Buzan and Segal, 1996, 1998). His argument was 'that if other great powers eventually learned to adapt and become Lite, then we should accept no less from China'. If it were to become rich, in Segal's view, China would 'eventually not only be forced to adapt to interdependence, it will also become enlitened' (Segal, 1997: 173).

In his writings and commentaries on how best the West should deal with China, Segal's main concern was to encourage policy-makers in the West and in the US especially to adopt policies that balanced the policy of engagement with one of containment that he called constrainment (Segal, 1996). In other words, Segal very much recognized the advantages of deepening the economic, social and political relations with China which, like others, he argued would lead in time to fundamental domestic change, which was necessary if China were to be integrated into the international community. But he argued consistently that such a beneficial change would only be possible if China were simultaneously deterred from using or contemplating the use of force to realize its irredentist claims and/or change the balance of power in its favour. He thought the polarized debate between those who wanted to 'contain' China and those who sought to 'engage' was misconceived. The former went too far in meeting the potential Chinese threat (that in the case of Taiwan and the disputed islands in the South China Sea was sometimes all too real) so as to provide no incentives for China to adopt more participatory international norms. It was only through the deepening of its interdependence with the outside world that China would change its domestic governance for the better. But the 'engagers' erred by conceding too much to a dictatorial Chinese regime without imposing upon it proper costs and penalties for using force to get its way. Hence he favoured 'constrainment', by which a 'carrot and stick' approach would be followed, in which engagement was matched by a tough-minded readiness to deter the Chinese from aggressive acts.

Such considerations provided a particular impetus to follow developments in Hong Kong and Taiwan. The impending return of Hong Kong to Chinese sovereignty was seen by Segal as a potential threat to the key institutions of the territory such as the rule of law, a clean civil service, press and academic freedoms, and so on. He stood full square behind the attempt by the last Governor, Chris Patten, to anchor these in a more democratic framework. His book on the subject dwelt on how the international dimensions of Hong Kong could help to sustain its liberal way of life beyond the reversion in 1997. His interest in Taiwan was stimulated by the democratization of the island in the 1990s despite the continuing threat from Beijing. Although he recognized that the dynamics of the democratic process in Taiwan could lead to a degree of unpredictability in the handling of relations with the Chinese Mainland, he nevertheless argued strongly in favour of firming-up the Western (principally the American) commitment to deterring the Chinese from imposing unification by force. He saw that as a necessary component of the policy of engagement. Any softening of the Western position would not only endanger Taiwan, but it would also have a profoundly adverse effect on the evolution of the reform process within China and on the international relations of the entire Asia-Pacific.

Towards the end of the 1990s, Segal became more uneasy about what he regarded as the uncritical adoption of engagement policies by many in the China policy and academic communities in the United States. He was also dismayed by the unthinking embrace of the myth of the Chinese market by business people in the United States and Europe. In his view, this uncritical approach to China risked bringing about precisely the opposite of what was intended. Far from encouraging China's leaders to face up to the hard choices entailed in meeting the true standards of market reform, Western governmental and business leaders were letting them think that they could have all the benefits without paying the price of genuine reform and pluralization. Treating China in this way would discourage pro-Western neighbours from looking to the West to deter a more assertive China. They might then have little alternative except to accommodate China by policies of appeasement. Moreover, craven Western policies could embolden China's leaders to overestimate their country's power and engage in adventurist policies that could undermine the stability of the entire Asia-Pacific region. What made Western policies even more difficult to bear was the sense that they were based on an entirely false appreciation of the true nature of Chinese power and influence. It was this that led to the article, 'Does China Matter?', around which this book is organized.

The Chinese response

Gerald Segal and his writing both intrigued and appalled Chinese officialdom. His intellectual frame of reference was not alien, even though he had no sinological affiliation. Neither his realism, nor his liberalism (as demonstrated by his concept of 'liteness') was unfamiliar. But the Chinese official classification of Western writers and commentators on Chinese affairs as either friend or foe always threatened to misinterpret a writer as direct and as honest and bold as Segal. From the viewpoint of Chinese officials Segal was discomfiting and difficult. He tended to touch on subjects that were seen as highly sensitive, and that affected notions of patriotic self-esteem. But at the same time he dealt with these matters in a policy-oriented way. They saw him as an influential voice among opinion leaders in the West whom they should cultivate, but at the same time as someone who might cause them embarrassment by being so close to the bone. They sought his views, but preferred to do so in private. Public encounters were more difficult.

Thus Segal's Adelphi Paper, *China Changes Shape* (1994), which argued that China was subject to a process of regional fragmentation, and which attempted to point out possible implications for Western governments, was, according to a well-informed Chinese source, seized on as a kind of *casus belli* by the then Chinese ambassador in London, Ma Yuzhen. He claimed that the monograph amounted to a form of advocacy for the break-up of China and to a call upon Western governments to encourage disintegration and to take advantage of the fragmentation. Segal, who had often enough been regarded as provocative, was now classified as 'anti-China' and denied access to the country. Not only was this a total misreading of the monograph, but it showed up Chinese officialdom in a very bad light indeed – as intolerant bullies. The attempt to muzzle or 'punish' Western scholars and commentators deemed to be hostile was not only misconceived, but in this case it also back-fired. Undaunted, Segal continued with his writings and commentaries without regard as to whether they were agreeable to the powerful. The true face of Chinese officialdom became apparent as means were sought to try to persuade Segal that it was up to him to find a way to give the Chinese 'face' so that they could relent and allow him a visa. Meanwhile many Chinese officials continued quietly to beat a pathway to his London office in the IISS to seek his views.

Many Chinese academics and researchers, however, took a different view. Although they too tended to disagree with many of Segal's arguments, they nevertheless sought to engage him in discussion and in normal academic interchange. Several seemed embarrassed by his treatment at the hands of their officials. Some tried to invite him to participate in conferences in China. Eventually, in the year before he died, he was able to visit Shanghai in response to yet another invitation, which on this occasion was not vetoed by the immigration officials. Of course no reason was given for the lifting of the bar.

However, the official restrictions and disapproval of Segal made it more difficult for Chinese academics to engage his arguments in their public writings. He was widely read in China, especially as he was such a prolific contributor to the main international newspapers and journals. The more sophisticated Chinese researchers appreciated his objectivity and his attempt to challenge the conventional wisdom. That is why they and their students always sought him out whenever they visited London. In sum, despite official disapproval, Segal was one of the Western voices that was certainly heard in Beijing, but it is difficult to gauge the extent of his influence.

Segal as a 'doer'

It is a testament to his enormous energy and commitment that Gerald Segal was not content solely with his prodigious output of publications, but he was also anxious to do things and make a difference. He was as extraordinarily active as an organizer of conferences, a promoter of fellow academics and a mentor to up-and-coming researchers. In 1987 he founded *The Pacific Review*, which rapidly became one of the premier journals on the region and he edited it until 1995. In 1996 he directed the Pacific-Asia programme of the Economic and Social Research Council which allocated more than £2 million among 15 projects throughout the UK, that spanned a huge range of issue areas from economics and social questions to politics and security. It proved to be a major fillip to academics throughout the country, some of whom addressed the region for the first time.

Segal also became actively involved in second- and third-track diplomacy to promote greater transparency and cooperation about security matters in Asia and to promote closer institutional links between Europeans and Asians. Thus he was a major force in first encouraging and then participating in the development of the Council on Security Cooperation in the Asia Pacific (CSCAP) – the organization of academics, officials and business people that was the informal counterpart of the intergovernmental ASEAN Regional Forum. He became a well-known figure in promoting security dialogues between the European and Asian security and foreign policy think tanks. He also played a role in facilitating the further development of ASEM (the biannual meeting of leaders from Europe and Asia begun in 1996) when it met in London in 1998.

Conclusion

Although Gerald Segal was far more of a generalist with an interest in Asia than a China specialist, arguably it is his writings on China that may have a more enduring interest. It is precisely because he approached China as a generalist in a non-sinological way within a framework of what he might have termed as mid-Atlanticist values that Segal had been able to make a truly distinctive contribution. He was not in thrall to the mystique of Chinese culture that seems to have captivated many who have spent years as its students. Neither was he seduced by a kind of sino-centricity that seems to have ensnared many of those whose academic careers have been structured around the depth of their knowledge of the country and who set high value by having continued access to the country and to the realms of its academe.

Interestingly, Segal spoke and wrote about political developments in Beijing and about China's external relations often with greater insight than those with sinological training. That may have had much to do with his unsentimental view of power and of politics with which it is imbued. But it would do him an injustice to think of Segal purely within the Realist framework. He was very alert to global trends and to the significance of socio-economic developments. This is apparent from his writings on other Asian matters. For example, he was dismissive of 'Asian values' as a conceptual category its own right, but he saw their articulation as congruent with the particular stage of development in the modernization of the economies and the transition of the particular Asian countries whose leaders were advancing these claims. As we have seen, Segal placed considerable emphasis on the significance of the domestic reforms of communist states to explain their foreign policy changes. Similarly, his concept of 'liteness' is directly related to changes in society, ideology and politics that countries undergo in the process of their enrichment. Thus Segal's answer to his own question would not be that China does not 'matter', but that it matters less as a truly powerful force in world affairs than as a country that could be truly transformed especially if the West were to approach it in a clear-eyed way. It would then be encouraged to follow the path of reform towards marketization, plurality and even democracy – i.e. 'liteness'. Perhaps, his follow-up article would have been 'How China does matter!'

2 Does China matter?

Gerald Segal

Middle Kingdom, middle power

Does China matter? No, it is not a silly question – merely one that is not asked often enough. Odd as it may seem, the country that is home to a fifth of humankind is overrated as a market, a power, and a source of ideas. At best, China is a second-rank middle power that has mastered the art of diplomatic theater: it has us willingly suspending our disbelief in its strength. In fact, China is better understood as a theoretical power – a country that has promised to deliver for much of the last 150 years but has consistently disappointed. After 50 years of Mao's revolution and 20 years of reform, it is time to leave the theater and see China for what it is. Only when we finally understand how little China matters will we be able to craft a sensible policy toward it.

Does China matter economically?

China, unlike Russia or the Soviet Union before it, is supposed to matter because it is already an economic powerhouse. Or is it that China is on the verge of becoming an economic powerhouse, and you must be in the engine room helping the Chinese to enjoy the benefits to come? Whatever the spin, you know the argument: China is a huge market, and you cannot afford to miss it (although few say the same about India). The recently voiced "Kodak version" of this argument is that if only each Chinese will buy one full roll of film instead of the average half-roll that each currently buys, the West will be rich. Of course, nineteenth-century Manchester mill owners said much the same about their cotton, and in the early 1980s Japanese multinationals said much the same about their television sets. The Kodak version is just as hollow. In truth, China is a small market that matters relatively little to the world, especially outside Asia.

Originally published in *Foreign Affairs* (78: 5) September/October 1999. Reprinted with the permission of the Council on Foreign Relations.

If this judgment seems harsh, let us begin with some harsh realities about the size and growth of the Chinese economy. In 1800 China accounted for 33 percent of world manufacturing output; by way of comparison, Europe as a whole was 28 percent, and the United States was 0.8 percent. By 1900 China was down to 6.2 percent (Europe was 62 percent, and the United States was 23.6 percent). In 1997 China accounted for 3.5 percent of world GNP (in 1997 constant dollars, the United States was 25.6 percent). China ranked seventh in the world, ahead of Brazil and behind Italy. Its per capita GDP ranking was 81st, just ahead of Georgia and behind Papua New Guinea. Taking the most favorable of the now-dubious purchasing-power-parity calculations, in 1997 China accounted for 11.8 percent of world GNP, and its per capita ranking was 65th, ahead of Jamaica and behind Latvia. Using the U.N. Human Development Index, China is 107th, bracketed by Albania and Namibia – not an impressive story.

Yes, you may say, but China has had a hard 200 years and is now rising swiftly. China has undoubtedly done better in the past generation than it did in the previous ten, but let's still keep matters in perspective – especially about Chinese growth rates. China claimed that its average annual industrial growth between 1951 and 1980 was 12.5 percent. Japan's comparable figure was 11.5 percent. One can reach one's own judgment about whose figures turned out to be more accurate. Few economists trust modern Chinese economic data; even Chinese Prime Minister Zhu Rongji distrusts it. The Asian Development Bank routinely deducts some two percent from China's official GDP figures, including notional current GDP growth rates of eight percent. Some two or three percent of what might be a more accurate GDP growth rate of six percent is useless goods produced to rust in warehouses. About one percent of China's growth in 1998 was due to massive government spending on infrastructure. Some three percent of GDP is accounted for by the one-time gain that occurs when one takes peasants off the land and brings them to cities, where productivity is higher. Taking all these qualifications into account, China's economy is effectively in recession. Even Zhu calls the situation grim.

China's ability to recover is hampered by problems that the current leadership understands well but finds just too scary to tackle seriously – at least so long as East Asia's economy is weak. By conservative estimates, at least a quarter of Chinese loans are nonperforming – a rate that Southeast Asians would have found frightening before the crash. Some 45 percent of state industries are losing money, but bank lending was up 25 percent in 1998 – in part, to bail out the living dead. China has a high savings rate (40 percent of GDP), but ordinary Chinese would be alarmed to learn that their money is clearly being wasted.

Some put their hope in economic decentralization, but this has already gone so far that the center cannot reform increasingly wasteful and corrupt practices in the regions and in specific institutions. Central investment –

20 percent of total investment in China – is falling. Interprovincial trade as a percentage of total provincial trade is also down, having dropped a staggering 18 percent between 1985 and 1992. Despite some positive changes during the past 20 years of reform, China's economy has clearly run into huge structural impediments. Even if double-digit growth rates ever really existed, they are hard to imagine in the near future.

In terms of international trade and investment, the story is much the same: Beijing is a seriously overrated power. China made up a mere 3 percent of total world trade in 1997, about the same as South Korea and less than the Netherlands. China now accounts for only 11 percent of total Asian trade. Despite the hype about the importance of the China market, exports to China are tiny. Only 1.8 percent of U.S. exports go to China (this could, generously, be perhaps 2.4 percent if re-exports through Hong Kong were counted) – about the same level as U.S. exports to Australia or Belgium and about a third less than U.S. exports to Taiwan. The same is true of major European traders. China accounts for 0.5 percent of U.K. exports, about the same level as exports to Sri Lanka and less than those to Malaysia. China takes 1.1 percent of French and German exports, which is the highest in Asia apart from Japan but about par with exports to Portugal.

China matters a bit more to other Asian countries. Some 3.2 percent of Singapore's exports go to China, less than to Taiwan but on par with South Korea. China accounts for 4.6 percent of Australian exports, about the same as to Singapore. Japan sends only 5.1 percent of its exports to China, about a quarter less than to Taiwan. Only South Korea sends China an impressive share of its exports – some 9.9 percent, nudging ahead of exports to Japan.

Foreign direct investment (FDI) is even harder to measure than trade but sheds more light on long-term trends. China's massive FDI boom, especially in the past decade, is often trumpeted as evidence of how much China does and will matter for the global economy. But the reality is far less clear. Even in 1997, China's peak year for FDI, some 80 percent of the $45 billion inflow came from ethnic Chinese, mostly in East Asia. This was also a year of record capital flight from China – by some reckonings, an outflow of $35 billion. Much so-called investment from East Asia makes a round-trip from China via some place like Hong Kong and then comes back in as FDI to attract tax concessions.

Even a more trusting view of official FDI figures suggests that China does not much matter. FDI into China is about 10 percent of global FDI, with 60 percent of all FDI transfers taking place among developed countries. Given that less than 20 percent of FDI into China comes from non-ethnic Chinese, it is no surprise that U.S. or European Union investment in China averages out to something less than their investment in a major Latin American country such as Brazil. China has never accounted for more than 10 percent of U.S. FDI outflows – usually much less. In recent years China has taken around 5 percent of major EU countries' FDI outflow – and these are the glory years for FDI in China. The Chinese economy is clearly contracting, and FDI into China is dropping with it. In 1998 the United Nations reported that FDI into China may be cut in half, and figures for 1998–99 suggest that this was not too gloomy a guess. Japanese FDI into China has been halved from its peak in 1995. Ericsson, a multinational telecommunications firm, says that China accounts for 13 percent of its global sales but will not claim that it is making any profits there. Similar experiences by Japanese technology firms a decade ago led to today's rapid disinvestment from China. Some insist that FDI flows demonstrate just how much China matters and will matter for the global economy, but the true picture is far more modest. China remains a classic case of hope over experience, reminiscent of de Gaulle's famous comment about Brazil: it has great potential, and always will.

It does not take a statistical genius to see the sharp reality: China is at best a minor (as opposed to inconsequential) part of the global economy. It has merely managed to project and sustain an image of far greater importance. This theatrical power was displayed with great brio during Asia's recent economic crisis. China received lavish praise from the West, especially the United States, for not devaluing its currency as it did in 1995. Japan, by contrast, was held responsible for the crisis. Of course, Tokyo's failure to reform since 1990 helped cause the meltdown, but this is testimony to how much Tokyo matters and how little Beijing does. China's total financial aid to the crisis-stricken economies was less than 10 percent of Japan's contribution.

The Asian crisis and the exaggerated fears that it would bring the economies of the Atlantic world to their knees help explain the overblown view of China's importance. In fact, the debacle demonstrated just how little impact Asia, except for Japan, has on the global economy. China – a small part of a much less important part of the global system than is widely believed – was never going to matter terribly much to the developed world. Exaggerating China is part of exaggerating Asia. As a result of the crisis, the West has learned the lesson for the region as a whole, but it has not yet learned it about China.

Does China matter militarily?

China is a second-rate military power – not first-rate, because it is far from capable of taking on America, but not as third-rate as most of its Asian neighbors. China accounts for only 4.5 percent of global defense spending (the United States makes up 33.9 percent) and 25.8 percent of defense spending in East Asia and Australasia. China poses a formidable threat to the likes of the Philippines and can take islands such as Mischief

Reef in the South China Sea at will. But sell the Philippines a couple of cruise missiles and the much-discussed Chinese threat will be easily erased. China is in no military shape to take the disputed Senkaku Islands from Japan, which is decently armed. Beijing clearly is a serious menace to Taiwan, but even Taiwanese defense planners do not believe China can successfully invade. The Chinese missile threat to Taiwan is much exaggerated, especially considering the very limited success of the far more massive and modern NATO missile strikes on Serbia. If the Taiwanese have as much will to resist as did the Serbs, China will not be able to easily cow Taiwan.

Thus China matters militarily to a certain extent simply because it is not a status quo power, but it does not matter so much that it cannot be constrained. Much the same pattern is evident in the challenge that China poses to U.S. security. It certainly matters that China is the only country whose nuclear weapons target the United States. It matters, as the recent Cox report on Chinese espionage plainly shows, that China steals U.S. secrets about missile guidance and modern nuclear warheads. It also matters that Chinese military exercises simulate attacks on U.S. troops in South Korea and Japan. But the fact that a country can directly threaten the United States is not normally taken as a reason to be anything except robust in defending U.S. interests. It is certainly not a reason to pretend that China is a strategic partner of the United States.

The extent to which China matters militarily is evident in the discussions about deploying U.S. theater missile defenses (TMD) in the western Pacific and creating a U.S. national missile defense shield (NMD). Theoretically, the adversary is North Korea. In practice, the Pentagon fears that the U.S. ability to defend South Korea, Japan and even Taiwan depends in the long term on the ability to defend the United States' home territory and U.S. troops abroad from Chinese missiles. Given the $10 billion price tag for NMD and the so-far unknowable costs of TMD, defense planners clearly think that China matters.

But before strategic paranoia sets in, the West should note that the Chinese challenge is nothing like the Soviet one. China is less like the Soviet Union in the 1950s than like Iraq in the 1990s: a regional threat to Western interests, not a global ideological rival. Such regional threats can be constrained. China, like Iraq, does not matter so much that the United States needs to suspend its normal strategies for dealing with unfriendly powers. Threats can be deterred, and unwanted action can be constrained by a country that claims to be the sole superpower and to dominate the revolution in military affairs.

A similarly moderated sense of how much China matters can be applied to the question of Chinese arms transfers. China accounted for 2.2 percent of arms deliveries in 1997, ahead of Germany but behind Israel (the United States had 45 percent of the market, and the United Kingdom had

18 percent). The $1 billion or so worth of arms that Beijing exports annually is not buying vast influence, although in certain markets Beijing does have real heft. Pakistan is easily the most important recipient of Chinese arms, helping precipitate a nuclear arms race with India. Major deals with Sudan, Sri Lanka, and Burma have had far less strategic impact. On the other hand, arms transfers to Iran have been worrying; as with Pakistan, U.S. threats of sanctions give China rather good leverage. China's ability to make mischief therefore matters somewhat – primarily because it reveals that Chinese influence is fundamentally based on its ability to oppose or thwart Western interests. France and Britain each sell far more arms than China, but they are by and large not creating strategic problems for the West.

Hence, it is ludicrous to claim, as Western and especially American officials constantly do, that China matters because the West needs it as a strategic partner. The discourse of "strategic partnership" really means that China is an adversary that could become a serious nuisance. Still, many in the Clinton administration and elsewhere do not want to call a spade a spade and admit that China is a strategic foe. Perhaps they think that stressing the potential for partnership may eventually, in best Disney style, help make dreams come true.

On no single significant strategic issue are China and the West on the same side. In most cases, including Kosovo, China's opposition does not matter. True, the U.N. Security Council could not be used to build a powerful coalition against Serbia, but as in most cases, the real obstacle was Russia, not China. Beijing almost always plays second fiddle to Moscow or even Paris in obstructing Western interests in the Security Council. (The exceptions to this rule always concern cases where countries such as Haiti or Macedonia have developed relations with Taiwan.) After all, the Russian prime minister turned his plane to the United States around when he heard of the imminent NATO attack on Serbia, but the Chinese premier turned up in Washington as scheduled two weeks later.

NATO's accidental May bombing of the Chinese embassy elicited a clear demonstration of China's theatrical power. Beijing threatened to block any peace efforts in the United Nations (not that any were pending), but all it wanted was to shame the West into concessions on World Trade Organization membership, human rights, or arms control. China grandiosely threatened to rewrite the Security Council resolution that eventually gave NATO an indefinite mandate to keep the peace in Kosovo, but in the end it meekly abstained. So much for China taking a global perspective as one of the five permanent members of the Security Council. Beijing's temper tantrum merely highlighted the fact that, unlike the other veto-bearing Security Council members, it was not a power in Europe.

In the field of arms control, the pattern is the same. China does not block major arms control accords, but it makes sure to be among the last to sign on and tries to milk every diplomatic advantage from having to be dragged to the finish line. China's reluctance to sign the Nuclear Non-proliferation Treaty (NPT), for instance, was outdone in its theatricality only by the palaver in getting China to join the Comprehensive Test Ban Treaty. China's participation in the Association of Southeast Asian Nations Regional Forum – Asia's premier, albeit limited, security structure – is less a commitment to surrender some sovereignty to an international arrangement than a way to ensure that nothing is done to limit China's ability to pursue its own national security objectives. China matters in arms control mainly because it effectively blocks accords until doing so ends up damaging China's international reputation.

Only on the Korean Peninsula do China's capacities seriously affect U.S. policy. One often hears that China matters because it is so helpful in dealing with North Korea. This is flatly wrong. Only once this decade did Beijing join with Washington and pressure Pyongyang – in bringing the rogue into compliance with its NPT obligations in the early phases of the 1994 North Korean crisis. On every other occasion, China has either done nothing to help America or actively helped North Korea resist U.S. pressure – most notoriously later in the 1994 crisis, when the United States was seeking support for sanctions and other coercive action against North Korea. Thus the pattern is the same. China matters in the same way any middle-power adversary matters: it is a problem to be circumvented or moved. But China does not matter because it is a potential strategic partner for the West. In that sense, China is more like Russia than either cares to admit.

Does China matter politically?

The easiest category to assess – although the one with the fewest statistics – is how much China matters in international political terms. To be fair to the Chinese, their recent struggle to define who they are and what they stand for is merely the latest stage of at least 150 years of soul-searching. Ever since the coming of Western power demonstrated that China's ancient civilization was not up to the challenges of modernity, China has struggled to understand its place in the wider world. The past century in particular has been riddled with deep Chinese resistance to the essential logic of international interdependence. It has also been marked by failed attempts to produce a China strong enough to resist the Western-dominated international system – consider the Boxer movement, the Kuomintang, or the Chinese Communist Party (CCP). Fifty years after the Chinese communist revolution, the party that gave the Chinese people the Great Leap Forward (and 30 million dead of famine) and the Cultural Revolution (and perhaps another million dead as well as a generation destroyed) is devoid of ideological power and authority. In the absence of any other political ideals, religions and cults such as the Falun Gong (target of a government crackdown this summer) will continue to flourish.

China's latest attempt to strengthen itself has been the past 20 years of economic reforms, stimulated by other East Asians' success in transforming their place in the world. But the discourse on prosperity that elicited praise for the order-sustaining "Asian values" or Confucian fundamentals was burned in the bonfire of certainties that was the Asian economic crisis. China was left in another phase of shock and self-doubt; hence, economic reforms stalled.

Under these circumstances, China is in no position to matter much as a source of international political power. Bizarre as old-style Maoism was, at least it was a beacon for many in the developing world. China now is a beacon to no one – and, indeed, an ally to no one. No other supposedly great power is as bereft of friends. This is not just because China, once prominent on the map of aid suppliers, has become the largest recipient of international aid. Rather, China is alone because it abhors the very notion of genuine international interdependence. No country relishes having to surrender sovereignty and power to the Western-dominated global system, but China is particularly wedded to the belief that it is big enough to merely learn what it must from the outside world and still retain control of its destiny. So China's neighbors understand the need to get on with China but have no illusions that China feels the same way.

China does not even matter in terms of global culture. Compare the cultural (not economic) role that India plays for ethnic Indians around the world to the pull exerted by China on ethnic Chinese, and one sees just how closed China remains. Of course, India's cultural ties with the Atlantic world have always been greater than China's, and India's wildly heterogeneous society has always been more accessible to the West. But measured in terms of films, literature, or the arts in general, Taiwan, Hong Kong, and even Singapore are more important global influences than a China still under the authoritarian grip of a ruling Leninist party. Chinese cities fighting over who should get the next Asian Disneyland, Chinese cultural commissars squabbling over how many American films can be shown in Chinese cinemas, and CCP bosses setting wildly fluctuating Internet-access policies are all evidence of just how mightily China is struggling to manage the power of Western culture.

In fact, the human-rights question best illustrates the extent to which China is a political pariah. Chinese authorities correctly note that life for the average citizen has become much more free in the past generation. But as Zhu admitted on his recent trip to the United States, China's treatment of dissenters remains inhuman and indecent.

Still, China deserves credit for having stepped back on some issues. That China did not demand the right to intervene to help Indonesia's ethnic Chinese during the 1998–99 unrest was correctly applauded as a sign of maturity. But it was also a sign of how little international leadership China could claim. With a human-rights record that made Indonesia seem a paragon of virtue, China was in no position to seize the moral high ground.

Measuring global political power is difficult, but China's influence and authority are clearly puny – not merely compared to the dominant West, but also compared to Japan before the economic crisis. Among the reasons for China's weakness is its continuing ambiguity about how to manage the consequences of modernity and interdependence. China's great past and the resultant hubris make up much of the problem. A China that believes the world naturally owes it recognition as a great power – even when it so patently is not – is not really ready to achieve greatness.

Does it matter if China doesn't matter?

The Middle Kingdom, then, is merely a middle power. It is not that China does not matter at all, but that it matters far less than it and most of the West think. China matters about as much as Brazil for the global economy. It is a medium-rank military power, and it exerts no political pull at all. China matters most for the West because it can make mischief, either by threatening its neighbors or assisting anti-Western forces further afield. Although these are problems, they will be more manageable if the West retains some sense of proportion about China's importance. If you believe that China is a major player in the global economy and a near-peer competitor of America's, you might be reluctant to constrain its undesired activities. You might also indulge in the "pander complex" – the tendency to bend over backward to accommodate every Chinese definition of what insults the Chinese people's feelings. But if you believe that China is not much different from any middle power, you will be more willing to treat it normally.

This notion of approaching China as a normal, medium power is one way to avoid the sterile debates about the virtues of engaging or containing China. Of course, one must engage a middle power, but one should also not be shy about constraining its unwanted actions. Such a strategy of "constrainment" would lead to a new and very different Western approach to China. One would expect robust deterrence of threats to Taiwan, but not pusillanimous efforts to ease Chinese concerns about TMD. One would expect a tough negotiating stand on the terms of China's WTO entry, but not Western concessions merely because China made limited progress toward international transparency standards or made us feel guilty about bombing its embassy in Belgrade. One would expect Western leaders to tell Chinese leaders that their authoritarianism puts them on the wrong side of history, but one would not expect Western countries to stop trying to censure human rights abuses in the United Nations or to fall over themselves to compete for the right to lose money in the China market.

To some extent, we are stuck with a degree of exaggeration of China's influence. It has a permanent U.N. Security Council seat even though it matters about as much as the United Kingdom and France, who hold their seats only because of their pre-World War II power. Unlike London and Paris, however, Beijing contributes little to international society via peacekeeping or funding for international bodies. China still has a hold on the imagination of CEOs, as it has for 150 years – all the more remarkable after the past 20 years, in which Western companies were bamboozled into believing that staying for the long haul meant eventually making money in China. Pentagon planners, a pessimistic breed if ever there was one, might be forgiven for believing that China could eventually become a peer competitor of the United States, even though the military gap, especially in high-technology arms, is, if anything, actually growing wider.

Nevertheless, until China is cut down to size in Western imaginations and treated more like a Brazil or an India, the West stands little chance of sustaining a coherent and long-term policy toward it. Until we stop suspending our disbelief and recognize the theatrical power of China, we will continue to constrain ourselves from pursuing our own interests and fail to constrain China's excesses. And perhaps most important, until we treat China as a normal middle power, we will make it harder for the Chinese people to understand their own failings and limitations and get on with the serious reforms that need to come.

3   China as a global strategic actor

Lawrence Freedman

China now shares with Russia the frustration of falling short of its strategic expectations, of promising to challenge the Western ascendancy in international politics and then failing, by some margin, to do so. With China, if anything the frustration might be even greater, in that unlike Russia its reputation as an up-and-coming state was boosted by an apparently stellar economic performance, with economic growth quadrupling over the quarter century since 1978, and investment in military modernization growing even faster. The limited role that China can now play in influencing the international system has to be explained in part by changes in the system itself, and the relative weight of the United States within it, which have little if anything to do with China. China has also been caught out by changes in the determinants of power. As the Second World War concluded, China's sheer size in terms of both territory and population might have been expected to turn it into one of the leading powers in the system: a strategic player, able to shape the system as well as be shaped by it.

As a country with a history of weakness, having been a plaything of the imperialists and then a victim of invasion and civil war, it was clear why military strength mattered to China. It wanted to reach a position where others were bound to take notice of its views and the oppressed masses of the world would have a clear and uncompromising voice. Under the leadership of Mao Zedong, the Chinese struggled to achieve true independence, so that they would not be beholden even to the Soviet Union. Into the 1960s China strained to catch up with the United States and the Soviet Union in nuclear capabilities to confirm this independence. Yet while defensively this effort undoubtedly improved China's security, at least after some anxious years, it provided no basis for an extension of the country's international influence.

The independence that came from its formidable defensive possibilities, promising to overwhelm and submerge any invader, gave China a special role in international affairs, allowing it to display a remarkable freedom of manoeuvre as it completed the journey from loyal Soviet ally to new

American friend. It could present itself as a rising star, but in fact its position was a reflection of the need to escape from isolation, to avoid falling between two poles rather than becoming a new pole itself. It was only its nuclear capability that gave it a claim to global reach, and so once nuclear capabilities became effectively marginalized in international affairs then its claims were correspondingly diminished. Meanwhile, the end of the Cold War removed the circumstances that had offered it some opportunity to play a strategic role. As conventional forces came back into fashion in the 1990s, the People's Liberation Army was so far behind that it could not hope to catch up with the 'revolution in military affairs' as proclaimed in Washington.

Neither has China ever quite realized the potential of owning one of the five permanent seats on the UN Security Council. This was allocated to China when the Nationalists were still in control. They held on to it until 1971, pretending to govern all of China from what was then known as Formosa (Taiwan). Only with reluctance was it forced to hand over the seat to the communists who had actually been in charge since 1949. Over this period the significance of this seat was devalued. While denied responsibility, the PRC accepted a role of irresponsibility, refusing to join international initiatives, for example the 1963 Partial Test Ban treaty, and generally putting itself at the head of all the subversive forces in the world. By the time that it did acquire the Security Council seat, which might have signalled recognition of the communist supremacy, the country's ideological message was starting to get ever more muddled. It had started on the journey from the purity of the Cultural Revolution to the materialist individualism of modernization, all under the same Party banner. As the UN underwent its post-Cold War revival, China's preoccupations appeared remarkably parochial: mainly concerned with preserving the principle of non-interference in internal affairs and the isolation of Taiwan.

China shares with other large and proud states emerging out of a colonial past, most obviously India, a keen sense of international hierarchy and an instinct for power politics. It has been unsentimental in its attitudes towards the use of force and the pursuit of vital interests. At the same time, until comparatively recently it has shown disinterest and often distrust in international treaties and the principles of multilateralism, fearing them as means by which it could be put on the spot. Over time, as its interests began to coincide more with those of its neighbours, or at least as it began to assert this to be the case, China began to understand how international organizations could be used to protect interests and put pressure on others. As a result it became more willing to sign up to international treaties and agreements, and indeed by the 1990s had signed up to 80 per cent of available arms control treaties (Johnston, 2003a: 12, n. 23). There has also been a shift in international perspectives. The big arms control agreements of the 1960s – concerning nuclear test bans and non-proliferation – were specifically designed to isolate China, while the more political security efforts of the post-Cold War era have been more inclusive in inspiration. So multilateralism has become a less threatening prospect. Nonetheless, this history perhaps explains why China has been unable to use its position in international organizations to promote a distinctive concept of the collective good, except rhetorically, and has instead assessed most issues according to its relevance for Chinese interests narrowly conceived. This reinforces the view of China as a regional rather than a global power.

This chapter explores these issues, taking in Gerry Segal's initial fascination with China's potential for turning a bipolar world into something more tripolar, and his concluding dismissal of China as a 'middle power'. It opens with a discussion of the meaning of power politics in these terms, flowing from a realist conception of the international system. I use realism here in a loose sense, more classical than 'neo', to refer to those theories of international affairs that adopt conceptual frameworks close to those of practitioners and focus on questions of power and interest. There is no need for this approach to be conservative, either ideologically or intellectually. It can cope with norms and values, acknowledge the role of domestic factors and generate radical conclusions. When it comes to the business of identifying international hierarchies, however, realism does tend to resort to traditional language and assumptions. The question posed in this chapter therefore presumes a rather constricted form of realism. This may be an appropriate way to consider a country once described as the 'high church of realpolitik in the post-Cold War world' (Christensen, 1996: 37; see also Johnston, 1995/1996: 7).

Measuring power

Much of the confusion surrounding attempts to assess the role of any particular player in the international system stems from the many, and by no means consistent, uses of the word 'power'. There are two ways of evaluating power from a realist perspective: the first as resources, which provides an indication of capacity, and the second in terms of the effects produced through the purposive use of that capacity. The first is easier to measure, but the second is more meaningful. There is a relationship between the two in that those resources that appear to be most effective acquire a more significant weighting over time as a measure of power. If it is believed that a state is well endowed in critical resources, then effects may flow from this position without much effort. Other, weaker states instinctively take them into account when they calculate courses of action. Wars provide the ultimate test of claims of comparative strategic advantage, which is one reason why those seeking to establish the shifting balance of power study them so avidly. The 1991 Gulf War was such a shock to the Chinese, amongst others, because it demonstrated just how advanced American military capacities had become, and just how ineffectual their capacity would be if tested in combat.

The tradition of measuring power as resources runs deep in international relations as a means of helping states navigate their way around a system that lacks a central authority. Traditionally it has been raw military strength that has been assigned the highest value, evaluated in terms of the quality and quantity of armed forces and also their geographical reach. Those doubtful about the influence derived from military strength, at least in isolation from other types of resources, will wish to take account of 'softer' forms (Nye, 1990), which can include cultural appeal, diplomatic competence, positions in international organizations, plus the capacity to dole out economic and technical assistance. Economic power, including advanced technology, manufacturing capacity, flexible labour markets and patterns of trade, is often presented as the foundation for all other types. There is now less confidence that military power can be turned into economic power or that without economic power, military power can be sustained.

States with sufficient resources to set them apart from the crowd are known as 'powers'. The 'great powers' are those whose interests must be accommodated if the international system is to be kept stable and war is to be avoided, that is those able to play a strategic role. Whatever the views of academic critics, the persistence of these labels in guides to international clout and status is notable. Great powers tend to consider their position in the international hierarchy as an interest in itself. Those at the top of the hierarchy acquire affection for the status quo. 'Rising powers', capable of challenging the status quo, are described as revisionist or radical. The 'status quo powers' know that if they come to be taken less seriously, should they start to slip, they may get less respect than they believe they deserve. Such circumstances generate insecurity and danger all round. If revisionists are tempted to test the status quo powers they may, in turn, believe that they must reassert their position. Of course a successful revisionist power soon acquires its own interest in a new status quo, even if its official ideology points to continued challenges to others. This was the basis of the Chinese critique of the Soviet Union during the 1960s. From an ideological position that posited an inevitable clash between the Communist and imperialist blocs, Moscow had concluded that it was possible to do deals between the two in order, as Beijing saw it, to preserve a duopoly of power.

The special position of the United States and Soviet Union was described in a category identified by William Fox during the closing stages of the Second World War when he noted the arrival of 'the superpowers', who combined great power with global reach (Fox, 1944). It was not enough to be a great power in one's own region. Superpowers were great powers in a number of regions. The term was coined before nuclear weapons confirmed the category, although Fox's initial focus on the imposing presence of superpowers in a number of regions may turn out to be of more lasting value than the later focus on the size of nuclear inventories. Initially Fox included the British Empire. Soon it was apparent that there were only two superpowers. After the Cold War the United States appeared to be in a class of its own or as a lone superpower, or as former French Foreign Minister Védrine put it, a 'hyperpower', able to combine hard power with soft power, projecting itself through the English language, free-market principles, its mastery of global images, and technological and cultural creativity (Védrine *et al.*, 2001; see also Wohlforth, 1999).

A likely feature of a hyperpower would be that it is beyond balance – that is, no other power, or even group of powers, can mount a credible challenge to its pre-eminence. It challenges the possibility of a balance of power as a means of maintaining some sort of global equilibrium and instead raises the possibility of hegemony. This was in contrast to the equilibrium of sorts that had been achieved during the Cold War. This stability was explained as a welcome property of a bipolar configuration of power (Waltz, 1979) with the corollary that alternative configurations might be less stable. Tendencies towards multipolarity had been identified long before the end of the Cold War, with China normally mentioned as one of the extra poles, and as the 1990s began it was assumed that a multipolar age was beginning (e.g. Tow, 1994). This helps explain why the actual tendency towards unipolarity has turned out to be so frustrating for powers other than the United States.

Still a coming power

This preamble is relevant to any discussion of the strategic position of China, because the precise location of China within the international hierarchy has been a continuing preoccupation among scholars and policy-makers, as well as for the Chinese themselves. Gerry Segal's dismissal of the 'Middle Kingdom' as 'a middle power' (Segal, 1999) was provocative because of the effort that had gone into building up China as a great power with a strategic role, and the associated assumption that it must be becoming even more important with each year of impressive economic growth. Yet, in the early 1980s, Gerry had also explored the extent to which China had led the world out of bipolarity into tripolarity. He observed that China was not as powerful as the superpowers. Nonetheless, then he continued:

> The view of the importance of China is based less on a calculation of Peking's available nuclear throw-weight, as on the tendency of the two superpowers to treat China as the next most important force in

the global system after themselves. It would be foolish to argue that China, even in these terms, has become an equally significant point in the triangular relationship, both in terms of the perceptions of Moscow and Washington and in terms of the facts of political life. China is the only power other than the superpowers with a fully independent nuclear force and an embryonic second-strike capability. It has in demographic and economic terms the potential to make credible its threat to engage in a protracted people's war if attacked. It is also largely autarkic and therefore is little bothered by the constraints of trade dependencies.

(Segal, 1982a: 10)

This passage helps explain why the young Gerry was less convincing about China's strategic importance than the mature Gerry. There are three distinctive problems in interpretation. The first is the assumption that a marginal position in the international economic system is a power bonus. To be sure, it avoids dependencies, but it also stunts growth (as certainly happened in this case), and so reduces the possibilities for a further expansion of capacity. In addition, dependencies tend to flow in both directions, so new forms of leverage over others might be created even as others may get some leverage over you. Second, the specific strengths mentioned were largely defensive. Leaving aside the question as to whether Britain and France were really behind in nuclear capabilities at the time, the value of a second-strike capability was as a deterrent, in persuading an aggressor that a nuclear first strike could not eliminate the likelihood of severe retaliation. People's War and economic autarky were also important in persuading an aggressor not to try a classic land invasion. What these capabilities could not do was create offensive options for China – to allow it to send and sustain forces well beyond its boundaries in order to influence distant military struggles. The Russians became petrified of the Chinese masses storming over their long, shared border and made a considerable military provision to prevent such an occurrence. In practice, China's military reach turned out to be quite short: it did well against ill-prepared Indians in 1962, but poorly against much tougher Vietnamese in 1979. Although much smaller in every sense, its main target of Taiwan remained – and still remains – exasperatingly out of its grasp.

As Wohlforth has observed, the expectations surrounding China parallel those from before the First World War about rising Russian power, in assuming 'that population and rapid growth compensate for technological backwardness' (Wohlforth, 1999: 36). In practice, the compensation is not apparent. China's nuclear capability remains modest, with the bulk of its weapons suitable for regional use, and around 20 of the obsolete D-5 suitable for intercontinental use, plus one missile-launching submarine (SSBN) which has had technical problems from the start. More modern

ICBMs and SSBNs are under development, but it will take time before they arrive. Chinese strategists would be bound to conclude that they still lack what was described during the Cold War as a second-strike capability – two decades after Gerry Segal wrote of one being close, and this must add to their anxiety about any serious US missile defences, which would reduce their options further.

Furthermore, large parts of China's conventional capabilities would be considered museum pieces in the West. However fast it introduces new equipment – a process limited by the inadequacies of its indigenous defence industry – only a modest proportion of its forces have any chance of being seriously modern in the foreseeable future, and even that will require a substantial contraction in numbers. Even with the contingency that most preoccupies the West – action against Taiwan – it is well away from having a reliable option for some time to come. It must at any rate conclude that it has its hands full with a complex regional situation, leaving aside Taiwan, with uncertain developments on the Korean Peninsula and an innate wariness about Japan.

The third problem, which is the most interesting feature of the young Gerry's analysis, is that so much depends on the power attributed to China by the United States and the former Soviet Union. With hints of an early constructivism, the argument is that China matters because others act as if it matters. The corollary of this is that when others decide that it does not matter so much, then that is also the case, however infuriating that might be to a Chinese leadership that was coming to enjoy a central position on the world stage. That was after all the double message of the mature Gerry's 1999 article. He was encouraging a sense of proportion about China, challenging not only the pretensions of Beijing but also those in the US who were exaggerating China's potential as a 'peer competitor'.

Many in the US defence establishment, bereft of a great power threat against which it was possible to plan, hoped that China might fill the gap, and provide a competitor worthy of their revolution in military affairs. This perception was reflected in the US quadrennial defense review of September 2001. The ancient Chinese strategists such as Sun Tzu were often applauded in the West as the originators of the stream in strategic thought that had culminated in the US defence transformation, involving guile and deception as much as direct combat. Aphorisms from *The Art of War* were much cited: 'to fight and conquer in all your battles is not supreme excellence; supreme excellence consists in breaking the enemy's resistance without fighting'. The sentiment was also assumed to appeal naturally to Chinese strategists, and there is evidence that ever since the shock of the effortless American victory in Desert Storm they have been keen to find forms of warfare that could find clever ways of getting round the enormous American advantage in firepower, an aspect of the RMA that was often taken for granted in the American debate (Pillsbury, 2000). Whether they were likely to succeed was another matter.

The most recent and most meticulous survey of China's military modernization (Shambaugh, 2003) leaves doubts. China's basic strength remains the ability to absorb any occupying force. The lesson of the 2003 Anglo-American campaign in Iraq is not that remarkable things can be achieved by three divisions, but that those countries that have rotted from inside collapse without much of a push. The basic lesson for China, and other putative 'rogues', is the importance of internal cohesion and legitimacy when it comes to resisting invasion. Iraq was not able to mount a People's War along Maoist lines: there is an interesting question, which is unlikely ever to be answered, about whether China could now mount such a defence, for it would be, above all else, a test of the government's legitimacy. Defence is not, however, the issue with China. If it is to be considered a great power it must be able to project power into distant regions, and even challenge the military hegemony of the US.

A postulated combination of rapid growth, cunning intelligence and an unavoidable level of geo-strategic competition encouraged alarmist interpretations of '*The Coming Conflict with China*' (originally an article and then a book, Bernstein and Munro, 1997 and 1998), in a surprisingly short time after similar predictions about Japan had been thoroughly discredited and the old Soviet threat had evaporated. The administration of George W. Bush was initially inclined to view China in something approaching these terms, and it was described as a 'strategic competitor'. But after the terrorist attacks of 11 September 2001, with so much else on its plate, the US started to describe China as a potential 'strategic partner', a half-way stage between enmity and amity, hovering close to indifference.

The careful wording of the 2002 National Security Strategy document illustrates the tension. On the one hand China, a 'strong, peaceful, and prosperous China', is welcomed, especially as the Bush administration believes that outcome requires democracy. The regret is only that such a commitment to political reform has yet to be made. Notably China has yet to accept that 'pursuing advanced military capabilities that can threaten its neighbors in the Asia-Pacific region' is a less reliable path to 'national greatness' than 'social and political freedom'. Even so, a 'constructive relationship' is sought, working closely in the many areas where interests overlap – of greater importance since 9/11 – while still encouraging political enlightenment, moderation on Taiwan and responsibility on proliferation issues (Bush, 2002: 27–28). As one top US official observed at the end of 2002:

> For thirty years, American strategists have debated how to 'bring China into the international system.' Well, today, to a considerable

extent, China is 'in.' But we have yet to make permanent China's full integration in shaping and maintaining an international order in which all can live in peace, prosperity, and freedom.

(Haass, 2002)

If a theme emerges from statements by successive US governments in recent years it is that China is moving in the right direction but not quite there, professing to be a good international citizen, but with a retained capacity for great irresponsibility. (See for example the citations in Johnston (2003a: 6–11).)

Power as effective influence

This leads on to the second use of the word power: as the ability to use resources effectively for political purposes. Some view is required of China's political goals. Are these geared more to the status quo, or have they been consistently radical, even revolutionary? Are these goals to be achieved largely in the Asia-Pacific region, or is China a real aspirant for global leadership? On some versions of realism, China is almost bound to seek to reshape the international system to suit its own needs, however long it takes, and to be constantly dissatisfied with American pre-eminence. Johnston has demonstrated that there is nothing inevitable about this challenge (Johnston, 2003a). Apart from anything else it is very hard to imagine what the alternative Chinese system would look like. It provides no ideological leadership to any segment of international society: the days are past when it could claim to be leading the Third World against the first two. It offers no alternative network of trade and finance, or serious thoughts, as Japan once had, about how it might dominate the existing network. It expects to be treated with respect, especially within its own region, but does not present itself as a candidate for global primacy. China may not like American primacy, which must constrain its ability to pursue its more concrete regional goals, but is wary of proposals for a new multi-polarity such as that espoused by President Chirac of France. Indeed, there is evidence, by no means conclusive, that the Chinese are beginning to leave the rhetoric of multipolarity behind in favour of a discourse high-lighting globalization (Johnston, 2003a: 30–37).

Furthermore, even when China seemed to carry more weight in the international balance of power, this was less because of its growing power but because circumstances provided it with a role as a swing state – one that could suddenly tilt the balance of power through a dramatic shift in allegiance. Its reputation as such a state lingered long after the circum-stances had passed. China has appeared in many guises and associations, moving through civil war from friend of the US to loyal ally of the Soviet Union but then on to rival for leadership in the communist world. It has been the most zealous enemy of Western imperialism, ready and willing to fight in Korea, but moving to become at one point a virtual ally, often jokingly described as 'NATO's sixteenth Member' (when there were only fifteen), before emerging again as a combination of military competitor and economic imitator.

Was this reputation as a swing state warranted, and did it work to China's advantage? The comparison with France is instructive. Both countries concluded during the course of the 1950s that they were uncomfortable with alliance if this would only represent a continuation of past humiliations. The test of alliance was whether it provided cover for the pursuit of national agendas, and both countries had reason to become disillusioned during the 1950s – France as a result of Suez in 1956 and China with the Offshore Islands crisis of 1958. In both cases they felt themselves facing nuclear threats without support from their primary ally. In neither case was this the sole reason for seeking their own national nuclear programme – factors of prestige and a general desire to assert independence were also significant – but it provided an added incentive. In both cases the principal ally became extremely suspicious of the motives, and soon made no pretence at sympathy and instead made every effort to frustrate their nuclear ambitions. Moscow and Washington alike saw these independent nuclear capabilities as undeserved rebukes and potential sources of dangerous confusion in the event of future crises, but both also failed in their attempts to abort them at an early stage. France and China alike saw the success with their nuclear programmes as the foundation for an increasingly assertive foreign policy and seemed to delight in drawing attention to the divergence from their former ally. Neither, however, was particularly successful in convincing others to follow suit, although they both had temporary victories at crucial moments, with far-reaching consequences in the first half of the 1960s – France in its courting of West Germany to provide joint leadership of Europe, and China with North Vietnam.

There was, however, one crucial difference. While France under General de Gaulle pushed hard, it knew when to stop. De Gaulle took France out of NATO's Integrated Military Command but not the Atlantic Alliance in its political aspects. He backed President Kennedy during Cuba while China was openly contemptuous of Khrushchev's performance during the October 1962 crisis. The Chinese leadership did not know when to stop. As the 1960s progressed, caught in the grip of the Cultural Revolution, it came to describe the Soviet Union as far more than a disappointing and overbearing ally but instead an ideological enemy, apparently preparing to invade China. For all the cultural critiques of the United States emanating from the cafés of the Seine's Left Bank, and the tensions of Vietnam, the political disagreements across the Atlantic were always contained. Neither, of course, did France have a long, disputed border with the United States.

The turning point for both France and China came with the Soviet invasion of Czechoslovakia in August 1968. By this time, de Gaulle's apparently impregnable position had been dented by the student-inspired events of that May. The consolidation of Soviet hegemony undermined the premises upon which much of his foreign policy had been based, of a growing fluidity in international relations as the Cold War lost its centrality and its bite. Soon de Gaulle left office, and his successors gradually smoothed down the rougher edges of his policy. For China the implications of Czechoslovakia were more serious. While it had no sympathy with the ideology of the 'Prague Spring', the crackdown demonstrated the limits to Soviet tolerance of dissent. In 1968 China's nuclear capability was not quite ready to provide a credible deterrent. In 1969 came the skirmishes across the Amur and Ussuri river. Taking the opportunity of Ho Chi Minh's funeral, and against a background of semi-official nuclear intimidation, Zhou Enlai agreed with Soviet Prime Minister Kosygin to calm things down. The Chinese engaged in their own re-appraisal, but they could not now undo the damage that had been done in terms of Soviet perceptions of this new and irrational threat to its east. While the French could rebalance their foreign policy, the Chinese were obliged to move in an even more dramatic direction.

This was the point at which China accepted that its situation was so parlous that it had to reposition itself within the international system, the start of the strategic triangle and the potential for tripolarity. It is important to note, however, that while the Chinese move was bold it was not so much a reflection of strength but of weakness. Henry Kissinger's reputation as a master strategist as President Nixon's national security adviser reflects the speed and decisiveness with which he recognized the opportunity and picked up on it, although Nixon's own role in the changing policy is now given greater weight. Kissinger also characterized the opportunity as one for triangulation, but quite narrowly. It was 'America's relationship with the Communist world' – not the world as a whole – that 'was slowly becoming triangular' (Kissinger, 1979: 191).

There was never true tripolarity. Washington could play off China against the Soviet Union, but so poor was their relationship that neither Beijing nor Moscow could seriously threaten the United States with the prospect of a reconstituted Sino-Soviet bloc. So the real beneficiary was the United States. It had not been able to gain much early benefit from the Sino-Soviet split. The Partial Test Ban Treaty became possible when Moscow gave up on being able to mollify Beijing, but at the same time the loss of Soviet influence allowed China to encourage the North Vietnamese to ignore the Geneva accords on Laos. It was only as it established relations with both and could be confident that these would be sustained (even while bombing Hanoi!) that the US could really take advantage. The Sino-Soviet fracture was too deep to mend, dogged by too much history and too much in dispute. The Soviet Union was the big loser, as it had first lost an ally, which had helped it establish a claim for being in line with the tide of history and speaking for the bulk of the Eurasian landmass, and then gained an enemy. The split with China demonstrated that factionalism, which always plagued the political left, did not end when they seized their own states. China's motives were defensive: it was aware that it was vulnerable to US–Soviet collusion. It was hardly a victory, other than for a modicum of rationality among the leadership. Against the claims of the 1960s it was a substantial retreat. It did facilitate the recovery of the UN seat and eased negotiations on other issues, but it did not create opportunities for the positive projection of power. The other essays in Gerry's 1982b edited book, including my own, conveyed considerable scepticism about the relevance of the triangle beyond the undoubted leverage that it had given Washington (Freedman, 1982; on this period see Ross, 1993).

Beyond *realpolitik*

The fact that relations between China and Russia improved notably as the Cold War came to an end might have been expected to improve their bargaining power in relation to the United States. Furthermore, expectations at this time were that the new world order would be multipolar. It was, after all, only a couple of years since Paul Kennedy had suggested that the US was likely to be hampered through imperial overstretch while it was overtaken by more dynamic, and largely Asian, economies (Kennedy, 1987). German unification was expected to create a new powerhouse in the centre of Europe, exercising a dominant influence on the continent's future. It might even, working closely with France, begin to fulfil past dreams of turning the European Community into a formidable unitary actor. Saudi Arabia commanded attention because it held such substantial oil reserves, while Russia and China remained in the equation because they were nuclear powers and had seats on the Security Council.

These expectations turned out to be premature because they assumed extrapolations of past trends. The Japanese economy stagnated. Unification turned out to be a burden rather than a boost for Germany (at least economically), and the rest of continental Europe was sluggish. Oil prices, and therefore revenues, remained low for the Gulf states. Meanwhile the American 'new economy' took off. Still, economic power had a wider distribution than military power. For two decades the US forces had been working to improve their conventional capabilities. The extent to which they had succeeded did not become apparent until the 1991 Gulf War, even allowing for the fact that the quality of the enemy may have flattered American strengths. Nonetheless, the ability of the US to deploy weapons of great precision and lethality over long distances, and to orchestrate military operations so efficiently, was extraordinarily impressive. Twelve years later, in the second bout that this time saw Saddam Hussein overthrown, the speed and decisiveness of the American advance was even more overwhelming. In the intervening years the Americans had mounted effective air campaigns over Kosovo and Afghanistan. They seemed weak or hesitant in ground operations against irregular forces. Operations against Iraqi resistance demonstrated the difficulties that high-technology forces could face against guerrillas, but not to the point of defeat.

This was difficult enough for countries who might consider themselves allies of the United States. In Europe, for example, only the United Kingdom stayed in touch with American capabilities, although still far behind. The growing gap between European and American defence capabilities caused considerable consternation, especially as it appeared to release the Americans from dependence upon allies. For countries that could imagine themselves on the receiving end of American military power, the position was much more alarming. In general, for the major powers this should not matter, because there was no reason why there should be a war with the United States. Washington focused on known 'rogues', such as North Korea and Iran. Yet China occupied a difficult space, and in American formulations was not, unlike Russia, quite into the comfort zone.

China was seen in Washington to be both an ascendant power and politically authoritarian. With the end of the Cold War, the role of China as a useful distraction to the Soviet Union on its eastern flank ended, while a sharper light began to be shone on its internal repression. The coincidence of the Tiananmen Square crackdown with the collapse of European communism left China more exposed than it might have been had European communism survived. The tendency to replace *realpolitik* in rationalizations of Western policy by human rights considerations has put a strain on several partnerships left over from Cold War times (for example, Saudi Arabia), and this has increasingly come to be a critical issue in relations with China (Foot, 2003). One reflection of this tendency has been the importance attached to humanitarian interventions. China has clearly been out of sympathy with this move. It places a high value on sovereignty, and has been wary of anything that might serve as a precedent with regard to Tibet. Its own involvement with UN operations has been minimal. An article in 2000 reported that when over 35,000 UN military personnel were involved in 18 different missions, China filled only 53 of the slots on five missions, although the authors did detect signs of greater pragmatism (Gill and Reilly, 2000). The total has now reached a still modest 355, and there is agreement in principle on joining the stand-by arrangements for future peace-keeping operations (Kim, this volume, Chapter 4). One would be hard put to say that China is pulling its weight. Lastly, concerns about China's role in the diffusion of capabilities for weapons of mass destruction also linger. While it has pledged itself to be responsible in this area there have been regular complaints about a readiness to trade in critical technologies, with Iran and Pakistan cited as particular customers of concern. The trickiness of this issue was illustrated by evidence that in order to avoid being blamed for helping North Korea with its nuclear efforts, China had encouraged Pakistan to exchange nuclear technology with the reclusive state. The problems thus created may help bring home to Beijing that as it has acquired a stake in the status quo, even indirect help for 'rogues' can soon backfire.

Beijing's preference for *realpolitik* as a guiding principle has been subverted by a need to adjust to these changing international norms, that happen to be backed by American power. *Realpolitik* at a time of American primacy argues as much for a low profile as resistance in the name of multipolarity. China has become reluctant to use its Security Council position to establish broad views on international issues. During the Cold War it had at least tried to speak with a distinctive, if ineffectual, voice as an advocate of Third World radicalism. For much of the 1990s its only interest appeared to be the continuing diplomatic isolation of Taiwan, leading to such unhelpful acts as failing to back the UN force in Macedonia, because Macedonia had decided to establish relations with Taiwan.

When, during the 1999 Kosovo War, its embassy was struck in a US raid, albeit inadvertently, here was another indicator of how China could get in the cross-fire generated by a more assertive United States, and its response was furious. It joined with Russia in condemning the NATO campaign, and then, when Moscow suddenly decided that Serbia was not worth further damage to its relations with the US, China was left alone. It took care not to make the same mistake in 2003. When France, followed by Russia, led the opposition on the Security Council to the move against Iraq, China said very little, not raising its head above the parapet, and was almost assumed to be an appendage of Russian policy. If France and Russia had reached a compromise with the United States, the assumption is that China would have gone along.

In between, China had been able to use support in the war against terrorism and its engagement with international trade to qualify the wary assessment of the Bush administration. China's problems with its own Islamic militants offered some basis for a common cause with the US. It signed up to a range of regional and international declarations and made no fuss about the American campaign in Afghanistan. This was despite the fact that the most important consequence of the war on terrorism is that it has brought American forces and strategic interests into operations close to China's periphery in Central Asia. The rumbling crisis over North Korea's nuclear provocations has added to the sense of rather direct engagement with the US. The previous time that China went to war against the United States was because of Korea, and Pyongyang has been doing everything possible to keep itself in the American firing line. Beijing's own irritation with the North's behaviour has led it to work more closely with Washington than it had originally expected, but there is always a risk that matters could get out of hand, with dangerous and difficult choices posed for all the regional powers. Added to this is the unfinished business of Taiwan. The dangers inherent in this conflict are dealt with elsewhere. For our purposes, the point is only that China is struggling to maintain its freedom of manoeuvre for the future. During the 1996 crisis, when the US sent two carrier battle groups to the area after the PLA had been firing missiles in the general direction of Taiwan, it became clear that the US would not ignore an attempt to turn two Chinas into one by forceful means.

Conclusion

All this confirms an image of China that is confined to a regional position not only by the limited reach of its military strength but also by a rather parochial sense of its interests. It has not become a new 'pole' in the international system, for even within its own region, where it occupies a formidable place, it has no natural allies and followers. Its sheer size commands respect and its economic potential gains constant attention, but after all that has happened over the past four decades there is scant interest in any ideological pronouncements, and its system of governance is assessed as at best anomalous and probably inadequate for the social and political challenges that lie ahead. The conclusion must be, therefore, that China is not a major strategic power except within its own region. It is not actively reshaping the contemporary international system but instead is being shaped by it, and in particular by those integrative forces summed up under the heading of 'globalization'.

There is, however, an important qualification to this judgement. There are few really strong powers in a traditional sense in the international system, and the United States is the strongest to an extraordinary degree. For this reason, many of the most difficult international issues are not really about competitions among the strong but the problems caused by the weak. The countries that have found themselves at the centre of recent storms – from the Balkans through the Middle East and into Africa – have been those whose internal divisions have led to enormous humanitarian distress and political oppression. It is, for the Africans, an unfortunate feature of their strategic unimportance that it is a constant struggle to gain attention for their continent's multiple problems. The same in no sense can be said for China's region, which is critically important to the rest of the world. The inner collapse of North Korea, further fragmentation in Indonesia, let alone upheavals within China itself cannot be considered purely 'local' matters because of their knock-on effects for the system as a whole. How the Asia-Pacific region functions over the coming years will be crucial for the stability and economic well-being of the global system, and on many of the big questions, such as the future of North Korea as well as its own ability to modernize politically as well as economically, China will be on centre stage.

China's economic dynamism is bound to add to its local influence, and in a twist of history, it is getting favourable mentions from regional leaders for its pragmatism amd materialism, at a time when the Americans are appearing dogmatic and excessively preoccupied with their 'war on terror'. Within their own region the Chinese are also starting to develop effective strategies – diplomatic as well as military – to cope with American primacy. They need to do this more than other medium powers because many of the tests facing the Americans happen to be found in and around the Chinese periphery. The case of North Korea indicates that Washington and Beijing can learn to work together on matters of common concern. So in the end China does occupy a position of great strategic significance, but that is not because of its global strength or its singular and radical ideology, but because of its location in a region that has the potential for future turbulence.

4 China in world politics

Samuel S. Kim

Segal's global China

In a characteristically forceful essay, Gerald Segal argues that Chinese power and influence is greatly overrated economically (as a market), politically (as a world power), and ideationally (as a source of ideas). At best, China is taken to be no more than a 'second-rank middle power', and as such it matters far less than most people inside and outside of China would have us believe (Segal, 1999).

Is Segal trying to trash with a single blow the thesis that the rise of China is a serious threat to the world? Quite to the contrary! In his article 'East Asia and the "Constrainment" of China', only three years earlier, he had argued that 'constrainment' is the more effective strategy for countering a rising China, because 'China is a powerful, unstable non-status quo power' (Segal, 1996: 108). The clear premise of both articles remains the same: that China as a dissatisfied revisionist (non-status quo) power is operating outside the global community across a wide range of international rules and norms. Accordingly, China matters only as a threat to 'international rules and norms' presumably reflecting 'Western interests', a threat that must be constrained, not appeased.

Along this line, Segal invokes the Cox report – a highly politicized document showcasing the right-wing Republican image of China as a rogue dragon – as 'truth evidence' on Chinese espionage in the United States. He views China as acting out on the global stage (the UN General Assembly?) the role of a 'theatrical power', a metaphor reminiscent of what some China-bashers once called 'gong bang diplomacy' (Johnson, 1984). Furthermore, Segal advances his argument on China's putative rogue-state behaviour in non-falsifiable terms: 'China matters in arms control mainly because it effectively blocks accords until doing so ends up damaging China's international reputation' (Segal, 1999: 32). With the warning theme of appeasement running throughout, Segal's *Foreign Affairs* article seemed ready-made for the neo-conservative, neo-imperial wing of the Republican Party in the United States, supporting their self-fulfilling prophecies about the Chinese threat.

Although there is no differentiation between China's global and regional role, Segal's global China matters far less than Segal's regional China. The notion that at best China is no more than a 'second-rank middle power' in world politics rests on the following:

- That 'Beijing almost always plays second fiddle to Moscow or even Paris in obstructing Western interests' in the UN Security Council (Segal, 1999: 31).
- That China matters militarily because it is not a status quo power, or that it is obstructionist in arms control negotiations (Segal, 1999: 32).
- That China's global political power and influence 'are clearly puny – not merely compared to the dominant West, but also compared to Japan' (Segal, 1999: 34).
- That China 'is a seriously overrated power' in terms of international trade and investment (Segal, 1999: 26).
- That China is a 'political pariah' in global human rights politics (Segal, 1999: 34).
- That China apparently matters even less in the domain of global environmental politics, given the absence of any reference to the environmental question in Segal's argument.

The scope of this essay is limited, however, to an investigation of Segal's key points and arguments in regard to China's role in world politics, and the basis upon which their validity can be confirmed, revised or repudiated. The focus here is limited to two major world-order issues and related global institutions or regimes for the purpose of exploring the extent and degree of China's integration into these institutions and its status quo or revisionist behaviour within them: the UN Security Council (UNSC) and the World Trade Organization (WTO). Of all the global multilateral institutions, China's permanent membership with the veto power in the UNSC and its WTO membership have become source and symbol of its great-power status, and, as such, a useful barometer of assessing how much China matters in world politics in terms of its global power, commitments, and responsibilities.

Parsing global China

I proceed from the premise that by dint of what it *is* and what it *does*, the People's Republic of China (PRC) is inescapably part of both the world-order problem and the world-order solution. Consider the potential trump cards that China holds in reserve:

1   demographic weight as the world's most populous country;
2   territorial size (the world's second largest);

3   a modernizing military with the world's largest armed forces (2.3 million troops in active service) and the world's third-largest nuclear weapons power;

4   veto power in the UNSC;

5   membership in virtually all the important global institutions, including most recently the WTO;

6   new economic status as the world's second-largest or sixth-largest economy, depending on how you count (see below), a status recently made manifest by France's invitation to China to attend the 2003 G-8 Summit; and

7   the world's second-largest generator of carbon dioxide emissions (after the United States).

The combined weight of these malleable and non-malleable factors virtually guarantees Beijing's seat in any global regime. As one of the Permanent Five (P-5) on the Security Council, its voice cannot be ignored in the conflict management process. No major military, social, demographic or environmental conflict can be managed multilaterally without at least tacit Chinese consent or cooperation. One of the key findings and conclusions of the most comprehensive collaborative study of China's participatory behaviour in eight select global regimes (sponsored by the Council on Foreign Relations, the publisher of *Foreign Affairs*) is that 'no significant aspect of world affairs is exempt from its influence' (Oksenberg and Economy, 1999: 5).

In a rapidly globalizing world, however, the notion of 'great power' – Segal's unspoken bogeyman – is subject to continuing redefinition and reassessment. While granting that there is no sure-fire 'scientific' way to define and measure state power and influence in world politics, the answer to the question 'does China matter?' should be framed and informed by several factors: the nature of power, the issue of globalization and how China's status quo (cooperative) behaviour in world politics is defined.

'Power' must be seen in synthetic terms. What constitutes 'great power' has changed significantly with the sudden and unexpected collapse of the socialist superpower and the diffusion and multiplicity of power in all its varying forms. The traditional military and strategic concept gives too much weight to a state's aggregate power and too little to the more dynamic and interdependent notions of power in an issue-specific domain – that is, power defined in terms of control over outcomes. As David Baldwin (1979: 193) argued more than two decades ago, 'the notion of a single overall international power structure unrelated to any particular issue-area is based on a concept of power that is virtually meaningless'. In a remarkable interview with Richard Ullman in 1999, George F. Kennan at the age of 95 intoned: 'I can say without hesitation that this planet is never going to be ruled from any single political center, whatever its military power' (Ullman, 1999: 6).

Second, virtually all states are subject today to the relentless twin pressures of globalization from above and without, and substate localization and fragmentation from below and within, especially in multinational states such as China. The globalization-cum-transparency revolution has fundamentally transformed the way that we think about security in several mutually interactive ways: by blurring the international/domestic divide, thus posing an unprecedented 'intermestic' challenge for national decision-makers; by sharply increasing the costs of the use of force (materially and normatively); by shifting our attention from national security narrowly defined to human security broadly conceived; by engendering multiple multilateral pressures to build coalitions with substate and transnational actors, including international organizations; and by generating relentless survival-of-the-fittest pressures on states to establish a synergistic congruence between domestic and foreign policies amid the changing functional requirements of globalization (Cha, 2000; Kim, 2000).

The third issue is how to define China's cooperative behaviour in world politics. The forces of globalization in the post-Cold War world have transformed both the context and the conditions under which Sino-global interaction can be played out. Indeed, globalization has greatly influenced not only the dynamics of power on the world stage but also the very meaning of power. While external assessments of the significance of a rising China vary considerably depending on the normative or theoretical perspective, China's own conceptualization and assessment has come to focus more on economic, scientific and technological factors than on military factors. Paradoxically, China's own assessments of trends in what the Chinese call 'comprehensive national power' (*zonghe guoli*) in comparative terms are increasingly pessimistic about its ability to catch up to the US, at a time when the rise of China as a great power has become nearly conventional wisdom among most scholars, pundits, and policy-makers in the West (Kim, 2003; Johnston, 2003b).

It is important to keep in mind, however, that a fair and balanced assessment of China's role in world politics begs the question, 'compared to *when* and to *whom*?'. The dubious premise that China's 'cooperation' with 'Western interests' and/or 'American interests' is the same as being or acting cooperative within the global community must be rejected. China today is more integrated into, and exhibits a greater degree and level of cooperation within, a multitude of global institutions than ever before, with a dramatic increase in Beijing's participation in UN-sponsored multilateral treaties and regimes. Beijing's global learning curve is made evident in a series of major policy shifts on a wide range of world-order issues, including arms control and disarmament, UN peacekeeping operations

(UNPKOs), global trade and market norms, human rights and environmental protection, albeit more in some realms than in others (Economy and Oksenberg, 1999). The shift in China's approach is highlighted by comparing and contrasting two official Chinese views of the United Nations as pronounced by the *People's Daily*: in 1965 the United Nations was blasted as nothing more than 'a dirty international political stock exchange in the grip of a few big powers,' whereas in 1995 the United Nations was touted as having truly become 'the largest and most authoritative intergovernmental organization in the world,' whose 'unique influence on international affairs cannot be replaced by any other international organizations' (Kim, 1979: 100; Wang, 1995; Kim, 1999: 47–48).

Segal's thesis that China as a powerful, unstable and dissatisfied revisionist actor operating outside the global community must be constrained, finds special resonance among American neo-conservative unilateralists. The irony here is that it is the United States, not China, who is more often outside the global community – speaking and behaving as an isolated superpower. In a 1999 article for *Foreign Affairs*, even a mainstream realist such as Samuel Huntington had to concede America's creeping unilateralism: 'On issue after issue, the United States has found itself increasingly alone, with one or a few partners, opposing most of the rest of the world's states and peoples' (Huntington, 1999: 41). In its first two years, the Bush administration seems to have accomplished an (un)diplomatic 'mission impossible' by turning creeping unilateralism into runaway unilateralism, rejecting multilateral treaties or treaties-in-the-making one after another (the ABM treaty, the Biological Weapons Convention, the Comprehensive Test Ban Treaty, the Kyoto Protocol, the International Criminal Court [ICC], a draft treaty on international small arms sales, etc.). In May 2002, the Bush administration took an unprecedented step in 'unsigning' the Rome Statute of the International Criminal Court by informing the UN Secretary-General of its decision not to become a party to the treaty, and that the US had no legal obligation arising from President Clinton's signature on 31 December 2000.

Indeed, the Bush administration has been asking China to follow what it says, not what it does. For example, in the *National Security Strategy of the United States of America* of September 2002 – the official inauguration of the Bush doctrine of pre-emption – the administration offers patronizing double-standard advice: 'In pursuing advanced military capabilities that can threaten its neighbors in the Asia-Pacific region, China is following an outdated path that, in the end, will hamper its own pursuit of national greatness' (Bush, 2002: 27). For the US to ask China to jettison the obsolescence of military power while spending and devoting more resources to its own military budget than the next couple of dozen or more countries combined can only be understood as a warning message from the world's only imperial superpower, with profound and unsettling implications for the future of Sino-American relations and the regional and global orders. In short, compared with America's runaway unilateralism, China seems like a responsible multilateral actor in global institutions.

Baseline criteria and indicators

China's integration into the global community and cooperative (compliance) behaviour within it may be measured by several criteria or indicators. The first is China's membership in international governmental organizations (which has increased dramatically from only two in the 1960s to 52 in the 1990s, about 83 per cent of the average of major Western democracies and about 160 per cent of the world average). Second, although the criterion for evaluating China's cooperative behaviour within the global community is complicated by the fact that global institutions and regimes command varying degrees of clarity and consensus on their respective norms and rules, participation in multilateral treaties may be considered a first-cut indicator of cooperative behaviour. The percentage of multilateral treaties that Beijing has signed and ratified relative to the number of such treaties for which it has been eligible can be accepted as prima facie evidence of its willingness to accept the established rules of the game. Whereas Beijing had signed about 10 to 20 per cent of all applicable arms control agreements in 1970, for example, by 1996 this figure had jumped to 85 to 90 per cent (Swaine and Johnston, 1999: 101). Finally, there is no substitute for inductive empirical analysis of China's norm-compliance or norm-defying behaviour once inside these global institutions, the main focus of this chapter. Has there been any case or situation when Beijing tried openly to undermine the established rules of the game in global institutions or regimes, or even attempted to block enactment of new accords and treaties in global institutions and conferences?

China in global institutions

China's global policy can be conceived as part of the triangle where domestic, regional and global policies interact in the pursuit of three overarching interests and demands: first and foremost, economic development to enhance domestic stability and legitimacy; second, promotion of a peaceful and secure external environment free of threats to China's sovereignty and territorial integrity in Asia; and third, cultivation of its status and influence as a responsible great power in global politics (Wang, 1999). There is an inordinate demand in China's international relations to accelerate economic development and to restore China's great-power status in the world, to make up for domestic security and legitimation deficits.

As Chinese Foreign Minister Tang Jiaxuan put it, China's diplomatic work 'should unswervingly be subordinated to and serve the strategic goal for the establishment of a well-off society in an all-round manner' (Tang Jiaxuan, 2002).

China in the UN Security Council

China's status as one of the P-5 with veto power in the UNSC is at once the most visible symbol and most valuable source of its great-power status in global high politics. Not surprisingly, the nature of Chinese support on the question of UN institutional reform, especially on the expansion of UNSC membership, is more rhetorical than real. But this is no different from the other four P-5 members. There is tacit agreement among the P-5 that any reform discourse is to be confined to the issues of membership expansion, with no collateral damage or diminishment of any kind to their veto power. Moreover, any institutional reform or restructuring proposition through formal amendment would encounter a rigorous and well-nigh impossible hurdle, given the requirement of two-thirds plus the P-5 (Article 108 of the Charter). Hence China faces no imminent danger that its veto power will be diluted through expansion of UNSC membership. Beijing has a vested interest, symbolically and strategically, in keeping the Security Council exactly as it is. Not only would an increase in the number of permanent members dilute its own high-profile role as a Group of One (G-1) and as the champion of the Third World, but any changes in the use of the veto power would also reduce Beijing's influence, since the veto power serves as a great-power status symbol as well as a highly useful and fungible instrument of renewable leverage in the service of China-specific interests.

The real question has to do with China's voting behaviour in the Security Council. There is little empirical evidence to support Segal's claim that 'Beijing almost always plays second fiddle to Moscow or even Paris in obstructing Western interests' or that China's global political power and influence are 'puny' compared to the West and Japan. Despite the ominous 'bull in the China shop' predictions during the exclusion pre-entry period, paralysis in the Security Council's decision-making process resulting from Chinese overkill with the veto has failed to materialize. As shown in Table 4.1, in more than three decades, from late 1971 to the end of 2002, China cast only four vetoes out of a total of 133 (3.0 per cent), as against 13 by the Soviet Union/Russia (9.7 per cent), 14 by France (10.5 per cent), 27 by the United Kingdom (20.3 per cent), and 75 by the United States (56.4 per cent). These figures exclude a 1981 Sino-US 'veto war' during closed-door deliberations on a recommendation on the appointment of the Secretary-General; those behind-the-scenes vetoes are not included in official UNSC documents.

Table 4.1 Voting in the Security Council, 1971–2002

Year	Total passed	Unanimous	Permanent members unanimous	Non-aligned unanimous	Total vetoes cast	Vetoes cast by permanent five
1971	6	2	2	6	4	SU = 2, UK = 1
1972	17	3	3	17	8	Cn = 2, UK = 4, US = 1, SU = 1
1973	20	7	7	19	4	US = 3, UK = 1
1974	22	11	11	17	4	F = 1, SU = 1, UK = 1, US = 1
1975	18	10	10	13	8	US = 6, F = 1, UK = 1
1976	18	9	9	12	9	US = 6, F = 2, UK = 1
1977	20	13	13	17	9	F = 3, UK = 3, US = 3
1978	21	7	7	21	0	
1979	18	3	3	17	2	SU = 2
1980	23	8	8	22	3	SU = 2, US = 1
1981	15	10	10	15	13	US = 5, F = 4, UK = 4
1982	29	21	21	28	9	US = 8, UK = 1
1983	17	10	12	15	3	US = 2, SU = 1
1984	14	7	8	12	3	US = 2, SU = 1
1985	21	16	16	21	9	US = 7, UK = 2
1986	13	10	10	13	12	US = 8, UK = 3, F = 1
1987	13	10	10	13	4	UK = 2, US = 2
1988	20	17	17	20	7	US = 6, UK = 1
1989	20	18	18	20	9	US = 5, F = 2, UK = 2
1990	37	29	36	29	2	US = 2
1991	42	36	40	36	0	
1992	74	64	65	67	0	
1993	93	85	87	89	1	Ru = 1
1994	77	65	70	67	1	Ru = 1
1995	66	60	60	66	1	US = 1
1996	57	50	50	57	0	
1997	54	50	50	53	3	US = 2, Cn = 1 (S/1997/18)
1998	73	69	69	73	0	
1999	65	57	58	62	1	Cn = 1 (S/1999/201)
2000	50	44	49	48	0	
2001	52	50	50	52	2	US = 2
2002	68	63	66	64	2	US = 2
1971–2002	1153	914	945	1081	133	China (Cn) = 4 (3.0%); USSR (SU)/Russia (Ru) = 13 (9.7%); France (F) = 14 (10.5%); United Kingdom (UK) = 27 (20.3%); United States (US) = 75 (56.4%)

Sources: Adapted from UN Docs S/PV.1599 (23 November 1971) to S/PV.4681 (20 December 2002).

The four Chinese vetoes have had little to do with playing second fiddle to Russia or France in obstructing or opposing 'Western interests'. The first two vetoes were cast in 1972 – one on the question of UN membership for Bangladesh and another on an amendment in regard to the Middle East. The Bangladesh veto was in effect a proxy veto cast on behalf of an ally (Pakistan), but two years later Beijing reversed itself, giving full and unqualified support for Bangladesh's UN membership. The second veto was cast along with the Soviet Union on an amendment to a three-Power draft resolution (S/10784) on the Middle East question. The impact of the second Chinese veto was substantially diluted by three facts:

1 it was a non-solo veto;
2 it was on an amendment rather than a draft resolution; and
3 the original draft resolution itself was vetoed by another permanent member (Kim, 1979: 206–208).

The third and fourth vetoes were cast in 1997 and 1999 on *sui generis* Taiwan-connected cases. The 1997 veto was on a draft resolution (S/1997/18) authorizing a small UN peacekeeping mission for Guatemala, vetoed because of that country's pro-Taiwan activities, but here again Beijing reversed itself, 11 days later allowing the Council to approve the United Nations Human Rights Verification Mission in Guatemala (MINUGUA). China's fourth veto was on a draft resolution (S/1999/201) to extend the mandate of the United Nations Preventive Deployment Force (UNPREDEP) in the former Yugoslavia Republic of Macedonia for a period of six months, as a punitive strike at Macedonia for establishing diplomatic relations with Taiwan in January 1999. None of the four Chinese vetoes had any paralysing consequences for the UNSC's decision-making process; none fits the case of playing second fiddle to Moscow or Paris; and none had much to do with obstructing or opposing 'Western interests', whatever that might mean.

In striking contrast, the United States stands at the opposite extreme, having cast 75 vetoes or 56.4 per cent of the total for the same period (1971–2002). Virtually all the American vetoes had to do with what Washington considered anti-Israel draft resolutions, or what the overwhelming majority of the UNSC membership saw as the expressed will of the world community on the brutalities of the Israeli government in the occupied territories. Although China's voting coincidence with the United States in the UN General Assembly has never exceeded 29.7 per cent (peak year of 1996), what is even more revealing is that the global/UN average of voting coincidence with the United States rose from 27.8 per cent in 1991 to 50.6 per cent in 1995 and then dropping down to 31.7 per cent in 2001. In 2002, Washington's serial unilateral pre-emptive strikes at the UNSC set off shock waves of anti-Americanism (more accurately, anti-Bushism) in the global community, including global human rights NGOs, turning the Segalese claim on its head – to wit, it was the United States, not China, opposing 'Western interests', in defence of its absolute sovereignty-cum-unilateralism and in support of Israel's colonialism in the occupied territories.

China has managed to exert considerable leverage, if not normative influence, in the decision-making process, not by hyperactive engagement or coalition-building leadership but by following an indeterminate strategy that has vacillated between tacit cooperation and calculated aloofness. Despite its 'principled opposition' to a wide range of issues in the Security Council, China has generally expressed this opposition in the form of 'non-participation in the vote' or 'abstention'. Given its longstanding assault on the veto as an expression of hegemonic behaviour, Beijing has made a concerted effort not to allow itself to be cornered into having no choice but to cast a solo veto.

In the post-Cold War era, however, 'abstention' has become in most cases a kind of normative veto, and an expression of 'principled opposition' without standing in the way of the majority will in the UNSC. From August 1990 to December 1999, for example, China cast no less than 41 abstentions as an expression of its principled opposition on such issues as the use of force, humanitarian intervention and the establishment of international criminal tribunals (Morphet, 2000: 161–162). Thus China is sometimes forced to affirm a resolution (as in the case of Resolution 827 on the international war crimes tribunal in Bosnia) which violates its most cherished principle of the non-violability of state sovereignty, with nothing more than the habit-driven ritualistic pronouncement of a 'principled position' (Thalakada, 1997: 94–95).

The most obvious explanation for such behaviour is the desire to retain maximum leverage as part of its indeterminate strategy of becoming all things to all nations on the many issues intruding upon the Security Council agenda. Like nuclear weapons, the real power of the veto lies not so much in its actual use as in the threat of its use or non-use. To abstain is to apply the Chinese code of conduct of being firm in principle but flexible in application, or to find a face-saving exit with a voice in those cases that pit China's *realpolitik* interests against *idealpolitik* normative concerns for China's international reputation. Of the P-5, as Barry O'Neill has argued, with some exaggeration, China is the most powerful member of the UNSC, because it holds its veto power from an extreme political position, standing alone (O'Neill, 1997: 75). Despite the habitual claim that support for and solidarity with the Third World is a basic principle in Chinese foreign policy, Beijing has emerged as perhaps the most independent actor in global group politics, a veritable Group of One.

In any event, the pattern that emerges with respect to China's voting behaviour in the Council, particularly regarding abstentions on Chapter

VII enforcement draft resolutions, is neither positive engagement nor obstruction, but situation-specific and self-serving pursuit of the maxi–mini strategy. As if to confirm Segal's claim that China has no soft power to leverage, there is growing angst among some liberal Chinese scholars that abstentions imply that China has no normative power or that China refuses to bear the responsibility as one of P-5 in global security politics. Pang Zhongying has publicly criticized China's excessive use of abstention as tantamount to abandoning China's responsibility – as compromising rather than enhancing China's identity as a responsible great power (Pang, 2002). At least two other International Relations (IR) scholars join Pang in indirect attacks on Chinese abstention by playing up the notion that China's great-power status as one of the P-5 requires nothing less than the corresponding responsibility and requirement of more proactive participation in UN peacekeeping operations (UNPKOs). Working positively in UNPKOs is not only China's responsibility as a great power, we are told, but also a requirement for China to join the global security mechanism (Wang, 1999; Tang Yongsheng, 2002).

With the demise of the Washington–Moscow–Beijing strategic triangle, however, China's responsible use of the veto power in the UNSC remains the only way that it can project its identity as a great power. This identity is willed yet conflicted, as Beijing is pulled in one direction by Third World states with whom it needs to build coalitions, and in another by those who are most powerful in the global system (Foot, 2001: 41). With the recent and unexpected revival of Taiwan's UN bid, the veto power has also been publicly touted as the powerful sword and impregnable shield that defend the integrity of the People's Republic as the only legitimate Chinese government in the world organization.

China's position on UNPKOs has evolved over the years in a dialectical situation-specific way, balancing its *realpolitik* interests with concerns for its international reputation as the champion of Third-World causes. During the pre-entry period as a whole (1949–1971), both ideology (in the form of the Maoist theory of just war) and experience (the trauma of the UN intervention in the Korean War) conditioned China's negative attitude toward UN peacekeeping activities. Once on the Security Council, China's position shifted and metamorphosed through three discernible stages:

1 principled opposition/non-participation (1971–1980);
2 support/non-participation (1981–1989); and
3 support with incremental and situation-specific participation (1990–present).

In December 1981, China voted for the first time for the extension of a UN peacekeeping force (UNFICYP, in Cyprus). In November 1989, in another shift, the Chinese government decided to dispatch five Chinese military observers to serve in the United Nations Truce Supervision Organization (UNTSO) in the Middle East, and 20 Chinese civilians to serve as members of the UN Transitional Assistance Group (UNTAG) to help monitor the independence process in Namibia (Liu, 1989).

China's creeping multilateralism is mirrored by Beijing's growing involvement in UNPKOs, particularly since the end of the Cold War (Wang, 1995). Recent Chinese writings and Chinese multilateral diplomacy show a greater willingness to evaluate UNPKOs according to their contributions to the 'conditions of peace and stability'. With a lesson from Kosovo (where China got badly burned) fresh in Chinese minds, Beijing opted for a more flexible conflict management approach in East Timor, where China for the first time contributed its civilian police in a UN peacekeeping and peacemaking role. One indicator of Beijing's incremental multilateralism with respect to UNPKOs has been the establishment and expansion of training programmes for peacekeepers – the Office of Peacekeeping in China, located under the General Staff Headquarters of the People's Liberation Army (PLA) (Gill and Reilly, 2000). Another sign of Beijing's greater commitment to UNPKOs is that in 1997 China decided in principle to take part in the UN's standby arrangements for UNPKOs, and in 2002 it actually joined the Class-A standby arrangements system.

China's active participation in two of the major UNPKOs – Cambodia and East Timor – suggests a range of situation-specific factors at work: geographical proximity, initial involvement with the authorization process in the Security Council, and host-nation consent (one of the two conditions for the first generation of UNPKOs). As long as these conditions are present, along with the absence of the Taiwan factor, Beijing's slow yet steady support for UNPKOs is likely to continue unabated in coming years. As if to showcase Beijing's growing interest and willingness in expanding its influence beyond the 'home region', China announced in February 2003 that it would send 218 'peacekeepers' from the PLA – 175 engineers and 43 medical personnel – to the Democratic Republic of the Congo in support of the United Nations Peacekeeping Mission (MONUC), thus more than doubling the number of its peacekeepers from 137 to 355 (RMRB, 2003). In an apparent victory for the Ministry of Foreign Affairs and more progressive elements in the PLA, Beijing was demonstrating its desire and willingness to boost its international role and reputation as a responsible great power.

China in the WTO-based global trade regime

Segal's claim that in terms of international trade and investment China 'is a seriously overrated power' – comparable to something less than Brazil – seems increasingly off the mark, as the economic data in Stuart Harris's chapter in this volume show. My chapter illustrates China's reactions to an increasingly globalized economic order, its revised understanding of its place in the global economy, and the influence that has accrued to China as a result of its enhanced economic power.

Nothing better illustrates China's stand on globalization and its willingness to embrace the norms of free trade than its protracted struggle to gain WTO entry. After nearly 15 years of often difficult negotiations, in late 2001 China finally became a member of the WTO under terms that gave in to longstanding Western demands for not only reducing tariff and non-tariff barriers but also opening long-closed sectors such as telecommunications, banking and insurance. Even before its official entry into the WTO, China's average tariff rate had declined from above 40 per cent in 1992 to just under 20 per cent in 1999. China agreed in its WTO accession to further reduce tariffs on industrial products to an average of 9.4 per cent and the average statutory tariff rate for agricultural products from 22 per cent to 15 per cent by January 2004 – far lower than nearly all developing countries. In a few important areas, China assumed obligations that exceed normal WTO standards – the so-called WTO-plus commitments (Lardy, 2002b: 2, 75). There is no denying that Beijing's determination to gain WTO entry at almost any price represents a big gamble in the history of China's engagement with the global community. Why then has Beijing taken unprecedented sovereignty-diluting steps to gain WTO entry?

While there is no simple answer to this, China's WTO entry nonetheless underscores the extent to which the forces of globalization have blurred the traditional divide between the international and the domestic, confronting China's leadership with an 'intermestic' challenge. What really convinced the Chinese leadership to proceed with the deal, despite or perhaps even because of mounting domestic opposition, was the commitment of Jiang Zemin and Zhu Rongji to globalization and a fundamental restructuring of Chinese industry. Politically, failure to reach an agreement would have left Jiang in a passive position with his domestic adversaries, including Li Peng. Jiang would have had a large and inefficient government-owned enterprise sector with no way to address its problems (Fewsmith, 2000: 273).

Indeed, Jiang and Zhu seem to have assigned to foreign trade, especially exports, an almost impossible multitasking social and economic mission: of alleviating the growing unemployment problem, increasing tax revenues and the state's foreign exchange reserves, fuelling steady economic growth, accelerating technology transfer, and above all enhancing the competitiveness and productivity of domestic enterprises. China's membership of the WTO is seen not only as providing one of the most important channels to participating in spontaneous economic globalization, but also as allowing Beijing more space to exert its influence on the management of economic globalization. The drive for status, not as a hegemonic or revisionist power but as a responsible great power, is made-to-order for mutual legitimation – China and the WTO need each other.

As revealed in Jiang Zemin's major speeches since 1997, the forces that most define China's national identity at the turn of the millennium are those associated with globalization. This shows the extent to which China has shifted from ideological or even nationalistic legitimation to performance-based legitimation. Such performance-based legitimation can be generated over the long term only through increased trade, foreign investment, and the more disciplined and rule-bound domestic economy that WTO membership is expected to bring about. Hence, China's embrace of the WTO-based global trade regime and norms of free trade has been largely a function of the Chinese Communist Party's determination to enhance domestic social and economic stability and regime legitimacy through export-driven economic development.

Judging from the first year of participation in the WTO, there is no evidence of revisionist behaviour by China, and no rejection in any serious manner of the dominant structures, rules and norms of the organization. Rather, Beijing appears to be in no rush to make a big splash, or, unlike India, any grandstanding to capture the high moral ground in the global trade regime. Neither is there any evidence of coalition-building leadership attempts, due in no small part to the nature of the WTO itself, with the established rules of entry and play, as well as the ineluctable fact that Beijing is still in the early stages of apprenticeship – trying hard to learn the ropes of the global trade regime. Besides, China's own complex and diverse economic interests, which are complementary with developed rather than developing countries, do not provide much room to be a revisionist or an obstructive player in terms of further liberalization on the Doha agenda. China is making every attempt to pursue and balance, in a cautious and consensus-seeking manner, multiple interests and goals related to the diversity of its economic interests, image goals and domestic political and social constraints (Pearson, 2002).

As in Putnam-like 'two-level games' (Putnam, 1988), China's WTO strategy is perhaps best understood as an ongoing negotiating process of choosing among competing policy options. Chinese central decision-makers, situated strategically between domestic and international politics, are constrained simultaneously by what the dominant WTO actors (i.e. the US and the EU) will accept, and what domestic constituencies will ratify. The major challenge is how or whether China's leadership is changing its domestic institutions fast or deep enough to become more 'compliant' with its WTO commitments. No doubt Beijing will exploit the loopholes in WTO rules to protect politically important economic constituencies at home. But this is no different in kind from the arbitrary use of anti-dumping rules by the US to protect important economic constituencies (e.g. the Bush administration's imposition of heavy tariffs on steel imports). However, China's primary compliance problem will not be a wilful disregard of WTO commitments by the central government, but rather the lack of capacity to implement its WTO commitments or non-compliance by hard-to-control provincial and local interests (Pearson, 2002; Johnston, 2003b).

Conclusion

Returning to Segal's question 'does China matter in world politics?', the answer seems at once obvious and somewhat paradoxical. Yes, China matters in world politics, albeit in varying degrees across time, and more in some issue areas than in others. According to the criteria and indicators spelled out above, the acceleration of Sino-UN linkages, with a steady increase in Chinese membership and participation in practically all the major global institutions, along with increasing Chinese accession to UN-sponsored multilateral treaties, has set in motion a process of mutual legitimation and empowerment between China and the global community as symbolized and structured by the United Nations and its affiliated institutions. On the one hand, no global institution can claim legitimacy and universality without the membership and participation of the world's largest country. On the other hand, because the UN is the most universal intergovernmental organization and the authoritative dispenser of international legitimation, its importance for China's quest for legitimacy and status remains undiminished. Indeed, as argued above, China's great-power status in the UNSC and its WTO membership have become the most important source and symbol of its great-power status.

As for China's participatory behaviour once inside global institutions, there is no evidence of any unsettling revisionist or norm-defying behaviour, except where sovereignty-bound Taiwan issues are involved. Despite some rigorous encounters in the global arms control and disarmament and human rights regimes in the early 1990s, China, unlike the United States, has yet to withdraw from any global institution that it has joined since 1971, and neither has it 'unsigned' any multilateral treaties, although there are still several outstanding multilateral treaties signed but left unratified. China's obstructive behaviour has become as rare as China's resort to veto in the Security Council, in no small part because Beijing's veto power – the anticipatory veto, as it were – serves as its trump card when needed. Once participating in global institutions, China has been acting for the most part as a system-maintainer, not a system-reformer or system-transforming revolutionary; it has played multiple games by following the established rules rather than by attempting to replace or repudiate them.

Thanks to the socialization effects and potential image costs, China has accepted by fits and starts the extant international norms and governing procedures of multilateral global regimes. Judging by the phenomenal growth of Chinese membership in international organizations (both IGOs and INGOs), its generally cooperative participatory behaviour, the emergence of epistemic communities at home, and a number of policy adjustments and shifts over such global issues as arms control and disarmament, UN peacekeeping, human rights, environmental protection and sustainable development, some Chinese global learning has occurred. The general pattern and direction of China's international behaviour has been a slow but steady movement from conflict to cooperation, albeit more in the global political economy than in global high politics. Post-Mao China has discovered that global institutions are, or can be made to be, empowering instruments in the service of newly redefined Chinese national interests. Herein lies the logic of China's maxi–mini diplomacy.

Since 1997, the concept of the responsibility of great powers has suddenly come to the fore, against the backdrop of those warning of the rising 'China threat'. The rise of China as a responsible large country in the international community can be considered one of the major changes in post-Cold War Chinese foreign policy (Zhang and Austin, 2001). China's growing globalism is all the more remarkable when viewed in a wider context: the historical backdrop of the tyrannies and grievances of the past, the abiding quest for national identity via civilizational autonomy and political and normative self-sufficiency, and America's creeping unilateralism during the Clinton administration turning into runaway unilateralism in the Bush administration. This is not to say that Chinese globalism is more important than Chinese nationalism, but only that the former is important in the service of the latter.

That said, there is no evidence of any concerted drive to exert coalition-building leadership at the global level. China is unlikely to exercise leadership in global politics in the near future, because regionalism takes precedence. China is still more of a regional power than a global power: its primary foreign-policy concerns and interests are more regional than global, and Chinese power and influence are concentrated in the Sinocentric Asia-Pacific region rather than in the world at large. In this, Segal seems to be more on target, with his unspoken premise that China matters more in East Asian regional politics than in global politics.

Perhaps the greatest challenge to China's leadership in the uncertain years ahead is how to prevent tomorrow's China from becoming yesterday's Soviet Union. In the early 1950s it was common to hear the rallying cry that China needed to start a tidal wave of learning from the Soviet Union so as to make today's Soviet Union tomorrow's China. Half a century later, many Chinese leaders and scholars have come to recognize the ineluctable historical (Toynbeean) truth that the degeneration of a large country or empire – such as the former Soviet Union and many Chinese dynasties – starts from the internal roots of ethnonational separatism, economic stagnation or political and social chaos, and they see the need to respond to the challenge of establishing a stable, orderly and healthy society as the top priority (Wang, 1999).

The paradox of China's drive for status as a responsible great power in the global community is that the more the centre devolves social and economic power to local and provincial authorities in order to concentrate on Asian regional security and sovereignty issues, the weaker will be its ability to comply with multilateral treaties. Equally significant in the longer term is a danger of domestic political backlash against China's WTO-plus commitments. China's emerging role in world politics therefore remains a major source of uncertainty in a turbulent post-Cold War world that is becoming increasingly integrated and fragmented. China is a major regional power but an incomplete great global power, with myriad world-class domestic problems. In the coming years, the way Beijing manages its economic reforms – especially in regard to state-owned enterprises, rising unemployment and social unrest, rampant corruption, widening inequality and ethnonational pressures from within – may be the decisive factor that will shape China's future as a complete great power. A weak and fragmenting China would be the worst of all possible scenarios, a disaster not only for China but also for peace and stability in the region and beyond.

5   China in the global economy

Stuart Harris[1]

Introduction

In this chapter, I discuss whether Gerry Segal's views on China's economic importance – a key component of his *Foreign Affairs* article – held when written and whether they still hold. Previously, Segal had largely confined himself to the political and strategic implications of a rising China. The more detailed consideration of economics in his article was therefore something of an exception.

Segal argued that 'China is a small market that matters relatively little to the world, especially outside Asia' (Segal, 1999: 25). Although in earlier exchanges with Gerry I argued against the China threat on the grounds that China would remain relatively unimportant for a considerable time, this was only partly on economic grounds. Segal was correct that the public debate had tended to overemphasize China's economic weight. Even so, at the time, his generalization was unduly dismissive. In part perhaps this reflected the influence of the 1997–1998 Asian economic crisis. Some of the pessimism then prevalent, especially in Europe, about the inability of Asia generally, and China in particular, to weather the crisis has abated. In any case, the economic argument now needs to be qualified. We now have a longer experience of China's management of its economy on which to base our evaluations.

Segal's conclusion that judgements of China's economic importance were based on its assumed potential remain largely true today but, while still often exaggerated, that potential is more evidently substantial and is being factored into both expectations and global economic decision-making. So China does now matter. Of course, although China's actual and potential importance is greater than Segal allowed, China's economic importance is still conditional on China continuing its reform process and its economic progress. Failure in those respects will give China an importance in much less welcome ways, creating political and social instability regionally, and inevitably globally. I would also note that China's own perceptions of that prospective economic importance reflect a greater recognition of its economic weaknesses than Segal acknowledged.

To answer the Segal question, 'does China matter?' I need to ask what determines whether a country 'matters'? Specifically, how does a country 'matter' in global economic terms? His article advanced a number of measures against which to judge China's importance: the proportion of world gross domestic product (GDP); income per head; inter-province trade within China; the proportion of world trade and of Asian trade; the share of US, European and Asian country exports; and the share of inward global and regional foreign direct investment (FDI). Segal concluded that Asia as a whole, apart from Japan, has little impact on the global economy, as illustrated by the Asian crisis, and that exaggerating China is part of exaggerating Asia.

Here, I address a number of the Segal criteria directly relevant to assessing China's global significance. There are, of course, other ways to consider China's economic importance – or whether China 'matters'. For example, will China's economy influence the global economy in providing either a locomotive or a drag on global economic activity? It was judged to have behaved responsibly during the Asian crisis by not devaluing its currency; how far will its actions in the future affect global currency movements, and how co-operative will it then be? Again, as some argue, does China's industrial development threaten living standards and jobs internationally?

A broader sense of China's economic importance is what it represents in terms of power and influence. Put simply, to what extent does China's economy enable it to influence others in directions that it wants them to go, or to avoid directions it opposes. This influence can be achieved, as with any country, basically by coercion, bribery or persuasion. Coercion is usually thought of in military terms, with economic strength as a critical basis for military strength, and this is an issue for some in the US, as I note later.

Economic coercion, however, including withdrawal of economic relationships, is an important potential weapon itself and a factor in Chinese thinking, with examples of its use in practice, as with its purchases of civil aircraft. I will ask how much freedom China has to coerce in an increasingly interdependent global economy. It is also relevant to ask not just about capabilities but about the use that China might make of its added power. That, however, is dealt with more extensively in other chapters.

China's economy

A country's share of global GDP is a traditional indicator of its overall economic weight. In 2000, on standard GDP measures, China was sixth in global rankings, after France but above Italy. (Adding Hong Kong and Macau puts it closer to, but still below, France.) Segal saw the sixth ranking of China in global GDP terms as indicating merely middle-power status. He noted that China's GDP was only 3.4 per cent (3.7 per cent in 2001) of global GDP, compared with the 31.2 per cent (32.5 per cent in 2001) of the United States. In a sense he was right. Yet Russia, ranking only seventeenth, is now effectively a member, as is Canada, of the G-8, purportedly comprising the major economic powers. And China is larger than both Canada and Russia on standard measures.

But there are analytical problems with the standard comparisons based on market exchange rates that are especially relevant to China's potential role in the global economy. For international comparisons, use is made increasingly of purchasing power parity (PPP) measures of GDP.[2] Segal acknowledged these measures, but negatively, referring to them as the 'now dubious purchasing power parity calculations'.

Since PPP measures are analytically important here, not just because of the global comparisons of GDP – I draw on them later in assessing China's potential – I need to detail what they represent. Standard comparisons of GDPs across countries convert national currency aggregates to a common currency – the US dollar exchange rate. Among the problems with this approach is that individual country exchange rates are affected differentially by various policy and other influences; moreover, major short-term swings occur in market-based exchange rate values, including that of the US dollar. Thus, such conversions can give an erratic picture, making it difficult to make valid comparisons of real product levels between countries.

Moreover, a large proportion of commercial exchanges which make up a country's GDP are not traded, and their prices may not follow – in the short to medium term – movements in the exchange rate. Thus the US dollar value of what the average Chinese can purchase in their own currency can mislead, especially by undervaluing their benefits from the cheaper labour-intensive non-traded sector. Consequently, for comparisons, economists increasingly use PPP measures, based on the cost of a basket of traded and non-traded goods and services across countries. This approach values the number of units of a country's currency required to buy the same quantity of comparable goods and services in the local market as one US dollar would buy in the US (Dowrick, 2002: 222; World Bank, 2003: 245).

In looking at a country's international purchasing power overall, its ability to service foreign debt or to import foreign military equipment, market or official exchange rates remain the relevant measures. Nevertheless, sufficient analytical work on, and using, PPP estimates has invalidated the Segal reference to them as 'dubious' for the comparative purposes to which he referred. PPP rates are generally accepted as superior for comparison purposes, especially where developing countries are involved. They are used extensively by the World Bank, the IMF and the OECD, and are regarded by the UN Statistical Commission as the appropriate basis for international comparisons of the economic size of countries and, on a per head basis, the economic well-being of their residents.

In the short to medium term, the differences can be large.[3] Notably, however, exchange-rate measures tend to undervalue systematically the GDPs of developing countries, including China. On a PPP basis, China's economy ranks second in the world after the United States – larger than Japan's economy. Its proportionate share of global GDP amounts to 11.2 per cent, compared with the 21.4 per cent for the US.

World Bank PPP data show some overvaluation of the exchange rates in some developed countries, and considerable undervaluation in many developing countries (World Bank, 2003: 234–235).[4] In the long run, market-exchange and PPP rates are likely to move towards convergence, and relatively fast-growing countries to experience real exchange-rate appreciations (Froot and Rogoff, 1995: 1648, 1683). If so, then this would raise their GDP values relative to those of developed countries beyond their growth rate in national money terms.

Garnaut (2002) demonstrated that, in the 1980s and 1990s, the GDPs of some rapidly growing Asian countries, converted at US dollar exchange rates, rose more rapidly relative to developed countries than differences in real growth rates would suggest. He notes, for example, that real income per head in Singapore rose from US$8,000 in 1985 to US$28,000 in 1996. The growth in GDP per head, in exchange-rate-based international comparisons, was well ahead of the real growth rate measured in national currency terms. The significance is that China may catch up with or surpass the GDPs of developed countries in US dollar terms more rapidly than national growth rate arithmetic would suggest.

Segal noted a disposition to mistrust the accuracy of China's growth rate statistics, arguing that official Chinese figures have exaggerated China's growth since the market reforms of 1978. There has been a considerable argument – inside as well as outside China – over what are the correct figures, to which a critical former Premier, Zhu Rongji, contributed. This was largely stimulated by the failure of the official figures to reflect the 1997–1998 downturn and the build-up of stocks of unwanted goods (Rawski, 2002b). Many observers judged that official figures could overestimate real growth by perhaps 1 or 2 per cent (Lardy, 1998: 9; Maddison, 1998: 155).

Rawski, a major critic of China's official growth data, notes that underreporting of the service and private sectors probably offsets over-reporting elsewhere, at least until 1997, and that the official figures from 1978 to 1997 may be about right. He had argued, however, that compared with official figures averaging 7.5 per cent for 1998–2001, the real figures are closer to half – or 3.8 per cent (Rawski, 2002a). Other evidence of greater growth than this in those years leads others, such as Lardy (2002b), to doubt this. A growing consensus suggests that the official figures may have a margin of error of a percentage point either way (*China Economic Quarterly*, 2003: 32). Overall, therefore, greater credibility now attaches to the official figures of average annual growth of 9.5 per cent from 1979–2001, with little doubt existing about what has clearly been substantial and sustained growth.

And Segal's other criteria? His dismissal of China's low income per head ranking noted that this was less than that of Papua New Guinea (PNG). This has changed; in 2001, income per head in China was significantly above that of PNG on conventional as well as PPP measures, closer to levels, for example, of the Philippines.[5] In any case, for present purposes, this measure is less significant in China's situation. While China remains a poor country despite its large economy, the size of China's population means that the government could collect taxes on a very much larger tax base if it wished.

China's economy has opened up significantly in the last two decades. It had reduced its trade barriers substantially well before it joined the WTO, and its membership is stimulating further liberalization. China's openness is usually indicated by the growing proportion that trade represents of China's GDP – exports amounting to some 22 per cent in 2002. Yet, these figures exaggerate the openness: on PPP measures of GDP, exports as a proportion of GDP constitute just under 6 per cent. This compares, on the same basis, with around 18 per cent for the UK, and 12 per cent for Japan. Comparable levels would not be expected, however, since this reflects a pattern common to large economies. Thus, on the same basis, trade is only between 7 and 8 per cent of GDP for the US.

Certainly, in the trade and investment field, China's global importance has grown. China is already a major trading nation, ranking sixth in 2002 as a global exporter, just behind the UK. China's trade, not including Hong Kong, in that year represented 4.7 per cent of global trade, compared with 2 per cent only 10 years earlier (over 7 per cent if Hong Kong is included). Its trade with Asia exceeds that outside the region, but the US is its major export market and the EU its third major market; Japan, however, remains its major trading partner. Although still small in services trade, it increased its share of global service trade exports more than threefold in 10 years to 2.3 per cent in 2001. Overall, in recent years, China's exports and imports have grown more rapidly than the global average, and are expected to continue to do so.

Segal set trade with the major trading countries as one of his criteria. Although growing, China's trade with the major traders is not especially substantial. Imports by China account for less than 3 per cent of US merchandise exports, but the US takes about a third of China's exports (as a share of US imports it now accounts for some 9 per cent as against 3 per cent in 1990). If Hong Kong exports (substantially from China) were included, this would add another 5.8 per cent to the share of US imports from China/Hong Kong. China is a smaller trader with the EU. Only 1.2 per cent of EU exports go to China (excluding intra-EU trade it rises to 5.5 per cent). The role of foreign enterprises in generating exports has been significant. Foreign invested firms now account for over 50 per cent of China's exports and, since US firms are major long-term investors in China, a significant share of Chinese exports to the US comes from US companies.

The importance of bilateral trading relationships, however, is not just the trade's value, but includes the dependency involved or how far other import sources or market outlets can be substituted. For China, the main areas of potential trade dependency include raw materials, such as iron and steel, grains, fibres and energy. In the first three, trade dependency is unlikely to be significant, since markets are open and the materials substitutable, if at some cost. This is also largely true for energy as well, but energy has some special characteristics, as discussed below. China is dependent upon access to markets for its exports of manufactured goods, and some vulnerability exists, given its substantial dependence on US markets.

China's ability to coerce economically is also limited, except on a symbolic 'punishment' basis to demonstrate displeasure. That might be significant for small countries. It is unlikely to be so for major countries. Other markets would be available for most exports from the US or Europe to China, and the issue unimportant unless private interests involved are politically influential. With China's substantial dependence on the US market, finding alternative markets for that volume of exports would be difficult and costly. Private interests, however, have in the past worked to protect China's exports to the United States from undue punitive action.

China has become a significant factor in the international capital market. Attention is normally directed to inward FDI movements, which in recent years have usually exceeded $40 billion annually. In 2002, with inward FDI around $50 billion, China became the largest recipient of global FDI, passing for the first time the US – normally the largest recipient. This, however, was largely because of a major dip in inward investment in the US. In addition, 'round tripping': Chinese domestic firms exporting and then importing investment capital to gain from preferred tax and intellectual property protection treatment for foreign firms, accounts for an element of the Chinese figures, with estimates ranging between 5 and 20 per cent. Although FDI is mostly from non-Japan Asian countries, part of Hong Kong's investment is from US and European affiliates in Hong Kong. Overall, however, the increased inflow reflected other factors, including expectations of economic opportunities due to improved regulatory frameworks flowing from China's WTO membership and inflows from Japanese, Hong Kong, Taiwanese and, to a degree, South Korean firms relocating to China to reduce costs. (See also Breslin, this volume, Chapter 8.)

Since the 1990s, Chinese entities – state-owned enterprises (SOEs), but also Chinese cities, provincial governments, government departments and other state agencies – have become significant fundraisers on overseas capital markets, commonly through international investment banks in Hong Kong. A 2002 estimate suggests that some US$40 billion was raised in international markets from 1993 to 2000, around $21 billion of it in 2000, and much of it in the US. A further US$20 billion was raised in US dollar-denominated international bond holdings (China Security Review Commission, 2002). Further sizeable sums have come from governmental sovereign bond raisings and raisings by the remaining International Trade and Investment Corporations (ITICs).

China has also become a substantial foreign direct investor – accounting by 1995, for around 2 per cent of global capital exports (World Bank, 1997: 26). As an outlet for its large foreign-exchange reserves, it is the second largest foreign holder of US Treasury Bonds after Japan, and a major purchaser of US government-backed mortgage finance bonds. It is also an important purchaser of government securities in London, continental Europe and Tokyo.

In trade, whether China matters is often seen from a different perspective. For major products China may still be largely a price taker rather than a price maker. China's extra supply of consumer goods on international markets does, however, have some downward effect on prices of labour-intensive products. Among other things, this helps to counter the expected upward pressure on China's exchange rate.

While adversely affecting competitors, this price effect raises the living standards of those consuming those products. For example, with China now dominant in the global bicycle market (supplying over 60 per cent of the global market), average prices have fallen substantially. This benefits bicycle purchasers, but there has been a geographic redistribution of bicycle production. Consequently, there are those, particularly in the US among industry lobbyists and leading politicians, who argue that China matters, but negatively through its adverse effect on employment in developed countries.

As with bicycle producers in Western Europe who have been given protection against Chinese competition, but more generally, they reflect widely held fears that China's low-cost exports threaten living standards and jobs in developed economies. The fear has been reflected, for example, in the abnormal safeguard measures in the US WTO settlement with China, and in US and French arguments pursuing labour standards in international trade negotiations.

Production relocation effects in developed countries often have large local effects but are small at the macroeconomic level. For example, as noted earlier, China's total exports are a small share of total US imports (9 per cent) and its imports are a small share of total US GDP (7 per cent); imports from China are therefore only some 0.6 per cent of US GDP. In a growing world and domestic US economy, the necessary adjustments are manageable by those able to adjust. In a sluggish world economy, the adjustments required are likely to be more severe and difficult for those slow to adjust. Nevertheless, since, like other countries, China exports essentially in order to import, the more it exports the more it can provide markets for imports that create employment in exporting countries.

More generally, as China's productive efficiency moves closer to that of developed economies, it contributes to increased global productivity and global real income, which will translate into greater spending and increased employment. Gains from trading between China and the rest of the world increase the living standards of China and its trading partners, for the former through higher incomes, and, in the latter case, more substantially through increased consumer purchasing power. It is not that employment elsewhere is not affected by China's exports of labour-intensive products, but that the overall magnitude of the effect is small, with larger effects due to other changes, notably technological change.

There could be more substance in principle in the concerns about 'massive' flows of productive capital from developed countries to emerging countries, and China in particular. Capital exported from developed countries is capital not invested in those countries, putting downward pressure on their real incomes. Krugman (1994) has shown, however, that in practice the domestic impact of shifting productive capital from developed countries to emerging countries is small. Developed country capital exports to China are not quantitatively large relative to capital investments made domestically in capital-exporting countries. Moreover, China's substantial purchases of bonds from the US and some other developed countries helps finance their trade and budget deficits.

A second argument doubts the world's capacity to absorb rapid increases in production of goods arising from 'the manic logic of capitalism' (Greider, 1997), to which the industrial emergence of the developing world, and notably China, contributes. This is a new variant of an old fear of production outrunning demand or 'global glut' (Broad and Cavanagh, 1988) but, as illustrated by the employment sharing efforts in France under Prime Minister Jospin in the late 1990s, is as present in European politics as in the US.

Yet, compared with the 1930s and Keynesian concerns at oversaving and underconsumption, many countries, including the US, now worry more about undersaving and overconsumption. While China's growth adds to global productive capacity in labour-intensive products, at present

China contributes only a relatively small proportion of the global supply of the goods it exports. That it will add to that supply more substantively in the future seems probable, given its entry into the WTO – helped, for textiles and clothing, by the eventual removal of quotas under the Multifibres Arrangement. With better macroeconomic policies than in the 1930s, however, the confidence that those gaining increased incomes in China from exports will spend them is more justified.

China's export expansion will not be limited to labour-intensive products. As well as increasing exports of consumer durables, China is already the third largest exporter of electronic equipment, and is widely expected to become the major exporter of information technology products within a few years. These are commonly dual-use products, however, with strategic implications that some will see as increasingly problematic.

These projected developments depend upon an international willingness to accept growing exports from China. This is particularly relevant for the US, where China's direct trade surplus remains substantial, although less so if Hong Kong is included. Moreover, what such a bilateral trade balance means in a globalized world is increasingly unclear, since US firms are major participants in exports to the US. Overall, however, China has maintained a reasonable balance between export and import growth. Its trade surplus is gradually diminishing, and it provides a substantially growing market for those exporting to it. The UN economic report for 2003 notes that, given a global economy showing only modest growth overall, China's domestic demand provided some stimulus to exports from other countries, but particularly in East Asia (United Nations, 2003).

Nevertheless, China is not yet a major engine of global growth in general, although, in 2002, 15 per cent of global economic growth and 60 per cent of global export growth came from China. Although China's direct economic impact is greater in the Asian region than in the global economy, it does have a global impact in specific areas. Particularly important is its growing demand for energy. China is a major consumer of primary energy – second only to the United States. Although a sizeable producer of oil – not far behind Iran – its growing energy demand has increasingly required oil and gas imports. It is extending its oil interests overseas, investing not just in the Middle East (notably Iran and Oman), but in over 20 countries outside the Middle East, including in Africa (Sudan), in the Western Hemisphere (Venezuela) and in Central Asia (Kazakhstan) and several developed countries, including the US.

From some 70 million tonnes of net imports in 2002, estimates of future oil import needs range widely from 130 million tonnes to nearly 400 million tonnes by 2020.[6] This could account for between 5 and 15 per cent of world oil trade, from its present 4 per cent. By 2030 China's oil imports, according to IEA's Executive Director, 'will equal the imports of the United States today . . .' (IEA, 2002), and China will become a strategic buyer on world markets. That will make energy sourcing, diversification and safety of its energy transport links even more influential and constraining on its foreign policy than it is already, given the vulnerability that import dependence implies.

China is a major coal exporter, second after Australia, but, more importantly, it is the second largest consumer of coal after the US. Its domestic use of coal makes it central to the global warming debate, and negotiations around the Kyoto Protocol processes, since it provides around 10 per cent of global carbon dioxide emissions. World Bank (1997) estimates of China's consumption of energy per unit of output (energy intensity) put it at three to 10 times that of the major industrial countries. Again, the qualifying perspective of the PPP measures is important here: on a PPP basis, Maddison (1998: 155) estimated China's energy intensity as higher than that of Germany and Japan, but around US and Australian levels, and greatly below that of Russia.

China's future global impact

How far China will matter in economic terms in the future will depend upon the extent to which China can maintain its economic growth ahead of the major developed economies. Economic and employment growth is also critical to China's internal stability. Officially, China aims to double its GDP over 10 years, from 2000 to 2010, implying average annual growth rates of between 7 and 8 per cent. Projections of China's economic growth range around these figures. World Bank estimates have ranged upwards from 6.5 per cent – while others believe higher rates are possible.

In the trade field, the World Bank estimated that by 2020, China would be the second-largest world trader, accounting for some 10 per cent of world exports, just behind the US (World Bank, 1997: 31). If its recent trade growth is sustained, it will certainly become an important influence on overall world trade growth.

There is widely held optimism that these economic growth and trade rates, or rates near to them, are achievable. Yet others have less confidence, perhaps most notably Gordon Chang (2001b). The main doubts tend to centre on the sources of China's economic growth; questions about currency reform; China's ability to continue to attract high levels of FDI; the financial management of a banking system with large non-performing loans; loss-making state-owned enterprises (SOEs); and large government debts. Also in question is China's political ability to absorb changes implied in China's reform processes, including SOE reform; its WTO commitments and their consequences; and income imbalances between coastal and inner provinces, to which agriculture reform is a major contributor.

How it manages these issues will largely determine how, and how far, China will 'matter' in the future, so I look briefly at each in turn.

Sources of China's growth

I noted earlier the ongoing debate about China's economic growth rate. Economists question whether the sources of China's growth have been simply short-term quantitative factors – more labour and capital – or reflect more sustainable qualitative changes – more efficient combinations of labour and capital. Some argue that growth came predominantly from quantitative increases in resources – capital and previously underemployed labour, implying that these were largely one-time gains and not a basis for sustained long-term growth. This argument is discussed in Smith (1997: 260–266); like other studies she showed that quality improvements, through market reforms and technological catch-up, were increasing overall productivity. Hu and Khan (1997), for example, argue that productivity growth accounted for nearly half China's growth. Scope for further growth through greater efficiency is still large with further reform, a continuing inflow of foreign technology and further opening of the economy to international competition.

One question is whether China will continue to benefit from two financial pluses – the substantial inflow of foreign capital and high domestic personal saving. Much of China's foreign capital inflow comes through FDI, although China has borrowed substantially from international institutions. Its ability to continue to attract large inflows of FDI depends upon domestic political stability and economic policies that attract foreign investors.

FDI was critical to China's past growth in supplying capital, in stimulating exports, and in providing technology transfer and entrepreneurial skills. Yet, although the inflow is large, it represents, in domestic terms, only some 10–15 per cent of gross capital formation. It was central to China's economic growth, however, when labour-intensive exports were a major stimulus to growth.

Initially, foreign companies had the advantage of access to funding and protection of intellectual property unavailable to domestic Chinese producers. FDI at that stage, moreover, was largely by small companies, mainly from non-Japan Asia, seeking to benefit from China's cheap labour for export, but not offering transfers of advanced technologies. In that role, FDI will be less critical in the future, given the increased competitiveness of China's domestic producers and their growing importance in its exports.

Changes have benefited domestic producers as reforms have developed, and particularly after 1997 (Huang, 2003). Meanwhile, larger European and Japanese companies have become more important investors, and technology transfer, if still limited, has increased. FDI will remain important to China now, therefore, through its contribution to China's overall productivity growth. The evidence suggests no early diminution in foreign investor interest in China, although one investment motivation noted earlier, WTO entry, has a once-only character.

Like FDI, maintenance of high domestic savings rates – the major source of China's investment capital – depends in part at least on China's domestic policies and reforms.

Currency reform

It reflects China's growing importance in the trade and capital markets that its exchange-rate policy is increasingly scrutinized by trading partners and competitors at global as well as regional levels (*Business Times* Online, 2003). Because of its competitive position in international markets, a belief is emerging that its exchange-rate influences significantly currency markets, notably US dollar and Japanese yen rates – disadvantaging those countries.

China's exchange rate is becoming more important in international currency markets. Yet, the Chinese yuan, tied to the US dollar, follows the dollar up and down. Periodically, it will be undervalued against other currencies as it was in 2002–2003 following the weaker dollar, and be marginally undervalued against the dollar itself. Yet, as recently as the 1997–1998 Asian economic crisis, China was credited with stabilizing the turbulent regional currency situation by not devaluing the yuan.

Arguments abound about the merits of China's maintaining a stable exchange rate. They include suggestions, usually by interested parties, that not only is it deflationary but that China deliberately manipulates an undervalued currency for competitive purposes. As noted earlier, some deflationary effect undoubtedly results from the lower prices of China's more competitive exports, while its purchase of foreign securities provides some counter to upward exchange-rate pressures. In the long run, the yuan is likely to appreciate in line with productivity growth. Garnaut's argument that the market and PPP rate will converge will probably hold eventually. In the short and medium run, however, that tendency could be outweighed by other domestic and international influences including further trade liberalization. While China's exchange rate already matters, for some time it is unlikely to matter sufficiently for any manipulation to be effective.

Meanwhile, the yuan is only fully convertible on current account, and is unlikely to be made convertible for capital transactions and to be floated until drastic reform to China's banking system and other financial institutions has been effected.

Domestic financial management and the banking system

While acknowledging China's growth potential, its capacity to sustain sufficient growth for domestic stability depends upon its success in managing effectively its full range of macroeconomic policies. So far, despite occasional missteps, it has been reasonably successful in its economic and financial management. Managing a soft landing after inflation flared in the late 1980s–early 1990s was an important achievement, as were the elimination of the dual exchange-rate system in 1994 and the relatively stable exchange-rate system maintained since then, and the exclusion of the military from most of its business interests. It has also had some, if incomplete, success in reforming the banking system, in reducing its SOE problem, in dealing with corruption and smuggling, and in reforming the taxation system.

Concerns have been expressed about China's debt problems. As already observed, capital inflow other than FDI has been sizeable, but the related debt burden does not represent a particular problem. China's outstanding official international debt amounted to about 11 per cent of GDP in 2000. The debt is basically long term, and China has massive foreign-exchange reserves.

Domestically, however, China has problems over the level of domestic government debt and of banking sector non-performing loans (NPLs). The official 16 per cent of GDP figure, if correct, would not raise undue concern. China has sustained domestic growth through deficit financing for a number of years, however, and that is expected to continue to absorb unemployment. Continued use of deficit financing to support China's expansionary fiscal policy could provide future difficulties. Moreover, other estimates of government debt, as in *The Economist* (2002), put it much higher, arguing that debt calculations should include the state-owned banking system's NPLs.

Estimates of the banking sector NPLs themselves vary, ranging from the official figure of around 25 per cent to over 50 per cent. Since the major banks are state owned, the NPLs are a contingent government liability. China's central bank accepts that NPLs and government contingent liabilities through state guarantees to banks amount to some 60 per cent of China's GDP. NPLs seem to be diminishing only slowly in the face of government reform efforts. Although an important management problem, given the government's ability to raise funds by selling government assets (including shares in the profitable among its SOEs), however, it is not ultimately a problem that could bring the system down (Lin, 2003: 91).

Normally, however, such banking-sector uncertainty would be expected to discourage high levels of private saving through the banking system. Expectations of government backing and limited alternatives to the banks as a depository of savings make this improbable in China. The benefit that China gains from its high level of personal savings is likely to continue. Every new loan to a loss-making enterprise crowds out potential good investments elsewhere. NPLs reflect a non-productive use of the capital involved by banks through lending to unprofitable SOEs, while the profitable and potentially employment-absorbing private sector still has difficulty obtaining credit. Gradual entry of foreign banks under China's WTO commitments will increase the pressure on local banks to compete effectively, but also on the government to offer them support if they cannot do so.

State-owned enterprises

The banking sector's problem of loans to non-performing SOEs arose substantially following attempted SOE reforms in the 1980s and early 1990s. Direct government financing of SOEs was replaced by bank loans, in a bid to enable them to operate and survive in the competitive environment of an increasingly marketized economy. This proved ineffective, for various economic and political reasons. Recent reforms have relieved SOEs of the burden of redundant employees and allowed changes to SOE ownership structures, including privatizing the smaller among them, making up about 80 per cent of the total number. These reforms appear to have been more effective (Garnaut *et al.*, 2001: 16; Wang Xiaolu, 2002). The SOEs now account for well under one-third of gross industrial output, compared with around three-quarters in 1980. Nevertheless, despite major labour lay-offs, SOE employment remains well above its industrial output share, as does the SOE share of total investment – reflecting a continued inefficient use of resources.

SOE profitability has increased due in part to extraneous factors – falling interest rates, rising oil prices for the oil enterprises and bad debt write-offs – but ownership structure and management reforms have also increased efficiency. Despite profit increases, with its high shares of resources and rates of return well below the non-state sector, the state-owned sector remains a drag on China's economic growth. The murky ties between the party, state, provincial governments and the SOEs slow reform and still help to channel bank credit to the loss-making among them. Despite significant improvement, therefore, without further structural reform in the state-ownership sector, scope for increased productivity and exports will be diminished.

Political support for reform

China is undergoing a massive industrial revolution, and its dynamics create considerable political and social stresses in China, as historically such dynamics have in other countries. Many demonstrations have been reported in northern and western provinces in particular, where unemployment due to SOE and other reforms is relatively severe. The reform process and failures of governance associated with corruption, unemployment and falling incomes in rural areas could be politically destabilizing unless adequately addressed by China's government. So, too, could accommodating pressures for 'democratization'.

Income inequality has continued to increase, even though in most years all incomes have risen (Wang *et al.*, 2002). Several factors contribute to the growing inequality. Essentially, China is condensing its industrial revolution into a historically remarkably short period. Moreover, some inequality is necessary to encourage labour movement from the interior to the coastal economy to meet the latter's long-term labour needs and to facilitate productivity growth through modernization in China's agriculture. Too great an income discrepancy creates social problems, however, particularly if – rather than arising from differential rates of income growth – it reflects absolute falls in real incomes in the interior, as has been the case in some provinces in recent years. Efforts to limit this problem continue. Considerable state infrastructure investment has been directed to the inner provinces; around 20 per cent of China's FDI has been going to the interior regions. This constitutes some 10 per cent of the interior economy, paralleling experience in other countries, notably the US (Huang, 2003).

A more comprehensive welfare system is an accepted need. Those receiving social security rose to over 12 million in 2002, but this is still small compared with the urban unemployed estimated at over 40 million (Wang *et al.*, 2002). Moreover, the pension system is in financial difficulties, and together with subsistence payments to the unemployed, constitutes an increasing claim on current budget expenditures

Conclusion

Segal's broad conclusion was that China's small market mattered little to the world. That conclusion now needs substantial qualification. China's vast population and size give it the basis for a major global political presence; its geographic spread – 14 land borders and a number of sea borders – ensures that its economic presence is widely felt globally as well as regionally; in addition, it is a relatively important economic partner of the US and other major powers outside of Asia. Continuation of China's growth at high rates of between 6 and 8 per cent in, say, the next two decades, is at least a plausible prognosis.

Consequently, while not yet a major engine of global growth, China does matter – not just regionally but globally – in economic terms. The more complex question is: how much does it matter? There are no readily applicable criteria, and judgements differ according to the starting perspective. Certainly, as Segal said, China is still only a middle power. But attitudes towards a middle power that will remain a middle power differ substantially from one likely to become a great power in economic terms. Few doubt China's potential to become a great power – even if it faces 'a long and winding road'. Perhaps as critical in determining how China is perceived and responded to, and despite doubts expressed by some commentators, China's leaders have shown a capacity to deal effectively enough with its internal problems to progress rapidly and at the same time to maintain stability. This gives it an advantage over Japan.

China's population will become substantially better off, but for some time to come will remain relatively poor. Consumer income will grow, however, and consumption will grow with it, further enlarging China's market. China's participation in the global capital market, while still relatively small, is growing in importance, politically as well as economically; and so is its increasing involvement in the global energy market.

Of the economic impacts of China's continuing economic growth, two seem to gain considerable attention: its role *vis-à-vis* global competitors, and the international market's ability to absorb China's increased production. Even though the former is inevitable, but not quantitatively large, it may still matter politically and lead to more disputes over China's exports in major markets.

For the latter, while China's development will increase global productive capacity, global incomes will also increase. While demand will increase along with supply, the location of distribution will change, with impacts outside East Asia likely on producers in countries such as India and Mexico. That the quality of China's exports is likely to continue to rise, as China's export structure moves towards dual-use electronic goods and machinery, will give rise at times to strategic issues and concerns.

For some US Congress members and some senior academics (Mearsheimer, 2001), fear of China's economic growth potential already warrants counter-action by the US. The hurdles that activists are likely to succeed in placing in China's way, however, are probably less important than the hurdles China faces domestically to maintain its economic development.

China's growth will require massive infrastructure investments in transport, power, water, urban systems, telecoms, and desertification and environmental controls. Its energy demands, and growing energy import needs, also require major foreign and domestic investments. And its needs to provide enhanced employment opportunities are great.

China has shown a capacity to surmount many of its major domestic challenges while maintaining reasonable budget disciplines. Further challenges, such as the essential reform of the financial system and the reform of SOEs are being addressed – if less effectively. Given the further reforms still needed, major problems of social discontent and control could emerge beyond those already being experienced. More basic requirements include effective management of crises such as AIDS and SARS. They also include no significant internal or external conflict. Conflict is more likely with a weak and unstable China rather than a strong China (Bobbitt, 2002: 781).

China's emergence as a major economic power participating fully in the working of international economic institutions already influences the global economic system. But China has been participating in the international institutions very much as a status quo country (see Kim, this volume) and, while not without qualifications, with a manifest national interest in supporting the fundamentals of the existing economic system. In assessing whether China matters, it is not enough simply to judge it on its activities and performance to date. It is worth also considering how much this contributor to regional stability and global growth could become a major global problem if it behaved in a destabilizing fashion.

Ultimately, therefore, while Gerry's injunction not to overemphasize China's importance remains useful, his article's conclusion that, in effect, China could be largely ignored, no longer holds in economic terms. China is no longer peripheral economically, and although far from the dominant giant often argued or feared, it does matter, and its concerns and interests do have to be taken into account. Moreover, as a rising power, where it will be in the future rather than where it is today is what influences policy thinking in most countries. For most governments, China is a country that matters not just regionally, but also at the global level.

Notes

1   Comments on an earlier draft from Ross Garnaut and the editors are gratefully acknowledged.
2   The World Bank's PPP measures are obtained by converting gross domestic product using conversion factors provided by the International Comparisons Programme – a joint effort of the World Bank and the UN regional economic commissions.
3   PPP-based comparisons are themselves not without problems of data, including an equivalent of the index number problem. Present calculation methods also tend to overstate the differences between market and PPP exchange-rate-based figures for developing countries, including China, but not enough to invalidate their use and general conclusions drawn from them (Dowrick, 2002).
4   PPP-based estimates do reflect differences in developed countries; in the case of Japan, for example, in 2001, GDP on a PPP basis was over 20 per cent less than that based on market exchange rates, presumably reflecting particularly the high price of non-traded goods in Japan.
5   For 2001, income per head for China was $890 (or $4,260 in PPP terms); for Papua New Guinea it was $580 (or $2,150).
6   The higher figure is an IEA's estimate (IEA, 2000: 199); the lower is an official Chinese figure.

6 China in East Asian and world culture

David S. G. Goodman

Despite the comment that China is 'overrated as ... a source of ideas', culture is not something that Gerry Segal explored in any depth in his article on 'Does China Matter?'. That article was of course not centrally concerned with either China's cultural interaction with the rest of the world, or even the politics of that interaction, but was primarily an argument cautioning other governments and government agencies about the need to ensure some perspective in dealing with the government of the People's Republic of China (PRC). All the same, to that end Segal's article stated that 'China does not ... matter in terms of global culture.' Specifically it argued that China has had limited cultural reach not only compared to 'the dominant West' but also in comparison to Japan; that during the last 20 years the government of the PRC has spent more effort in resisting and controlling the domestic impact of external cultural influences than in attempting to create any specific external influence of its own; and that China does not play as great a role for Chinese around the world as does India for the Indians.

Not all these arguments confront established orthodoxy by any means. During the last 20 years the PRC has retreated from its role as a purveyor of world revolution and has devoted considerable effort to the domestic management of 'Western' cultural manifestations. At the same time, the argument about the relative strengths of Chinese and Japanese influence and authority outside their borders is clearly more contested. Japan, it is true, has had considerable impact in East and Southeast Asia during the twentieth century, both because of its colonial programme in the 1930s and its later economic development programme. However, China has an even older, and longer sustained cultural influence in the region that might still be said to run deep. On the surface at least, Segal's argument about the 'Overseas Chinese' would seem to be even more necessarily contested. It is often asserted that the Chinese outside the PRC constitute a significant social, economic and even political force in their own right; and moreover that there is considerable potential for these 'Overseas Chinese' to ally with the PRC to create a new future Chinese superpower.

In considering each of these three arguments, this chapter has two aims. The first is to examine in greater detail the points being made by Segal. The second is to attempt to go beyond the original position about how the rest of the world should approach its engagement with the government of the PRC to consider Chinese culture's wider interactions with the external world. In undertaking this analysis it draws on and highlights additional perspectives on China's cultural influence.

Segal's article is concerned primarily with the international politics of the government of the PRC as seen from the Atlantic Community, for whom it was written. It has been absolutely the norm for Chinese governments during the last hundred years to equate Chinese society with the Chinese state, specific governments and even political parties, and this equation is reflected in Segal's article (Fitzgerald, 1994). All the same it is clearly possible to distinguish between the party-state of the PRC as a source of cultural activity, and Chinese society more generally. In similarly deconstructive mood, China's cultural influence in Europe and North America is almost certain to be different from its influence in East and Southeast Asia, and countries where a significant proportion of the population may be Chinese. It is important to ask 'to whom' China matters as a source of cultural influence, as well as to what extent.

Essentially this chapter highlights two crucial aspects of China's cultural politics for the future, which do not always pull in the same direction. The first is the role of East and Southeast Asia in China's worldview. East and Southeast Asia are China's principal region of influence, in cultural terms no less than in economics and politics. Moreover, there is a clear, if sometimes less tangible relationship between, on the one hand, any PRC claims to world leadership and its role in its immediate region, and, on the other, China's claims to leadership of East and Southeast Asia and the influences of Chinese culture. The second is the contradiction between the cultural goals of the government of the PRC and the current political system's ability to deliver progress towards those goals. As in economics and politics, the Chinese Communist Party (CCP) wants to see China acknowledged as a cultural superpower. At the same time, the CCP's role in the determination of cultural production makes this extremely unlikely: there is often an inherent contradiction between narrow political nationalism and the wider appreciation of Chinese culture.

China as a world culture

Segal's contention that China has limited influence and authority, not only by comparison with Europe and Atlantic cultures, but also in comparison with Japan, seems puzzling if not downright perverse. There is of course no gainsaying the universal impact of American culture, as Coca Cola, McDonalds, MTV, TV soap operas and Hollywood bear more than adequate witness. European influences are also apparent not only in the widespread acceptance of democratic liberalism, nationalism and capitalism, but also in the appreciation of food and wine, music and literature, especially as standards of living and real disposable incomes rise.

All the same, in his haste to argue, Segal did not interrogate the complexity of the 'global culture' that he criticized China for having failed to engage. The description of 'global culture' can of course be limited to an Atlantic eye's view of the spread of the influence of the United States. Alternatively, global culture might be seen in more pluralistic perspectives, recognizing the development of other (if less dominant) cultural influences on the world as a whole. There are after all manifestations of Chinese culture – traditional medicine and exercise regimes, literature and films, not to mention the variety and impact of Chinese cuisine – to be found almost universally. Moreover, some cultures have greater influence in some countries and on some parts of the world than others. This wider appreciation of global culture would seem a particularly wise strategy in this case, given that in the long term China is always more likely, not least for linguistic reasons and the relatively greater ease of communications, to have greater impact within East and Southeast Asia.

While there is no denying the twentieth-century impact of Japan on East and Southeast Asia, first through its colonial expansion and then later since the 1950s through the scale and extent of its economic activities, Chinese culture seems more certainly to be at the heart of regional activities in a number of ways. Confucianism or at least Confucian traditions are often regarded not only as the major characteristic of China but also of East Asia, and some parts of Southeast Asia – especially those where Chinese migration has been considerable. Difficult as it is to identify and generalize about culture, where Japanese culture is usually regarded as inward looking and only interested in Japan itself, not least by the Japanese themselves (Hendry, 1987) China sees itself fundamentally as a world culture.

Segal's comments about the lack of influence of Chinese culture certainly stand in stark contrast to received wisdom. Even when acknowledging the limits to the generalization, almost every other commentator since Fairbank has long identified East Asia in terms of the common elements of Chinese cultural heritage (Fairbank *et al.*, 1960). Indeed, for many, the apparent economic success of the early 1990s was at least in part attributable to this background. In its triumphalist report of 1993, the World Bank hailed the 'economic miracle' of an East Asian development characterized by 'rapid growth and decreasing inequality' (World Bank, 1993). While the World Bank did not explicitly mention the importance of cultural factors, other commentators making similar arguments and later building on the World Bank Report quite explicitly emphasized the role of Confucianism in the emergence of regional economic success

(Levy, 1992: 15). Although there was some variability in the Confucianism identified in this way, common characteristics tended to include a stress on social order and the family.

Imperial China was certainly the source of considerable cultural, as well as political, influence throughout East Asia. It contributed elements of Confucian statecraft and a popular Confucian religion, as well as Confucian ethics in family and personal relations, to the surrounding states. Buddhism came to Mount Wutai in North China (in today's Shanxi Province) from India, and moved from Shanxi to Korea and Japan. Unsurprisingly, given the role of texts in both Confucianism and Buddhism, Chinese characters became a common script, and as in China, being able to read and write Classical Chinese became the mark of the educated throughout the region. Trade among the countries of East Asia was at times extensive, leading among other things to shared cultures in paintings and ceramics.

Segal's article does not deny these earlier Imperial cultural influences, and neither is there anything in his other writings to suggest that was the case. His argument in 'Does China Matter?' is that China no longer continues to exert such influence and authority in the region. He had a constant aversion to the China exceptionalism sometimes associated with academic observers of China. This was a discussion that could never be resolved. Segal was talking about China as the government of the PRC: while sometimes the China-experts might accept that equation, often they differentiate between Chinese society and culture on the one hand and any particular state or government on the other.

In the twentieth century it is undeniable that the influence and authority of the Chinese state declined under Empire, Republic and (perhaps more variably) the PRC. However, this did not always lead those in the East and Southeast Asian region to reject the influence and importance of Chinese culture. Necessarily, in the era of modern nationalism, the previous and sometimes much earlier regional position of Imperial China led later to both resentment and resistance. At the same time, even where political contestation between states resulted, this did not lead to the total rejection of Chinese culture. For example, while there has been a noticeable decline in Japanese appreciation of Chinese culture during the last 20 years, the attraction for things Chinese remains strong, including not just material culture but also religious ideas and influences.

Even at the level of more popular culture there would appear to be little to support Segal's contention. Every visitor to the countries of East and Southeast Asia relatively rapidly comes up against various manifestations of Chinese culture, if only because of the apparent ubiquity of the migration chains across the region that started in about 1000 AD. There are Chinese communities across the whole region, including not only the more obvious commercial classes of Southeast Asia, but also the substantial and more recent Chinese communities in Japan, and to a much lesser extent in Korea.

These communities have developed Chinese schools, Chinese temples and Chinese shops. In many cases they have developed their own local Chinese literatures, and their presence has often led to linguistic and culinary influences. Every capital city has a Chinese district, as do many smaller towns and cities, and there are both Chinese language media and even social and political organizations. Of course, the degree of Chinese cultural manifestation is variable. There are countries, such as Indonesia, where it is only during the last few years that open Chinese public behaviour has once again become possible.

In contrast, manifestations of Japanese culture are considerably more limited. Despite the massive scale of Japanese investment in the countries of East and Southeast Asia, there seems to be only a limited purchase for Japanese culture. Certainly the cuisines of Korea and more particularly Taiwan bear clear influences from the era of Japanese colonialism. In Taiwan's case this remains even celebrated to some extent, reflecting the extent to which many local and indigenous people in Taiwan feel (particularly in retrospect) that Japan brought liberation as well as conquest. Certainly, too, a number of Japanese cartoon characters, most notably Hello Kitty, have become fairly widespread throughout the region, especially among the young. For the most part though, Japanese cultural manifestations are limited and tend to be celebrated (including in China) only in themselves rather than leading to a wider influence for Japan.

On the other hand, Segal's contrast of China and Japan is useful in helping to understand the scope and role of Chinese culture. In a number of ways, it could be argued that there is no meaningful Chinese culture, or at least not in the ways that countries like Japan currently have national cultures. Since the late nineteenth century and the Meiji Restoration the Japanese state has constantly intervened to create a national consciousness and identity, and this codification of Japanese culture was an essential part of post-Second World War reconstruction with the development of new '*nihonjinron*' (theories of Japaneseness) (Nakane, 1986). In contrast, the concept of 'Chinese culture' has always been and remains one of limited utility – lacking in coherence and essentially contested (Shih, 2002), particularly in the last 20 years within the PRC (Guo, 2003). The explanation of this phenomenon lies in the relative novelty of 'China', unresolved debates over the meaning of Chinese nationalism, and last, but by no means least, the size and scale of the area ruled by the Chinese state.

Despite claims by the CCP and the PRC, in their constitutions and other foundational statements, to present solutions to problems faced by 'the Chinese people' and 'China's sovereignty' during late Imperial China as a result of 'foreign capitalist imperialism and domestic feudalism' (Hu, 1991: 1), these are essentially *ex post facto* rationalizations of events.

'China' did not come into existence until the establishment of the Republic, and the various terms for it in Modern Standard Chinese (most notably *Zhongguo* and *Zhonghua* – both referring to the 'Central Plains' which were the location of pre-modern moral authority) are late nineteenth-century neologisms. Before the establishment of the Republic, the Empire was designated only by the ruling dynasty. There was no sovereign Chinese state. The Empire was the world, ruled over by the Emperor – the 'Son of Heaven' – and defined not by boundaries but by allegiance to the Emperor (Shih, 2002: especially 2 ff.).

Neither were there any 'Chinese people', let alone citizens, before the twentieth century. The idea of a nation was anathema to an Empire that had prided itself on its social and cultural diversity (Hevia, 1995). The inhabitants of the Empire spoke different languages, had a variety of belief systems, ate vastly different diets and cuisines, and lived different life-styles. This variety should be no great surprise, given the size and scale of the Empire. Although China is often implicitly compared to a European nation-state, the more appropriate comparison might be with Europe itself. One result is that there was a far stronger individual identity to native place and locality than to the Empire, which became apparent as the polit-ical system began to change at the beginning of the twentieth century, and with the emergence of a strong provincialism (Levenson, 1967a: 158). Another result is that there was both an Imperial Culture and a series of local cultures. The Imperial Culture centred on the Court and the arts related to education (necessary for Imperial service): essay and poetry writing, calligraphy and painting. Material and social cultures (including language) were essentially localized.

The movement to recognize and develop a Chinese nation dates only from the first decade of the twentieth century, and is usually attributed to Zhang Taiyan, who sought to encourage feelings of solidarity to over-ride the country's intense provincialism (Rankin, 1986; Wong, 1989). It coincides with the first tentative attempts to create and use a standard colloquial Chinese language, seen by its promoters as essential in educating people and bringing them together. The nationalist project gained momentum with the collapse of the Empire, the establishment of the Republic, the May Fourth Movement of 1919, and the subsequent estab-lishment of both the Nationalist Party and the Chinese Communist Party. In general, its success is seen in the extent to which people across the various provinces now privilege China rather than their own locality (Goodman, 2002) and have in the process absorbed public beliefs about the longevity of the Chinese nation, the Chinese state and the Chinese people, all in only about 80 years.

At the same time, Chinese nationalism has achieved nowhere near the unanimity of purpose achieved in Japan. From the beginning, the concep-tualism of Chinese nationalism has been a domestic political issue, argued

over by political parties, groups and associations – each of whom claimed
to be the authentic Chinese voice, equating the fate of the Chinese nation
with their own fate (Fitzgerald, 1994). During the Republic there was
an uneasy relationship between nation and region (Gillin, 1967; Kapp,
1973; Fitzgerald, 1998) that still largely remains unresolved. In the era
of Mao-dominated politics, the PRC tried to minimize regionalism in its
explanation of Chinese nationalism, although, during the 1990s, considerably more pluralism has become recognized and to a considerable
extent encouraged (Goodman, 2002: 853). Even more pertinently for the
definition of Chinese culture, there has been an almost continuous debate
on the extent to which Chinese heritage should be accepted or rejected
in the definition of the nation, as well as about the precise content of
that heritage. Paradoxically, in terms of the 1990s wider-world debate
about an East Asian development model, interpretations of Confucianism have been extremely varied (Levenson, 1958; Louie, 1980) and
issues of its significance and meaning for Chinese nationalism and the
definition of Chinese culture have remained matters of intense debate in
the eras of Deng Xiaoping, Jiang Zemin and Hu Jintao (de Bary, 1991;
Guo, 2003: 91).

The consequences of this history and practice are a definition of Chinese
culture that is both complex and contested – not to say occasionally
elusive. Contemporary Chinese culture inherits both the imperial imperative to be a world culture and the twentieth-century requirement of a
more specific nationalism, with the two often in tension. Equally, there
is a tension between, on the one hand, a political nationalism that seeks
to emulate Japanese nation-building and emphasize a revolutionary break
with the past (and indeed often the CCP's revolution) and, on the other,
a cultural nationalism that constantly refers to China's past – if with little
agreement about the content of that past. In addition, there is the somewhat circular attempt to define Chinese culture in terms of the practices
and beliefs of those who are now taken generally to be 'Chinese' – the
descendants of those whose origins can be traced back to having lived
under the rule of one of the imperial dynasties, regardless of their current
place of residence. In among all these competing influences there is also
the discourse of race, that seeks to define Chinese culture in terms of the
Chinese people and their civilizing influence (Dikotter, 1992).

The party-state and culture

Segal's argument about China's cultural engagement with the world is
that, in the period since 1978, the government of the PRC has been more
concerned to limit external cultural influences coming in than with the
development of its own external influences outside its borders. It is certainly
the case that in the post-Mao Zedong reform era the PRC ceased its

attempts at the export of revolution, perfunctory though those were at times. Equally it is the case that in the wake of the Tiananmen crackdown of 1989, the CCP and the PRC held the Voice of America and the BBC responsible for inciting the youth rebellion that had preoccupied Beijing throughout May of that year. In the wake of June's clearing of Tiananmen Square, the party-state took action to attempt to limit European and US media activities in the PRC. It is also the case that state authorities are anxious, and possibly over-anxious, about the impact that American and European culture may have on the PRC. The early 2003 request for the Rolling Stones to remove 'Let's Spend the Night Together' from their repertoire, or alter the words, during a planned series of concerts (that eventually did not take place because of the SARS outbreak) is one trivial, yet clear and recent, example of such anxiety leading to action. More serious has been the system of Internet 'blocking' (exclusion of access to sites) introduced within the PRC since 2001 (Zittrain and Edelman, 2003).

All the same, it would be a mistake to draw the conclusion from these observations that, since the beginning of the 1990s, the PRC had either withdrawn into its shell, or significantly altered its belief in the need for external cultural outreach. The development and international promotion of the Chinese film industry (notwithstanding attempts at censorship), Beijing's eventually successful bid to host the Olympic Games (after an initial defeat by Sydney) and the domestic promotion of the Chinese soccer team's participation in the 2002 World Cup are all major events that suggest the PRC's commitment to international cultural interaction.

Far from abandoning international involvement, the regime's external promotion of China has simply changed, with the replacement of an agenda of international revolution by the more nationalist endeavour of acceptance as a major world power; and through the PRC's supplementing Europe and the United States as its major focus of attention with activities targeting its interactions with East and Southeast Asia. In particular, the PRC has concentrated on the international promotion of Chinese culture, although that may be no easy matter, not least because of the tension between the goals of political and cultural nationalism.

The most recent changes in the PRC's cultural outreach have been shaped by three events: the reform programme engineered by Deng Xiaoping in 1978 that resulted in significant changes in the relationship between politics and culture; the end of the Socialist Bloc in the USSR and Eastern Europe; and almost simultaneously the Tiananmen crackdown of 1989 and the various reactions abroad. Political reform in the late 1970s led first to a radical change in the system of censorship (from prior approval to the possibility of *ex post facto* condemnation) and the commercialization of publishing that gradually but dramatically opened up the space for representation of Chinese culture (Hendrischke, 1988;

Goodman, 2001). By the 1990s, there was essentially an open discussion of the representation of Chinese culture, if confined largely to personnel within the party-state (Dirlik, 1996). Central to the discussion of Chinese culture has been the issue of whether national identity is to be conceptualized as a revolutionary break with Imperial China, or as a return to the essential (often moral) purity of the past (which might also in some senses be regarded as a break with the more recent revolutionary past) (Guo, 2003: 75).

One of the historical ironies during the 1990s was that whilst the party-state held external media responsible for the problems that it faced during May and June 1989 in Beijing, its longer-term reactions to those events eventually resulted in considerably greater external cultural influences, and especially on the young, being manifested within the PRC. The difference, however, was that these new external cultural influences came initially from the Chinese communities of East and Southeast Asia, and then more generally from that region, and were more immediately concerned with popular rather than political culture. During the early 1990s Cantonese popular music (Canto-pop) from Hong Kong and pop music from Taiwan flooded into the PRC. These were rapidly followed by other manifestations of youth culture from around the region, including magazines, clothes and music from Japan, South Korea, Singapore, Malaysia, Thailand and even Vietnam.

The cause of this sea change was at least in part the situation of relative isolation in international circles that the PRC found itself in following 4 June 1989. Western European states and America turned their backs on almost all interactions with the PRC for varying periods of 6 to 18 months. The USSR was in the process of removing the communist monopoly, both domestically and in Eastern Europe. Faced with the prospects of isolation, the PRC turned to improving its relations with the states of East and Southeast Asia. Relations with most of these (with the exception of Japan) had been poor or formally non-existent for some time before the 1990s because of the Cold War and those states' concerns about communism and revolution, and the PRC's role in their promotion around the region.

For a variety of reasons, this *rapprochement* would probably have eventuated sooner rather than later in any case. The PRC's changed economic outlook after 1978, as well as its abandonment of its commitment to international revolution, the impact of changed PRC economic development policy on international investment in East and Southeast Asia, which was rapidly being perceived as a problem by several of the states of the region (Indonesia, Malaysia, Thailand) who felt that funds were being directed away from them and towards the PRC; and the collapse of the European Socialist bloc, all contributed to this development. Nonetheless, the events of 1989–1990 provided a catalyst for change in the PRC's foreign policy that also led to formal diplomatic relations with South Korea and several members of the ASEAN bloc, notably Indonesia and Singapore, and improved relations with others, including Malaysia and Thailand.

During the 1990s, trade and cultural interactions with the countries of East and Southeast Asia grew so significantly that several commentators started examining the porousness of the PRC's borders and the possible consequences for the development of the Chinese state (Goodman and Segal, 1994). Somewhat paradoxically, given the hostility that used to characterize attitudes in the countries of Southeast Asia towards their local Chinese communities, the PRC's appeal to the region has been based on its promotion of Chinese culture, as well as on trade. The obvious explanation of this paradox would seem to be the PRC's (not inaccurate) reading that much entrepreneurial expertise in the rest of East and Southeast Asia was in the hands of Chinese business people.

Tourism within the PRC from East and Southeast Asia was an obvious starting point for the development of the promotion of Chinese culture, for all, but particularly during the early 1990s directed at encouraging Overseas Chinese to visit (and presumably invest) in their ancestral places. While tourism to the PRC from the United States and Europe eventually regained its pre-1989 levels and began to grow again, the expansion of tourism from East and Southeast Asia grew even more rapidly during the 1990s. Another channel for the encouragement of Chinese cultural influence in East and Southeast Asia has been the development of Chinese language publications, in particular the overseas edition of *People's Daily* (*Renmin Ribao*): the CCP's official daily. This has been remarkable not only for its open circulation in Southeast Asia, which well within living memory would previously have been impossible, not to say dangerous, in most cases, but also because the overseas edition of the *People's Daily* is printed in the full-form Chinese characters (sometimes described as 'traditional' characters) that are still generally used to write Modern Standard Chinese outside the PRC. Given the CCP's commitment to simplified Chinese characters – a potent symbol of political nationalism and the need to create a fundamental break with past practice – this represents a considerable compromise to the end of extending cultural influence.

All the same, there are clear limits to the extent to which considerations of a wider Chinese culture might take precedence over the narrower concerns of political nationalism in the PRC. A most obvious and recent example of this kind of contradiction was the award of the 2000 Nobel Prize for Literature to Gao Xingjian. Gao is primarily a dramatist and was well known in the PRC during the 1980s for *Wild Man* and *Busstop*, performed there at that time. He is also a painter and writer of fiction, including *Soul Mountain*, which bore the prize citation. Since 1987 he has lived in Paris, and is now a French citizen, although he writes all his plays and fiction in Modern Standard Chinese. While then Premier Zhu Rongji congratulated Gao as a French citizen, others within the party-state poured scorn on Gao's achievement as not representative of contemporary Chinese literature (citing other preferred writers still living within the PRC) or as a politically motivated attack on the PRC (BBC News Online, 2000; *People's Daily* Online, 2000). A more enlightened cultural nationalism might have interpreted the award as a triumph for Chinese culture. That it did not, underlines the continuing place of the CCP's own particular politics in the determination of Chinese culture.

The PRC and the Overseas Chinese

Segal's argument that China does not play a significant role for Chinese around the world is at first sight a remarkably off-beat, unorthodox and provocative comment. Moreover, relative statements about the strength of India's connections with Indians as opposed to China's with the Chinese could really only have been made by someone living in Britain. In general, migrants almost always maintain connections to their country of origin, even if for long periods they may only be emotional or psychological, whether they be Chinese in Sydney or Indians, Pakistanis, Bengalis or Sri Lankans in Britain. In the UK, China does not loom large in the academic, let alone the public consciousness. Migrants and their descendants from the Indian sub-continent significantly outnumber any kinds of Chinese residents. Even so, there were politically inspired disturbances of political order in London's Chinatown during the late 1960s that took their cue from Mao Zedong's Cultural Revolution. On the whole, elsewhere in the world where Chinese are the more numerous migrant community (of the two), the links with the PRC are more in evidence, if more recently for social and economic rather than for political reasons.

The 1990s saw two major stimuli to thinking about international networks of Chinese. The first was the sizeable out-migration of young Chinese from the PRC in the aftermath of the entry of the PLA into Tiananmen Square in June 1989, although not solely occasioned by that event. The second was recognition of the phenomenal growth of the PRC economy, fuelled by its international links, that led to considerable attention in both academic publications and the mass media on the varieties and extent of Chinese networks around the world.

In the early 1990s a number of commentators beyond the borders of the PRC seized on the importance of the Chinese living elsewhere – the 'Overseas Chinese' – as an important engine of economic growth. In a contemporaneously influential article, *The Economist*, for example, high-lighted the leading roles of the 55 million (according to its calculations) Overseas Chinese in both their countries of residence and in the more recent development of the PRC. The influence of these Overseas Chinese was identified not only in East and Southeast Asia, where they were (and remain) concentrated, but also in substantial numbers in the US (1.8 million) Canada (0.6 million) Australia and New Zealand (1.8 million) Latin America (1 million) and Europe (0.6 million) (*The Economist*, 18 July 1992, p. 21).

In their own countries of residence, these Overseas Chinese were represented as wielding disproportionate, significant and often controlling economic influence, while they were also identified as the vehicle of economic change for the coastal economies of the PRC (Baldinger, 1992; Yamaguchi, 1993). The latter function was most obviously demonstrated for those societies of East Asia that are predominantly Chinese – Hong Kong, Singapore and Taiwan – and where, during the late 1980s and early 1990s, whole industries moved from their original base into the PRC (Asia Research Centre, 1992). Elsewhere, the spotlight fell on the small Chinese populations in a number of different countries in Southeast Asia and their apparently much larger economic impact. In Cambodia, where 5 per cent of the population were said to control 70 per cent of the economy; in Indonesia where 4 per cent of the population were attributed with a 73 per cent economic control; in Malaysia where 29 per cent were said to control 61 per cent; in the Philippines where 2 per cent were regarded as responsible for 60 per cent; and in Thailand where 10 per cent were held to control 81 per cent of the economy (Goodman 1998: 143).

The Economist provided perspective on the scale of influence of the Overseas Chinese by aggregating data:

> Overall, one conservative estimate puts the 1990 'GNP' of Asia's 51m overseas Chinese, Taiwan and Hong Kong included, at $450 billion – a quarter bigger than China's then GNP, and, per head, at about 80% of the level of Spain or Israel.

According to *The Economist*, Overseas Chinese economic success was attributable to two factors. One was the ties of personal acquaintance, trust and obligation said to be at the core of Chinese society. The other was the high rate of savings of the Overseas Chinese; worldwide, the Overseas Chinese probably hold liquid assets (not including securities) worth $1.5 trillion–2 trillion. For a rough comparison, in Japan, with twice as many people, bank deposits in 1990 totalled $3 trillion (*The Economist*, 18 July 1992: 21).

Building on this kind of analysis, other commentators claimed that the interactions of China and the Chinese in East and Southeast Asia had laid the foundations for a new economic 'superpower' to rival the US, Europe and Japan (Howell, 1992; Weidenbaum, 1993; East Asia Analytical Unit,

DFAT, Australia, 1995). Still other commentators went spectacularly even further, to argue that ethnic Chinese identity might supersede the need for states and lead to a reduced role for inter-state activity within the region (Ong and Nonini, 1997: 323). In the words of one author, there was every possibility that a 'Chinese Commonwealth' will emerge as a development from a China whose 'very definition ... is up for grabs' (Kao, 1993).

These portrayals of the potential relationship between the PRC and the Overseas Chinese are the essential context to Segal's related comment in 'Does China Matter?'. Although undoubtedly overstated and probably somewhat misdirected, Segal pointed to the need for perspective and the danger of reading too much into the emergence of a 'Greater China'. Such ideas are inherently interesting and challenging, but they fundamentally misunderstand the structures of Overseas Chinese transnationalism. The unity of the Overseas Chinese in East and Southeast Asia is a categoric construct, more a function of analysis than evident in their economic and political behaviour.

The concepts of either a Chinese Commonwealth or Overseas Chinese unity (with or without the PRC) may be useful devices for drawing attention to the processes contributing to the PRC's economic development during the early 1990s, and may even have some appeal to certain kinds of Chinese nationalism. It may indeed be a particularly useful rhetoric for encouraging Chinese outside the PRC to invest or engage in other business activities there. In 1992, for example, Fu Yuchuan, Director of the Overseas Chinese College of Hainan University, made one such attempt: 'The chances are becoming greater for the 24 million Chinese who have attained citizenship in Southeast Asian nations to come to realize once again their common heritage and cultural traditions, as economic cooperation grows' (*China Daily*, 22 October 1992).

At the same time, there are clear social, political and economic limits to the notion of Greater China, which are sometimes too easily overlooked by many commentators. The social limits are acute, not least since there are many common (flawed) assumptions by Europeans about the homogeneity of 'the Chinese'. The essentialization of the Chinese in the PRC as a single culture has, as already noted, more to do with the emergence of twentieth-century nationalism than with any social homogeneity. When the various Chinese of Southeast Asia outside the PRC are brought into consideration, the meaning of being Chinese in a social sense becomes very broad indeed. Many of the Chinese of the region speak no Chinese language at all and are significantly assimilated in their host societies, through state action and discrimination, no less than through length of stay. Migrating from the Chinese mainland during the colonial era, they rapidly became the business class of Southeast Asia – although it is hotly debated whether this was for cultural or structural reasons –

a settled minority in each country who effectively operated as the region's domestic capitalists (Mackie, 1988). Earlier reservations from the host societies were compounded during the latter half of the twentieth century by political discrimination that resulted as a response to the establishment of a Chinese communist party-state.

To cope with hostile circumstances, the Chinese of Southeast Asia turned at a very early stage in their migration to more reliable particularistic ties requiring relationships of long-term reciprocity: common place of origin, shared language, family and kinship (Lever-Tracy *et al.*, 1996). While these may be in a general way common characteristics of the Chinese in the region, in practice they necessarily reflect competition and division rather than any unity of action, purpose or mythical conspiracy. For each Chinese cooperation and interaction is within the security of shared reference groups, rarely moving beyond those boundaries to engage others described as 'Chinese'. Such relationships with shared reference groups became particularly important during the late 1980s and early 1990s, as the Chinese resident in East and Southeast Asia became involved economically in the PRC – preferring to interact with their families' place of origin on the Chinese mainland.

Even in East Asia, there is little social homogeneity about the Chinese of either Taiwan or Hong Kong. Taiwan is the most obviously heterogeneous, with a major social division between 'mainlanders' who arrived with the defeat of the Nationalist Party on the mainland of China in 1949 and much longer Taiwan-based communities of Hokkien- and Hakka-speakers. That division has been the basis of politics since the early 1990s – although without an exact translation of support – which has certainly developed different attitudes to the meaning of Chinese identity. In Hong Kong, society and politics are more divided along socio-economic lines, but even in that case language groups and ancestral homes in China create recognizably separate communities, which are especially active in the business world. Despite, or perhaps because of, the dominance of Cantonese speakers, there are organized communities of Shanghainese and Indonesian Chinese (those who fled Indonesia during the 1960s) who exercise disproportionate influence.

As these comments on social diversity suggest, there are clear political limits to the development of a Greater China. Hong Kong became part of the PRC in the middle of 1997, but Taiwan remains apart. Moreover, Taiwan's political relations are not simply a function of the PRC's domestic politics but also of its own, where significant sections of the population are unlikely to seek closer relations to a Beijing government of whatever persuasion, and others are hostile principally to a communist party-state. For their part, the comparative advantage of the Chinese of Southeast Asia would be lost through closer association with the PRC. They gain precisely because, as entrepreneurs, they are outside and separate from the PRC.

Chinese identity has clearly been important in a general way in the development of relations between the Chinese of Southeast Asia and the PRC, but the extent of divided loyalties can be easily overstated. To quote Lee Kuan Yew, in many ways the founder of Singapore, 'We are Ethnic Chinese but our stakes are in our own countries, not where our ancestors came from' (Cragg, 1996: 17).

Then too, the economic scale of Greater China is often exaggerated. The PRC is clearly a growing economy, if from a very low base which has led to impressive rates of growth for a very long period of time, with considerable potential. All the same, during the early 1990s the wealth of the Overseas Chinese was significantly overstated. The calculation of that wealth rested, without explicit acknowledgement, on only one part of the proposed Chinese Commonwealth, namely Taiwan, which contains more than 80 per cent of the aggregate domestic product of the hypothesized entity, and which is more usually (*pace The Economist*) not recognized as Overseas Chinese territory. Take Taiwan and Hong Kong out of the calculation of an Overseas Chinese Empire in the making, and what remains is a small but relatively buoyant Singapore economy, and a series of Chinese entrepreneurs in Southeast Asia, who speak individually for themselves rather than for the Chinese of Southeast Asia. Moreover, there is remarkably little economic integration among these various non-PRC constituent parts of a potential Greater China. Their major point of contact is in the PRC, where there are clear limits to the potential for further spectacular growth of Chinese Southeast Asian involvement.

Culture, the state and the region

The PRC would certainly appear to be more limited in its role in the determination of Chinese culture than its own self-view would sometimes seem to imply. Not least, this would seem to result from discussions and debate about the structure and dimensions of Chinese culture, and subsequent policy uncertainty. Moreover, the hyperbole surrounding the emergence of the idea of Greater China provides adequate evidence of the need for greater balance in assessing the role of the government of the PRC in regional, and, by extension, world affairs. By the same token, however, it also provides evidence of the impact and importance of Chinese culture beyond the borders of the PRC, particularly in East and Southeast Asia, and the significance of that region to the international position of the PRC.

The dynamics of cultural influence are such that, while the party-state may be divided on the definition of Chinese culture, and may not provide the only source of cultural authority, the PRC may still nonetheless both benefit from the wider appreciation of China and attempt to build on it to other ends. This usage of Chinese culture has clearly been an important part of the PRC's strategy since the early 1990s – particularly in its dealings with governments and entrepreneurs in East and Southeast Asia. For their parts, governments and entrepreneurs have most of the time responded positively to the greater interaction. Entrepreneurs have found a degree of ease and possibly psychological comfort in dealing with more familiar partners in the PRC. Governments have found themselves in agreement with a PRC that, as the discussion over the emergence of 'Asian values' demonstrated, shares a common sense of regional community in many aspects of international politics. The key issue here is not the importance of the PRC to the societies and countries of East and Southeast Asia, but the extent to which it will in the longer term come to be regarded as the regional leader, and the consequences of that interaction for the PRC's role in global politics.

7 China and the East Asian politico-economic model

Jean-Pierre Lehmann

For Dr Supachai Panitchpakdi, Director General of the World Trade Organisation (WTO), former Deputy Prime Minister and Trade Minister of Thailand, with a doctorate in economics from Erasmus University in Rotterdam, China matters a lot. In the preface of the book on China and the WTO that he co-authored with *Business Week* Asia Regional Editor Mark Clifford, he stated:

> Whether it's looking out over the next few years or the next quarter-of-a-century, how the world's most populous country handles the many development challenges it faces will go a long way toward determining what kind of world we inhabit.
>
> Pick an issue – the environment, the military, international affairs, the global economy – China's choices will have a major impact on Asia and the world.
>
> If China makes the wrong decisions, the result will be chilling, not only for the country's 1.3 billion citizens, but for many people beyond its borders as well.
>
> Conversely, a China that successfully makes the transformation to a relatively affluent, open society will be both an inspiration to other countries and a locomotive that will help to power the world's economies.
>
> (Panitchpakdi and Clifford, 2002: v)

Brahm Prakash, Director of the Poverty Reduction Division at the Asian Development Bank (ADB), made an even more striking assessment: 'China is the great hope. China can now be seen as the saviour of the global economic system' (quoted in Thornhill, June 2002). From querying, as Gerry Segal did, whether 'China matters', to proclaiming it the forerunner of how the twenty-first century will evolve, as Supachai Panitchpakdi avers, or indeed as the 'saviour' of the global economic system, as Brahm Prakash proclaims, there is quite a distance.

On the economic front, there can be little doubt that what China achieved in the last decade mattered a great deal, most of all, but not exclusively, to those most affected, i.e. the Chinese people, and especially those who previously lived beneath, or just at, subsistence level. In the course of the 1990s, China's economic reform programme resulted in lifting out of poverty a population roughly equivalent to twice a re-unified Germany – about 160 million people. Millions more have seen their incomes rise considerably. There remain many people in China living in dire poverty (as defined by the World Bank, at $1 per day at purchasing power parity): approximately 106 million, overwhelmingly concentrated in the rural areas. Nevertheless, China must be given credit for having lifted more people out of poverty more quickly than any country. At a time when the UN and many of the world's most eminent minds are grappling with the challenges of extreme poverty, this is no mean feat.

While the figures are awesome – as they always are in China – in some respects China can be seen as simply the latest among East Asian countries in undergoing highly successful economic development. In what the Japanese used to refer to as the 'flying geese pattern', Japan took off in the late 1800s, to be followed in the post-Second World War era first by the so-called Asian NIEs (newly industrialized economies), South Korea, Hong Kong, Singapore and Taiwan, and then by some of the more successful Southeast Asian countries, notably Thailand, Indonesia, Malaysia and, latterly, Vietnam, culminating in China joining the flock.

Having said all that, the fat lady has not sung yet. The lifting of millions of Chinese out of poverty at one level can be seen as simply undoing all the harm that successive Chinese governments have done to their citizens over the last 200 years, prior to the launching of Deng Xiaoping's economic reform programme in the late 1970s. In 1800, China's share of world GDP was over 30 per cent; by 1913 it had declined to 10 per cent and then by 1950 to 5 per cent. Of course, foreign wars and imperialism account for part of this economic disaster, but so do the abysmal governments China has had, and its frequent civil wars. As Guy Pfeffermann (2003) points out: 'the Chinese economic story is largely one of economic destruction and recovery'. In other words, the answer to China's economic performance depends not so much on the government proceeding to do what was right, but more that it stopped doing what was wrong.

Whether the momentum can be sustained once the post-destruction recovery has occurred is an entirely different question. And this is where Supachai Panitchpakdi and Gerry Segal do agree: the answer to whether China matters or not lies in whether it will realize its potential.

Nigeria, Venezuela, Iran and Burma are among countries where economists, foreign investors, international financial institutions and policy-makers placed great hopes at one time or another in the last few decades – only to see them dashed. China could join that undistinguished category.

To provide a sense of whether the potential will be realized and China will indeed emerge as a beacon of the twenty-first century – whether China matters – several questions will be addressed:

1 Is there a model of East Asian political economy? And, if so, is it sustainable?
2 What lessons can be learned from the condition that Japan has been wallowing in for the last dozen years or so?
3 Will East Asia undergo a political transformation?
4 What are the scenarios for China?

An East Asian model of political economy

Publications on the Asian economic model and 'Asian values' proliferated in the 1980s and 1990s, later to be replaced by those attempting to explain the causes of the 1997 Asian financial crisis. It is more intriguing to analyse why countries fail, or under-perform, than why they succeed. Countries are composed of individuals whom everywhere in the world share pretty much the same aspirations: to improve their lives and especially to improve the lives of their children. Countries do not under-perform or fail economically because their citizens wish that to happen. Economic growth is – or should be – a 'natural' pattern of human affairs. In very rich countries, like Switzerland or Norway, economic growth may slow down, as the incremental addition of revenue is very marginal. In medium-income countries and especially in poor countries, growth should be occurring as a matter of natural course because people's needs and aspirations are barely satisfied.

The argument that this has got something to do with 'culture' is nonsense, as was the whole Asian values concoction. North Koreans and South Koreans are products of exactly the same culture, but, while today the latter have a very high standard of living, both quantitatively and qualitatively – more South Koreans purchase classical music as a proportion of their CD purchases than any other country in the world – the former are, literally, starving both materially and spiritually.

While it is institutions and governance that are the most important determinants for creating an entrepreneurship-friendly environment conducive to growth, the fact does remain that in the course of the last five decades or so, outside the West, the only countries that have been really successful economically are in East Asia. The picture elsewhere has varied from lacklustre to catastrophic. According to the UN 2003 Human Development Report, no fewer than 54 countries, comprising 12 per cent of humanity, suffered negative economic growth in the last decade – some disastrously so – while another 71 countries, accounting for another

26 per cent of the world's population, either stagnated or experienced very low growth.

Although there are a few basket cases in East Asia – Burma, Cambodia, Laos and North Korea – the region is unquestionably noteworthy for having the greatest concentration of stars. There is no Latin American, African, Middle Eastern, Eastern European or South Asian Republic of Korea or Taiwan, and while the other big hulk of humanity, India, has been doing better recently, it is no China (Das, 2001, and *The Economist*, 25 January 2003).

In seeking to explain this phenomenon, there are many schools, but for the sake of the argument here, they can essentially be divided into two. One school, that we will call the 'universalists' – of whom Gerry Segal was one – argue that basically the East Asian governments provide infrastructure and a stable macro-economic policy, while otherwise just letting the market work; hence the driving force of growth is the private sector and entrepreneurialism (Rowen, 1998). The second school, the 'particularists', who are more numerous and also probably more influential (at least in the field of Asian studies of political economy), argue that East Asian economic development has taken place primarily due to the state (Wade, 1990). One of the most prominent among the 'particularists', Chalmers Johnson, coined the term the 'developmental state' (Johnson, 1982). Government is the driving force, with industrial policy the instrument that it wields. In this particular East Asian paradigm of political economy, economic development is not an end in itself, but the means to achieve political and especially nationalist and mercantilist ends.

This perspective provides a specifically East Asian theory and model of economic development, but also presupposes that globalization is not possible, indeed positively dangerous: East Asians play by different rules and with different goals, thus there cannot be a global market economy, only a global economic battlefield (Fallows, 1994).

Empirically, there is a case to be answered. With hardly any exception, dictatorships virtually everywhere in the world – in Africa, in the former Soviet Union, in most of Latin America, in the Middle East – have engendered economic disasters. The only exceptions lie among countries in East Asia (Lehmann, 1985). Perhaps the most blatant contrast can be drawn between Argentina's Juan Perón and South Korea's Park Chung-hee. Both were military dictators, but whereas the former destroyed his country's economy, propelling Argentina from having been one of the planet's richest economies to Third World status, the latter is recognized as the architect of the South Korean 'economic miracle', propelling a country from being one of the poorest in the world – in 1960, South Korea's GDP per capita was lower than most African countries – to becoming one of the richest.

The East Asian dictatorship = development equation, tempting though it may be to some East Asian (and possibly other) political elites, is of course bogus. Some Asian dictatorships have not produced the economic goods, for example the Philippines under Marcos, while others have been catastrophes, including North Korea under the Kims *père-et-fils* and Burma/Myanmar under the bunch of militarist thugs who have been running, in fact ruining, the country for the last couple of decades.

The fact remains, however, that there have been a sufficient number of economically successful, in some cases highly successful, East Asian states led by authoritarian leaders, with no comparable examples elsewhere in the developing world, to warrant the hypothesis that there may be a pattern: South Korea under Park, Chun and Roh; Taiwan under Chiang Kai-shek and Chiang Ching-kuo; Singapore under Lee Kuan Yew; Indonesia under Suharto; Malaysia under Mahathir; Vietnam under its recent leadership; and China under Deng Xiaoping and Jiang Zemin. There is no similar pattern anywhere else.

The point also to underline is that with the current possible exception of Indonesia since Suharto, to date most of these economic success stories have been sustained. In other words, while it is true that in the 1960s the Brazilian economy under the military dictatorship at the time did phenomenally well, it turned out to be for only a limited period. Economic crisis and hyperinflation quickly eroded the progress that had been achieved. Indeed many dictatorships fall because of economic failures, as was the case in the collapse of the communist Central and East European states. The edifice that Park Chung-hee built, on the other hand, has endured.

If there is indeed such a pattern that constitutes a paradigm of East Asian political economy, to which China corresponds, the implications for Asia and indeed for the world could be awesome indeed. The hypothesis being made by political scientists and a number of political leaders – indeed in many cases, the conclusion reached – that liberalism and democracy have 'conquered the world' (Mandelbaum, 2002) could prove to be utterly wrong. If a Sino-centric East Asian authoritarian paradigm of political economy is indeed the formula for success that the non-Western planet should be adopting in order to be lifted out of poverty, this is going to be a very different century from the one anticipated by a good number of authors, notably Gerry Segal and Barry Buzan (Buzan and Segal, 1998).

China would then matter a great deal, although not necessarily in the manner that could be greeted with anything approaching unmitigated contentment. This could indeed presage a new era and the definite decline of the West, the reversal of the course of history that has seemed to prevail towards liberalism, the many vicious attacks on it notwithstanding, since the Enlightenment (Fukuyama, 1993).

Part of the answer to this question may lie in a closer examination of what has taken place in Japan recently, as the country 'celebrates' the 150th anniversary of its opening by the black ships of Commodore Perry in 1853.

The Japanese model

Although the Japanese model of economic management was a fashion of the 1980s, trotting it out in 2003, after Japan has been experiencing twelve years of recession, may seem bizarre. Yet one may wonder whether it is not in fact now that Japan has sunk, seemingly irretrievably, into the socio-economic doldrums, rather than in the days of its anabolic steroidal economic performance, that the 'real' lessons from the Japanese experience may be drawn and applied to the questions arising in respect of China.

By the early 1800s, Japan was quite an advanced society. Its level of literacy in 1850 was in advance of most countries, including in the West, and well ahead of many developing countries today (Dore, 1964). It had also developed by the early nineteenth century a relatively sophisticated economy and possessed a powerful merchant class, which, among other things, spawned and sponsored a rich and colourful urban culture – the famous woodblock prints, the theatre, poetry, ceramics, etc.

The socio-political turbulence that marked the first few decades of the nineteenth century had all the makings, apparently, of a bourgeois-capitalist revolution (Lehmann, 1982). With the appearance of Western gunboats and the spectacle of China's disintegration by foreign armies during and following the Opium War, Japan experienced what historians have labelled a 'nationalist revolution' in the so-called 'Meiji Restoration' of 1868, rather than a bourgeois-capitalist revolution (Beasley, 1973).

Instead of taking over the reins of power as occurred in North America and several countries of NW Europe, the Japanese industrial class became economically influential, but politically dependent and ideologically subjugated. On top of a capitalist infrastructure, the Japanese state was concocted as a militarist–obscurantist empire. Economics were made entirely subservient to politics. The Meiji slogan was *fukoku-kyōhei* – rich country, strong army – underscoring the militaristic mercantilism that characterized the Japanese state within two decades of its modern 'revolution'.

These contradictions ultimately led to the emergence of fascism and imperialism (Maruyama, 1963). In the course of the heady years of its fast-changing socio-political landscape emerging from its industrial revolution, *c.*1870–1940, Japan abandoned feudalism (as a political administrative structure, although not necessarily though in terms of social values), and espoused nationalism, state-capitalism, militarism, fascism and imperialism, but never, apart from a very brief and ephemeral glimmer, liberalism (Arima, 1969). This was 'capitalism with Japanese characteristics'.

It was the only non-Western nation to have withstood Western colonialism and to have joined the West as an industrial and imperial power. All other non-Western countries, and indeed many Western countries, that embarked on ambitious 'modernization' programmes failed; including, China, Thailand, Egypt, Tunisia, Mexico, Brazil, Russia and Spain.

Japan's 'success', however, seemed ill-gotten in the ashes of Hiroshima and Nagasaki. In 1945, Japan would have been deemed a failed state. As immense luck would have it, however, with the outbreak successively of the Cold War, the Chinese revolution and the Korean War, the United States had to engage Japan in rapid 'nation-building'. It is interesting that, although many point today to the US occupation and reconstruction of Japan as a 'success', in terms of the comparisons or implications that can be drawn in respect of Iraq, from a longer-term perspective one might wonder whether the post-war reconstruction of Japan may not have been a failure, or at least partly a failure (Dower, 1999).

After an initial period of socio-economic turbulence, the American Occupation authorities 'restored order' to Japan, by jailing leftists and militant trade unionists, re-established pre-war and war-time senior officials in their former positions, released war-criminals from prison (one of whom, Kishi, later became prime minister) and pumped into the Japanese economy masses of capital and technology. In order further to fuel the Japanese economic engine, the yen was set at an artificially low exchange rate to promote exports, while the US encouraged the Japanese government to protect its infant industries (Tsuru, 1992). With the external economic stimulus given by the successive outbreaks of the Korean and Vietnamese wars – in which Japanese industry played a key role as source of procurement – and the consumer boom resulting from the 1964 Tokyo Olympics, the Japanese 'economic miracle' was born and took off.

The initial purpose of the US Occupation Forces in Japan had been to achieve the so-called 'three Ds': demilitarization, de-industrialization and democratization. The second 'D' was quickly abandoned in favour of re-industrialization. In the pre-war years Japan's leading *zaibatsu* (financial conglomerates) had 'strategic alliances' with American conglomerates, notably the Mitsui Group with General Electric and the Mitsubishi Group with Westinghouse. General Douglas MacArthur, Supreme Commander of the Allied Pacific, wrote to the Chief Executive Officers of the respective American firms, instructing them to resume their alliances and specifically to transfer technologies to assist the Japanese industries to recover rapidly. US geopolitical Cold-War strategy required a strong Japanese economy.

On the first 'D' (demilitarization), following the outbreak of the Korean War, Secretary of State John Foster Dulles sought to obtain Japan's participation, but its political leaders realized they had far too good a thing going: with the US-mandated constitution of 1946, in which Article 9 prohibited Japan from engaging in war, and with American military protection, Japan did not need to spend money or men to protect its interests. The erstwhile hated enemy, the US, would do it for them. Japan got the best possible deal following the war, with the US offering virtually everything – opening its market, providing total security, transferring technology – and asking for virtually nothing in return, except of course that Japan should obediently toe the American foreign policy line.

As to the third 'D', democratization, well, that took somewhat of a back seat to the geopolitical strategic imperative of strengthening the Japanese economy. When the Soviet empire was collapsing and Central European countries were regaining their independence and undergoing political transition, as a Japanese senior official told me, Japan had nothing to offer these countries by way of stewardship. Japan, he remarked, had never had to fight for liberal democracy; democracy was handed to Japan on a silver platter marked 'made in the USA'. While Japan became a capitalist power, indeed in its day a quite formidable capitalist power, in the post-war as in the pre-war era it eschewed liberalism (Miyoshi, 1991; Williams, 1994; Lehmann, 2000).

The morass in which Japan has been wallowing for the past dozen years is primarily the result of a crisis of political paralysis. The economic woes, at least in the initial recessionary years of the early 1990s, were relatively mild, yet the system had not been calibrated for reform or rejuvenation. Indeed, even at the economic level, as Shigeto Tsuru (1992) wrote in his prophetic book on Japanese capitalism, Japanese economic policy-makers do not understand the basic capitalist concept of creative destruction and indeed oppose it. Japan is a politically ossified society. And since corporate, financial, bureaucratic and political vested interests are so intertwined, it makes it almost impossible to 'abandon' bankrupt companies if they are well connected (Lincoln, 2001).

The basic ideology on which the Japanese economy is based also makes change difficult. There is a pretty unanimous view that probably the greatest fillip that the Japanese economy would benefit from is to open up to imports, inward investments, and also to talented human resources, especially from other parts of Asia. But the entire Japanese economic psyche and structure – the so-called *keiretsu* (industrial groups with cross-shareholdings) system, lifetime employment, and the position of government agencies as promoters and defenders of industrial champions – had been developed in a strongly mercantilist mindset, whereby exports are good and a sign of economic machismo, while imports are harmful. Similarly, outward investments are positive, inward investments are negative. The sense of exclusion that drives the mercantilism obviously renders difficult to impossible the assimilation within Japan and especially Japanese corporations of non-Japanese.

When contemplating the contemporary morass into which Japan has fallen, outsiders are struck not only by the political paralysis, but also by the intellectual paralysis. There is very little debate in Japan on fundamental issues. Civil society is extremely weak: social and environmental oriented NGOs are conspicuous by their absence, the mainstream press is very dependent on and hence tame vis-à-vis the establishment, and social science and history faculties in Japanese universities, with some crucial exceptions, tend to be quite mediocre (Hall, 1997). This is all in part due to the legacy of the Occupation. In aborting its political reform programme and focusing on rebuilding the Japanese economy, the Japanese establishment was allowed to get away without too much fundamental questioning and ultimately relatively little political change. The retention of Emperor Hirohito as head of state, instead of being tried as a war criminal, illustrates this (Bix, 2001). Thus, the emperor-system dominated what became a conspiracy of silence. The danger in asking any question, no matter how seemingly 'innocent', is that one cannot be sure of its trajectory; there is a risk it could reach the Emperor – hence better to avoid asking questions. Post-war Japan, therefore, developed in a state of amnesia (Buruma, 1995).

Japan did grow economically, but it never grew politically. With very few exceptions, including notably the late Masao Maruyama, one of the very few intellectuals in the 1930s and 1940s who dared become a political dissident, there has been scant contribution to political thought by Japanese authors. In the 1960s, 1970s and 1980s, as the Japanese economic juggernaut ploughed full-speed ahead, while scandal after scandal engulfed the ruling Liberal Democratic Party, the flippant quip by many Japanese and foreign pundits was: 'great economy, lousy politics'.

For several decades, however, the success that Japan enjoyed did have a considerable impact on other East Asian political leaders. Japan seemed to offer a viable, indeed highly effective, alternative to the 'Western' model of liberalism. In the Western scheme of things, liberalism encompasses both political and economic freedoms. In the East Asian Japan-based scheme of things, it seemed that granting a degree of economic freedom in order to provide the basis on which the private sector could grow was sufficient without having to worry about political freedoms. This was part of the reasoning behind Malaysian Prime Minister Mahathir's 'Look East Policy' and also behind Deng Xiaoping's announcement in 1978 that China had much to learn from Japan. At the initial stages of South Korea's political liberalization, the conservative factions hoped that Korea's 'democracy' could be contained by securing a permanent ruling party, as with the LDP in Japan.

However, at the dawn of the twenty-first century, what the Japanese 'model' seems quite conclusively to show is that a divorce between politics and economics is, ultimately, not sustainable. There is probably virtual unanimity, both within and outside Japan, that the only means to get its economic engine re-booted is to engage in very extensive political and institutional reform. The current (at the time of writing) Prime Minister, Koizumi, assumed office on the promises of extensive reform. So far, very little has happened. It is both fascinating and totally depressing to witness a society where most of its people want reform, where even some of its political leaders want reform, but that is institutionally and intellectually so ossified that it is incapable of reform.

This raises many questions, but two in particular. One is whether externally induced regime-change can achieve its desired ends. The second is whether Japan provides a model of East Asian political economy, the development-oriented state, which either takes the form of authoritarianism or an ersatz democracy, but that ultimately ossifies due to its inability to reform and rejuvenate, and whether China fits that mould. I will concentrate on the latter question, while leaving the first one in abeyance.

East Asian political transformations

Thomas Bebbington MacAulay's infamous *Minute on Indian Education* of 1835, in which, among other things, he wrote, 'I have never found [anyone] who could deny that a single shelf of a good European library was worth the whole native literature of India and Arabia', has been interpreted, indeed vilified, as the ultimate illustration of insensitive and insulting Western cultural colonialism. And of course it is, as well as being wrong. Had MacAulay, however, limited himself to the literature of political philosophy over the course of the last three hundred years or so (at the time of his writing), and added China to India and Arabia, he would not have been far off.

It is true that European political philosophy of the Enlightenment has some roots in Confucianism. When the scholarly Jesuit missionaries went to China in the sixteenth century, the most prominent of who was Matteo Ricci – known in China as Li Ma-tou – they discovered and were highly impressed by Confucianist social and political thought. They translated or paraphrased extracts into Latin, which were read by European scholars and philosophers, who found them intellectually refreshing and stimulating. What they found especially enticing was Confucianism's secularism, its emphasis on social order, but also its alternative basis of legitimacy of monarchical rule according to the mandate of heaven, as opposed to the more rigid and dogmatic divine right of kings (Shackleton, 1965).

Although inspiration may have come from China, however, from the moment of the Enlightenment and for the ensuing centuries, European (including, subsequently, American) political thought, philosophy and theory have had pretty much of a global monopoly. There are no Asian or Arabic equivalents to Hobbes, Locke, Montesquieu or Voltaire, to name only a handful from a rich pantheon that extends across half-a-millennium.

The modern West, eventually the modern world, was propelled by the dual Industrial and French revolutions. As the West's economies underwent revolutionary change, and as their nations gained global power and supremacy, there was a huge outpouring of debate and publications on their political cultures, structures, principles and ideologies. Why it was that China, having achieved great advance in technology and administration in previous centuries, should have remained comparatively backward and not conquered the earth, has much to do with the stagnation that occurred at the political and intellectual levels (Pomeranz, 2001). The greatest outcome of Western political thought emanating from the Enlightenment, and that came to be the very foundation stone of secular liberalism, was the rule of law. Although the rule of law was obliterated in the Western political theories and regimes that opposed liberalism – fascism and communism – ultimately it came to define what was described as the 'Western system', and set the West apart.

China's political thought in the modern age – from the time of the Taiping Rebellion (Spence, 1996) down to modern authors and political theorists, including Kang Youwei, Liang Qichao (Levenson, 1967b), the intellectuals and writers of the May 4th Movement (Chow, 1960), Lu Xun, Sun Yat-sen (Schiffrin, 1968; Gasster, 1969), and ultimately Mao Zedong – consisted above all in attempts to respond to and adapt aspects (and reject other aspects) of Western political thought. (This was also true of Arabic scholars of political philosophy (Hourani, 1970).) There is nothing that could be described as truly originally indigenous Chinese political thought over the last 120 years or so (Jenner, 1992). Neither, however, since the collapse of the imperial system in 1911, have Chinese political leaders and theorists gone – at least so far! – in the direction that certain leading Japanese political writers espoused in the course of the late 1800s, and that has remained influential to this day, which sought to reject all Western political thought, by adopting obscurantist chauvinistic nativism (nor has China gone through its variation of 'Islamism'). The reference to 'Chinese characteristics', as in 'socialism with Chinese characteristics', is no more than cosmetic.

Most of China's tumultuous modern history can be written as a search for adapting Western economic and political means to achieve national ends – specifically those of restoring the country's grandeur and place in the world and achieving wealth and power (B. Schwarz, 1999).

This has generally been true of all of East Asia. Certain East Asian political leaders, for example, Lee Kuan Yew of Singapore and Mahathir

Mohamad of Malaysia, may have been extremely skilful political masters, but they are not political theorists. Indeed what seems to have been the key to success for Lee's undoubted remarkable achievement in transforming Singapore from a backwater to a model city-state was his visionary pragmatism (Lee, 1998, 2000). More theoretical Asian political concepts, for example 'Pancasila Democracy' in Indonesia, are neither particularly erudite nor robust.

Apart from Japanese economic nationalism and mercantilism, therefore, there is nothing in terms of political economy in East Asia that can be defined as indigenous with strong regional roots. In many East Asian countries the adoption of liberal Western systems, when these have occurred, has been somewhat superficial. Singapore uses the rule of law a great deal, but primarily as a means for the authoritarian state to silence and impoverish its critics. Getting a fair trial in Malaysia while being on the wrong side of Mahathir is an improbable outcome. The Philippines has masses of lawyers and may be arguably the most 'Western' of the East Asian societies, but the extremely high level of corruption and the feudal nature of its society prevent it from being labelled truly democratic. Thailand seemed to be going in a generally positive direction as the tempo of military coups receded, but the seeming abuse of power exercised by the current Prime Minister, Thaksin, may be reversing the political clock. The many politically repressive regimes that remain in East Asia, in North Korea, China, Vietnam, Laos, Cambodia and Burma, are clearly a terrible indictment and proof of the region's political backwardness.

At the very many conferences, seminars, and workshops that I attended with Gerry Segal in or on East Asia, the point he would relentlessly seek to drive home was that the region was handicapped by weak institutions and rotten politics. Strong economies, which they were at the time, could not compensate. The strong economies could only be ephemerally so if the politics remain rotten and the institutions remain weak. Rotten national politics and weak institutions would also undermine regional stability, since their aggregation leads to a rotten regional political climate and structure and a very weak regional institutional framework. For example, while none of the Southeast Asian countries would come out smelling of liberal roses, the total and quite cynical absence of political principle was illustrated in the extension of membership of ASEAN to Burma/Myanmar. Only latterly have some members of ASEAN taken a somewhat more robust attitude towards the military junta in light of its attack on and detention of Aung Sang Suu Kyi and members of the party that she leads in May 2003.

Thus, although East Asia has been for over a quarter-of-a-century the global economic star, so far as the political landscape is concerned, it is far less brilliant. In reference, for example, to the Freedom House Index for 2003 (http://www.freedomhouse.org/research/freeworld/2003/averages.

pdf) two East Asian countries (North Korea and Burma) are among the handful with the worst score (7). Three East Asian countries (China, Laos and Vietnam) score among the penultimate worst (6.5). The others are dispersed throughout the scale, although mainly at the lower ends: Brunei and Cambodia (5.5) feature, along with North Korea, Burma, China, Laos and Vietnam, among Freedom House's definition of 'Not Free'. Singapore and Malaysia just manage to scrape in the 'partly free' category at respectively 4.5 and 5, Indonesia is at 3.5, East Timor at 3, and the more established democracies – the Philippines and Thailand – only score a 2.5. There is not a single East Asian country that features among the 34 countries that obtained the top mark (1). They include all of the G-7 and most of the OECD countries, with the exception of Japan. Japan, which in principle has been a democracy for almost six decades, stands, at 1.5, in the company of very recently politically emancipated countries, such as Latvia, Lithuania, Bulgaria, Czech Republic, Estonia, Slovakia and Poland (the only EU country in this category is Greece). Taiwan and South Korea, both of which have been democracies for little over a decade, score a 2, which is of course infinitely better than it would have been not so long ago, but shows that even in comparison with many former communist Central European countries, the recent East Asian democracies still have considerable progress to make.

The other disappointing, albeit not surprising, score that needs to be noted in passing is that of India – also 2.5. India may be, as its promoters claim, the world's biggest democracy, but the quality does not seem to match up with the quantity. Although there is in fact a great deal of innovative and stimulating political thought emanating from India – Sunil Khilnani (1997) believes that in the future the most prolific sources of leading thought on Western political philosophy will be coming from non-Westerners – as the Indian Economics Nobel Prize Laureate Amartya Sen (1999) has written, India is at best an imperfect democracy. Indeed, India can be held up to prove the converse of the defective 'East Asian model'. In the case of East Asia, the defect comes from the fact that strong economics and weak politics and institutions cannot be sustained. In the case of India, poor economic performance over the decades, arising in great part from the absence of proper attention to and investment in social development – there are more illiterates in India than in the whole of the rest of the world put together – has impeded the country's political development. The structures and the competencies are there, the principle of the rule of law is strongly embedded, but there is such poverty, such underdevelopment (e.g. in infrastructure) and, partly no doubt for these reasons, such endemic corruption, that India can hardly be a beacon, even unto itself.

Thus, one might reach the conclusion along neo-Marxian lines that the twenty-first century variation of the 'Asiatic mode of production' prevents the countries of the region from fulfilling their potential and becoming robust political, economic and social states.

The four winds of change

There is scope, however, for a degree of optimism. Four diverse winds of change have been occurring in the last few years that may be converging to generating a political transformation and even possibly a political economy paradigm shift in East Asia.

The first is that Japan has failed to exercise leadership in East Asia, and its erstwhile model has been rendered obsolete. At the Asian Pacific Roundtable conference hosted by ISIS (Malaysia) in Kuala Lumpur in June 1998, the year after the East Asian financial crisis had broken out, there was a plenary session entitled, 'Why is Japan so Hopeless?'.

The second is along the lines of the maxim that nothing succeeds like failure in proving that something is wrong. The East Asian financial crisis knocked the ballast out of the Asian values hot-air flying machine. It showed that no society can walk on air over a protracted period of time. In the longer run, sustained growth and development cannot be achieved without institutional reform and especially institutional reinforcement (Godement, 1999). While in the buccaneering heady days of full-throttle East Asian growth, institutions, rules, transparency, accountability and all these things might have seemed sissy, in the more sober days of financial collapse they appear pretty indispensable.

The third is globalization and especially the establishment of the WTO in 1995 (Legrain, 2001). This has been, without doubt, the strongest possible external stimulant. The WTO is all about the rule of law. The reforms that China, for example, has had to undergo in order to gain accession have had a very positive effect (Martin and Ianchovichina, 2002). China may still rank just above the bottom in freedom rankings, but it would have been at the very bottom only a couple of decades ago. China, at least maritime urban China, is a far more open society than it was and tends to become more so with every year that passes. The Chinese have a lot to thank the WTO for in achieving these recently won freedoms (Fan, 2002) – as many Chinese know. Contrary to the anti-democratic monster portrayed by some of the more vociferous 'protest community' movements in the West, in East Asia, and indeed in much of the developing world, the WTO has been perceived and indeed has acted, even if unintentionally, as a force of democratization.

The fourth are a series of political developments that have occurred in a few places in East Asia. The transformation of South Korea and Taiwan into liberal democracies is a great achievement, the importance of which cannot be underestimated. In jettisoning their military dictatorship and fascistic norms, they emulated the example of Spain following the death of Franco. But their merit is arguably all the greater. Spain's transformation was much aided and abetted by the prospect of joining the European Union. Spain (like Portugal) had become increasingly incongruous also in being a fascist state in a democratic neighbourhood. For South Korea and Taiwan, the neighbourhood can hardly be described as democratic, there was no particular external incentive – *à la* joining the EU – and indeed given the menace both face (North Korea and the PRC respectively), every argument could have been used (and was used by diehard reactionaries, but ultimately unsuccessfully) to maintain them under a form of political-security siege. South Korea and Taiwan score 2.0 on the Freedom House Index, a very great leap from where they would have been not so long ago.

What is also very important to note – and this is where both South Korea and Taiwan stand out in positive contrast to Japan – is that democracy in both places was achieved through internal social forces, including through the efforts of political elites but also by many courageous students, intellectuals, workers and professionals. Significantly, it was not handed over on a silver platter made in the US. The South Korean and Taiwanese people fought and died for their freedom. Also both South Korea and Taiwan experienced political leadership change as a result of the ballot box – something that has not occurred in Japan since the establishment of the Liberal Democratic Party in 1955. There were some changes in leadership that occurred in the early 1990s. Prime Ministers Hosokawa, Hata and Murayama were not from the LDP – although the first two were former members of the LDP, while Murayama was a veteran socialist. Coalition governments were formed that included the Socialists and the Buddhist Komeito Party. None of the political machinations, however, were submitted to the electorate. They were all backroom deals, carried out without any reference to '*vox populi*'. By the time elections had to be called, an LDP prime minister, in the person of Hashimoto, was back at the 'helm'.

Hong Kong seems to be going through a political rising, and it is also reasonable to make the prediction that the Singaporean 'nanny state' will be undergoing liberalization. Lee Kuan Yew himself has recognized that this is necessary, if only to make Singaporean society more creative (Lee, 2000). Although there have been no risings and riots in Singapore, many young Singaporeans have been voting with their feet; Singapore has been increasingly suffering from an acute brain drain as energetic bright young Singaporeans depart.

Whether these four winds will ultimately transform the continent will depend to a considerable extent on what happens in China and what happens from China – the two being quite closely interlinked.

What seems clear, however, is that there is a 'model' of East Asian political economy, which features a strong outward-looking economic development and export-oriented state, promoting and protecting government-connected private enterprise. In other words, the government provides a business-friendly environment to those businesses that are government friendly. What is equally clear is that in the longer term it is not sustainable. Either the mould has to be broken – as has occurred in South Korea – or inevitably at some stage the economy will enter into prolonged stagnation – as has occurred in Japan (Pilling, 2002).

Scenarios for China

At the Asia-Pacific regional level, China has come to matter more and more. One question that arises is whether China will fill the leadership vacuum that has characterized East Asia for the last several decades. Although Japan is by far the biggest regional economy and benefits from a close alliance with the United States, it has been hindered from exercising leadership for a combination of three reasons:

1   its economic size has not resulted in great market opportunities for East Asian exporters, as its market has tended to remain closed;
2   its ambivalence on issues related to war responsibility and guilt – along with the penchant of its political leaders to blurt out on a regular basis highly incendiary remarks – has continued to alienate its neighbours; and
3   the absence of any political leadership role.

Emotions and policies in Asia on this subject – including not only the countries of East Asia, but South Asia as well, illustrated by the recent visit to Beijing of Indian Prime Minister Vajpayee – are, as can be expected, highly mixed. On the economic front, China is clearly seen as a threat: in exports, but also in respect to inward foreign investments – with the country being perceived as taking more than a lion's share at the expense of its neighbours. But there are also very high expectations of China becoming a regional economic locomotive, as can be seen in the manner in which, for example, the ASEAN countries are gearing to establish a free-trade area with China (Pangestu, 2003; see also Breslin, this volume). One of the most affected is Taiwan – hitherto the information technology powerhouse of East Asia – which watches in dismay as lots of its money and many of its brains cross the Straits to settle in the PRC. In the Shanghai area alone, there are over half-a-million Taiwanese engineers and entrepreneurs (Einhorn and Himelstein, 2002). Certainly there are far more Asian (and other foreign) investors, entrepreneurs, managers, engineers, etc. settling in China than ever occurred or would even be imaginable in Japan. In that sense, as William Overholt (2002) and others have argued – China is a far more open economy than Japan.

Although the regional economic perspective is mixed, on balance most observers agree that it is positive. On the political, geopolitical and cultural regional levels, as is the case in relation to these spheres in the country itself, the situation is far more nebulous. Whether China becomes a constructive regional force or a destructive one, will obviously reflect domestic developments.

As things currently stand on the domestic political front, the country that China seems most to resemble is neither South Korea nor Japan, but Indonesia during the decades of Suharto's rule. The Suharto regime in Indonesia did not, as some argued, collapse because of corruption. It had been corrupt since 1965 when it took over power, and it managed to last more than three decades. The point rather was that the sole legitimacy of the regime and the ruling party Golkar resided in its ability to provide economic growth. As the national economic cake kept getting bigger, the fact that the Suharto family was helping itself to chunky slices mattered relatively little. Once the cake began to shrink, however, the legitimacy of the regime and its party disintegrated. The absence of strong institutional roots grounded in legitimacy meant that the political edifice collapsed as soon as the economic earthquake hit (A. Schwarz, 1999).

The Chinese Communist Party (CCP) finds itself in very much the same conundrum. There is no legitimacy left on the basis of ideology. Whereas China used to define its guiding doctrine as Marxism–Leninism–Maoism, the only thing left in the current regime is Leninist organizational structures. There is no ideology and no principles.

The conundrum and the paranoia are vividly illustrated in China's policies and attitudes in respect to information technology (IT). While it recognizes that it needs IT as a critical component of its engine of growth, it is also very wary, by definition, of the spread of 'information' (Laperrouza, 2002). As CCP cadres ruefully if jokingly suggest, it would be great if they could get the technology without the information.

As Chinese steadily increase their levels of economic freedom, as a middle class emerges, the drive for greater political freedoms may well grow, boosted perhaps by a failure to meet social expectations, whether among recent university graduates – it is reported that 50 per cent of university graduates in China in 2003 failed to obtain jobs (Chua, 2003) – or among the dissatisfied peasantry. Currently and for the foreseeable future the factor that is likely to cause the most social unrest and instability in China is the huge discrepancies in wealth that are occurring (Zhang and Jae, 2002/2003)

All of this rapid economic and social development is taking place in an ideological and moral vacuum and with weak institutions – especially in respect to the rule of law. Socialism with Chinese characteristics is indeed emerging as perhaps one of the rawest forms of capitalism that the world has witnessed.

The internal core challenges and dilemmas that China faces are also mirrored in the challenges and dilemmas at its periphery, especially in respect of Taiwan, Hong Kong, Tibet and among the Muslim minorities in the province of Xinjiang. Thus the centre, Beijing, increasingly finds itself under attack both from within and from without.

As these forces proliferate and intensify, there are ultimately two directions that China can take. One is to evolve towards a more tolerant, open, pluralistic, liberal and accountable political society, with strong and increasingly independent institutions and responsible governance. The other is to withdraw into its bunker, becoming more dictatorial, more opaque and more belligerent.

The post-Second World War Japanese route – what might have appeared as East Asia's variation of a 'Third Way' – is not tenable. As has been shown, the Japanese model of a closed, illiberal, mercantilist political economy is ultimately doomed to stagnation. Although there has been hardly any reform in Japan, nor has there been social unrest. This is due to the great wealth Japan has been able to accumulate. The nation of Japan today is living off its riches, a bit like a propertied person of leisure who can sustain a rich life-style by taking paintings off the manorial walls and selling them. Japan is, comparatively speaking, basking in recessionary luxury. It is the next generation that will have to pay a very heavy price (Lehmann, 2002). China is not there and will not be there for a very long time. So the East Asian Japan inspired 'Third Way' is a non-starter.

Timing here, however, may be sooner than one thinks. As anyone visiting Beijing over the course of the last few years knows, the hosting of the Olympics in 2008 has enormous political significance. Olympic Games in East Asia – Tokyo in 1964, Seoul in 1988 – are not just about throwing a few javelins around, but are primarily about positioning the nation in the global community. For Japan, 1964 represented its 'return' as an upstanding member of the world community after its defeat and humiliation in the Second World War – the following year it joined the OECD. As for South Korea, the 1988 Olympics (also followed by the country joining the OECD) provided a strong boost to political reform, among other things allowing the country to enter the international arena as a constructive and credible player, turning its back on the 'hermit kingdom' it had been for most of its history.

Various things – various 'what ifs?' – can happen on the road to Beijing 2008 over the course of the ensuing years. An intensification of protests in Hong Kong: will Beijing dispatch the PLA to 'restore order'? A massive demonstration of the Falun Gong in China: will the tanks be brought out? A 'provocation' by Taiwan: will the missiles be hurled across the Straits?

What seems reasonably certain is that while the Chinese people were prepared to forgive – but not forget – one Tiananmen, they are unlikely to forgive a second Tiananmen. China's responses to these and other challenges will determine the course that it will take in the twenty-first century and the impact that it will have on the Asia-Pacific region.

China, it is often claimed, is principally fired by nationalism. This may be true. The question, however, is whether it is enlightened constructive nationalism that we are talking about, or obscurantist destructive chauvinism (Bunnin and Cheng, 2002). The former can coexist with liberalism without any great difficulty. The latter leads to fascism. Thus will China evolve along a Taiwanese or South Korean route, or will it go down a Japanese 1930s/1940s route? The answer to that question obviously matters a great deal.

The changes that have occurred in China have been quite remarkable and have taken almost all observers by surprise. This includes the Taiwanese, many of whom now openly wonder what kind of society China will become and the implications for Taiwan. If China continues along a 'Taiwanese' road, greater economic freedoms leading to greater political freedoms, then, as they joke, they are likely to have a scenario not of 'one nation – two systems', but 'one system – two nations'.

The global political environment also of course needs to be taken into account. When Japan embarked on fascism, it was internationally quite fashionable. Japan was in the company of Germany, Austria, Italy, Spain, Portugal, among other nations. This is not true today. Although liberalism is constantly and everywhere under attack, it still retains a quasi-monopoly position as a universal political ideology. In the last decade, liberalism has swept across a good deal of the world and could continue to do so. It will be rough: the benefits of liberalism do not accrue quickly, and many societies, although they may adopt its outward forms, remain reluctant fully to embrace its central tenets. But all alternative models have clearly not been able to deliver prosperity on a sustained basis. Economic freedoms cannot, in the long run, be divorced from political freedoms.

In China today, not only is there a gap between political freedoms and economic freedoms, but also an ever-growing divergence between the country's economic system and its political system. This, among other things, makes the Chinese political scene somewhat surreal, as was illustrated by the recent political successions. As Ian Buruma vividly shows in his excellent study of Chinese dissidents (Buruma, 2001), this quality applies not only to the communist establishment, but also to that of the dissidents. Given the size and diversity of China, it is even more dangerous to generalize than is the case with most countries. The extraordinary changes notwithstanding, there have been millions of Chinese who have been left behind – what one can term 'losers', and there are millions who suffer all kinds of deprivations (Becker, 1999). Still, along with the four external winds of change that I mentioned above, there is an internal wind of change. Chinese leaders are acutely aware of the mess that their predecessors made in the past and the immense sufferings that these failures have caused to the people of China; hence the need to try to get it right this time (Lehmann, 2001). This is by no means obvious. There are many and constant challenges facing China. Some of the challenges, no matter how acute, are at least familiar: this is true, for example, of problems of environmental degradation or the great and growing income gaps. But many are also unexpected; for example the recent SARS epidemic and the uprising in Hong Kong. Furthermore, though the Chinese Communist Party retains monopoly political control at the national level, there are many and growing dissensions within the Party. It is not at all clear that the Chinese Communist Party has the institutions or the people needed to cope with these challenges. The imperatives for opening up the power base to diverse forces, perspectives and competences will become increasingly urgent.

As every visitor to China knows, the reforms of Deng Xiaoping notwithstanding, it is the portrait of Mao Zedong that still hangs proudly on Tiananmen Square. It was there that in October 1949, as Mao proclaimed the 'Liberation' of China, he pronounced: 'Never will China be humiliated again'. For China to become a great nation in the twenty-first century, its only option is to adopt – even if incrementally – the institutions and ideas of liberalism. For such a scenario to occur, much will depend not only on what happens in China, but also how China is received and addressed in the outside world.

8 China in the Asian economy

Shaun Breslin

Introduction

Even Gerry had to admit that China might be more important for the East Asian regional economy than for the world at large. Nevertheless, he argued that this importance was often overstated, and questioned the way that figures were interpreted or used to inflate China's economic significance for its neighbours. Thus, for example, while the growth rates of Chinese trade with regional neighbours were indeed large, he argued that these growth rates did not show the real significance of China as they had grown from a very low starting level. Furthermore, he argued that 'China's massive FDI boom, especially in the past decade' was often built on recycled investment from within China itself seeking to benefit from tax breaks and other incentives for 'foreign' investors. In effect, Gerry argued that China mattered to the region much less than initial impressions (and statistics) seemed to suggest.

In the sceptical spirit of DCM, this chapter accepts that too great an emphasis has been placed on growth as an indicator of China's importance. It will also elaborate on Gerry's concern that 'recycled' investment exaggerates the significance of regional FDI into China. However, this chapter will also take issue with some of Gerry's key assumptions. In particular, it suggests that his assessment of the importance of China as a market for other regional economies underplayed the significance of China for other regional states. China's real significance is not as a market for producers in other regional states, but as a production site for exports to more lucrative markets in the developed world. Crucially, I suggest that Gerry was overly 'statist' in his analysis – partly in terms of his conception of actors, but more clearly in his emphasis on the nation-state as the major unit of analysis. So this chapter argues that economic actors in other regional states still play an important role as intermediaries between China and the global economy, with a key determinant of this intermediary role being the evolution of fragmented post-Fordist production processes. Taken as a whole, China clearly does matter in the regional economy – but, while China's growth presents an opportunity for some in the region, it also poses serious challenges to others.

Intra-regional trade

> China matters a bit more to other Asian countries. Some 3.2 per cent of Singapore's exports go to China, less than to Taiwan but on par with South Korea. China accounts for 4.6 per cent of Australian exports, about the same as to Singapore. Japan sends only 5.1 per cent of its exports to China, about a quarter less than to Taiwan. Only South Korea sends China an impressive share of its exports – some 9.9 per cent, nudging ahead of exports to Japan.
>
> (Segal, 1999: 26–27)

Times have changed since Gerry was writing using figures for 1997. To be fair, Gerry was trying to explode the myth that a newly rich China provided a great new market for foreign producers – the lure of unlocking the Chinese market that has inspired foreigners since George III sent a delegation to China in 1793. And in this respect, Gerry was right. China has not proved to be the market for imported consumer goods that many hoped for, and notwithstanding the implications of World Trade Organization (WTO) entry, 'potential' and 'China' are still two words that often go together.

It is also true that the more mature and lucrative markets of Japan (despite a decade-long recession), North America and Europe are still the major prizes for most regional states following export-led growth strategies. Nevertheless, as Table 8.1 shows, all regional states now have strong trading relationships with China. And this is not a result of trade diversion away from Western markets, but trade fragmentation.

Following Naughton (1996), any analysis of Chinese trade should start by dividing this trade into two. On the one hand, we witness a relatively closed and protected domestic trading regime with considerable barriers to entry designed to limit international competition and protect domestic producers. The government has used import plans, licences and quotas and retained some of the highest import tariffs in the world to protect key domestic sectors – although we should note that tariffs were steadily reduced throughout the 1990s. In addition to these 'normal' trade barriers, a number of other factors limited access to the Chinese market. Incomplete currency convertibility resulted in restricted access to foreign currency, and meant that converting and repatriating profits was difficult if not impossible; the lack of transparency in China's policy-making (and in particular, the monopoly of the state news-agency, *Xinhua*, in the dissemination of economic information) placed outsiders at a disadvantage; intellectual and property right infringement was costing millions to

Table 8.1 The importance of China as a trade partner, 2002

Country	Exports to China as % of total exports	Exports to China and HK as % of total exports	China's export ranking	Imports from China as % of total imports	Imports from China and HK as % of total imports	China's import ranking
Cambodia	1.29	1.64	6	5.97	14.00	3
Indonesia	5.41	7.48	5	8.41	10.92	1
Japan	7.67	13.43	2	16.55	19.83	2
South Korea	12.09	18.43	2	9.42	10.30	3
Malaysia	4.34	8.96	4	5.15	7.71	4
Myanmar	5.37	6.48	4	19.77	22.31	1
Philippines	3.76	8.80	3	4.48	9.96	3
Singapore	4.37	13.26	3	6.20	8.60	4
Taiwan	7.41	31.10	1	6.90	8.41	3
Thailand	4.40	9.46	3	5.98	7.31	3
Vietnam	6.80	8.57	2	11.91	15.51	2

Source: International Monetary Fund (2003) *Direction of Trade Statistics Yearbook* (Washington, DC: IMF).

copyright owners; and the differential application of the fiscal system where local companies typically negotiated tax-free deals with the local government, effectively provided a hidden fiscal tariff for foreign companies.

Furthermore, US trade officials claimed that the lack of full price reform in China acted as a hidden state subsidy for those Chinese producers in the state sector, or private enterprises that retained close and warm links with the state administration. They paid cheap state set prices, while external actors were forced to pay the higher market rate (Barshefsky, 1999). Chinese enterprises were also supported through massive subsidies, which often took the form of 'loans' from government or the banking system that will never be repaid. Although WTO entry should theoretically change the situation, the extent of domestic protection helps explain why China has not yet proved to be a significant market for regional (and extra-regional) exporters.

But on the other hand, and in stark contrast to the domestic trade regime, China has created a remarkably liberal internationalized trading regime built on encouraging FDI to produce exports for external markets. Indeed, at WTO entry, around half of all imports came into China tariff free in the form of components that were processed and subsequently re-exported as finished goods (Lardy, 2002b). Here, foreign involvement was encouraged as it did not compete with domestic industries, and provided the opportunity for rapid capital accumulation. This policy has been a major contributing factor in explaining the rapid growth of Chinese exports. In 2002, foreign-invested firms accounted for just over half of all Chinese trade, and if we added domestic Chinese producers who produce under contract for export using foreign components, then the figure gets closer to 60 per cent. So while Gerry was right that China does not matter that much as a market for regional producers, China matters much more for those regional economic actors who see China as a production platform for exports that will eventually end up in the West.

It is for this reason that Table 8.1 gives two sets of figures for trade with China – one for trade with the PRC, and one that also includes trade with Hong Kong. It is true that including Hong Kong in Chinese trade does tend to inflate the importance of China as a trade partner for regional states. On average, once a good leaves China, there is a 24 per cent extra value added in Hong Kong before it is re-exported to its final destination (Chang, 2001a: 3). Nevertheless, while we might have expected Hong Kong's position as a link between China and the world to decrease as a result of China's opening, the opposite is the case. In the decade from 1991, around half of Chinese exports were re-exported via Hong Kong (Hanson and Feenstra, 2001: 2), and the value of Hong Kong's re-exports to and from China grew by an average of 10 per cent per annum.

This is partly a result of growth 'spillover' (Chia and Lee, 1993: 236). As the production of exports in Hong Kong has become increasingly expensive, it has migrated over the border into the Pearl River Delta of Guangdong Province. It is also partly a result of the political conflict between China and Taiwan, which means that much cross-Strait trade is still routed through Hong Kong. But the most important reason is the increasing fragmentation of production across national boundaries. As will be discussed in more detail later, companies in Hong Kong (and elsewhere in the region) have marketed themselves as having the knowledge and the necessary connections to make a success of doing business in China. As such, they have exploited their historical position as a link between China and the world to forge a position as a link between new China and the global economy.

Intra-regional FDI

Gerry argued in his article that official figures overstate the real extent of 'foreign' investment due to the significance of 'round-tripping'. This refers to the process of domestic Chinese actors sending money to Hong Kong that is then invested in China (often through a shell company) to take advantage of the considerable tax breaks and other incentives afforded to 'foreign' investors. The very nature of the process makes it difficult to be exact about its extent. Following Lardy (1995: 1067) and Harrold and Lall (1993: 24), a consensus emerged that round-tripping accounted for around a quarter of all investment in 1992. More recent research by Bhaskaran (2003) and Wu *et al.* (2002: 102) put the figure at between 25 per cent and 36 per cent.

But, even armed with this knowledge, it is difficult to come to any other conclusion than China matters a great deal when it comes to FDI flows. China became the second biggest recipient of FDI in the world after the United States in the 1990s, and FDI has grown more than twenty-fold since the beginning of the reform period. In 2002, China actually surpassed the US as the world's major recipient of FDI (*People's Daily*, 2002). Cumulative FDI in China in the reform period exceeded US$400 billion at the start of 2003, and China accounts for something like 20 per cent of global FDI in developing countries. The overwhelming majority of this FDI is in productive capacity, with the purchase of stocks, bonds and so on accounting for less than 5 per cent of total foreign capital inflows since 1978 (Chen Chunlai, 2002: 2).

Around 65 per cent of FDI takes the form of contractual or equity joint ventures with Chinese companies, although the fastest growth is in wholly foreign-owned enterprises which now account for roughly one-third of the total. The majority of FDI is for the production of textiles,

Table 8.2 Accumulated FDI stock in China by source countries, 1983–1999
(1980 US$ million)

	1983–1991	1992–1995	1996–1999	1983–1999
NIEs	61.75	74.12	61.71	66.17
Hong Kong	58.01	58.98	44.37	50.89
Taiwan	2.62	9.81	7.15	7.68
Singapore	1.12	3.29	6.35	4.76
South Korea	0	2.04	3.84	2.83
ASEAN	0.49	1.92	1.85	1.74
Japan	13.48	6.64	8.38	8.24
US	11.31	7.4	8.61	8.43
Western Europe	6.51	4.39	9.52	7.40
Latin America	0.11	0.52	6.09	3.53

apparel, footwear, toys and electronic goods. It is this last sector where FDI is growing fastest, with a particularly striking growth of FDI in computer-related manufacturing for export. Of the top 20 foreign-invested exporters in China, 17 are in electronic-related manufacturing.

Table 8.2 provides an indication of these FDI flows into China by origin, showing the importance of investment from the region in comparison to extra-regional sources. This table needs some annotation for clarification. First, the figures only show FDI until 1999 because of the subsequent astonishing rise of investment from Latin America into China, which in 2002 exceeded the value of investment from North America. Almost all of this Latin American investment comes from the British Virgin Islands (now the second largest investor in China) and the Cayman Islands (now eighth). The explanation for this rise in investment is found in the fiscal regimes of the Virgin and Cayman Islands. Investors from other countries incorporate in these tax havens in order to lower (or eliminate) their fiscal commitments (Palan, 2002: 152). Given the nature of such tax-evading investment, it is difficult to be precise about its real origin. However, based on interviews in the region, it seems that the overwhelming majority of this investment comes from Taiwan, with a smaller amount from Hong Kong. As such, the size of the investment from Latin America since 1999 distorts the real balance of investment, and disguises the real continuing importance of FDI from Taiwan and Hong Kong.

China's re-emergence in the global political economy has served the interests of some regional producers very well. Increasing production costs in Hong Kong, Taiwan and South Korea coincided with appreciating regional currencies, which increased the cost of exports on the US market. As such, both those Japanese producers that had originally invested in regional NICs to produce exports, and indigenous producers from the NICs themselves, were searching for new lower-cost production sites.

Of course, much of this investment went to other ASEAN states that were themselves seeking to attract investment to produce exports. But China became an increasingly attractive option as a result of four key phases in domestic Chinese policy. The first, from 1978 to 1986, marked a very limited opening of parts of China to the global economy, with international contacts limited to the Special Economic Zones (SEZs) and specially selected open coastal cities (Hamrin, 1990; Howell, 1993). The second phase, from 1986 saw the further opening of China, and the creation of a soft environment beneficial to foreign investors. This included lowering fees for labour and rent, establishing tax rebates for exporters, and allowing limited currency convertibility to allow investors to repatriate some profits. The government also extended the joint venture contracts beyond the original 50-year limit, and created a legal basis for wholly foreign-owned enterprises. This move considerably increased the attraction of investing in China to produce exports for other markets. While foreign-invested enterprises only accounted for 2 per cent of exports and 6 per cent of imports before 1986, the figure had increased to 48 per cent and 52 per cent respectively by 2000 (Braunstein and Epstein, 2002: 23).

The third turning point came in 1992. From 1989, Premier Li Peng instituted a retrenchment policy, with a limited reversal of reform in an attempt to bring inflation under control. China's international image was also tarnished by the 1989 Tiananmen crackdown, and the resulting 'conservative' wind in policy. In a tour of southern China in 1992 (the *nan xun*) Deng Xiaoping effectively set policy in an *ad hoc* manner, praising the emergence of proto-capitalist practices in open areas and calling for a new policy of rapid economic reform and further opening. In 1993 FDI in a single year outstripped the combined total of the entire preceding years of reform put together, and, following the devaluation of the renminbi in 1994, producing for export in China became increasingly attractive.

The fourth key change came with China's entry into the WTO at the Doha Ministerial meeting in 2001. Following WTO entry, China attracted a record of US$52.7 billion in foreign direct investment in 2002. Chinese officials forecast that FDI will double to reach US$100 billion in every year of the Eleventh Five-Year Plan period (2006–2010) (*People's Daily*, 2003). In particular, WTO entry is expected to increase investment aimed at accessing the Chinese market, particularly in banking, tourism, commerce, hospitals and education, as China gradually lifts its restrictions on foreign investment in line with its WTO agreements. Nevertheless, the evidence from the first year of WTO entry is that export-based investment continues to dominate.

The de-territorialization of production

In earlier periods of reform, it was possible to make a rather blunt division of FDI into China by place of origin. Western firms primarily tended to invest in China to access the Chinese market, while East Asian firms tended to invest in China to produce exports. Of course, there were exceptions to this rule, but the dichotomy more or less held firm. In more recent years, the evidence for a continued dichotomy has become somewhat mixed. On one hand, from sports shoes, to children's toys to electronic goods, Western trademarks are now common on goods that carry the 'made in China' stamp. On the other, investment figures still show the predominance of Asian investment in China.

An answer to this apparently contradictory information lies in increasingly fragmented production processes, and the role of regional firms as intermediaries between China and the global economy (Gereffi *et al.*, 1984). With different parts of the production process located in the most cost-effective location for that stage of production, we have a situation where the production of a simple plastic Barbie doll can involve seven different national jurisdictions. As a result, we need to disaggregate investment figures and consider the implications of post-Fordist production networks and transnational (and multinational) capital flows. By doing so, the significance of 'national' or 'territorial' conceptions of investment and trade declines, and a greater emphasis is placed on the role of non-state actors in 'commodity driven production networks' and 'contract manufacturing companies' that are both transnational in nature.

Anita Chan (1996), for example, has investigated investment in the biggest sports shoe factory in the world in Guangdong Province. This factory is a joint venture with Taiwanese investment that produces sports shoes for Reebok, Nike and Adidas. Liaw (2003) has similarly traced the significance of the Pou-Chen company in Taiwan which produces 15 per cent of the world's sports shoes in its factories in China (and now Vietnam) for a host of foreign companies – Nike, Reebok, New Balance, Adidas, Timberland, Asics, Puma, Hi-Tec, Lotto, LA Gear, Mitre, and so on.

Companies in Hong Kong have similarly sought to exploit their position as intermediaries between China and the world, stressing their considerable expertise and specialist knowledge – technical, cultural and linguistic – of China (Yu *et al.*, 2001: 6–9). Increasingly, companies like Li and Fung act as 'matchmakers', linking Western investors with Chinese factories (Hanson and Feenstra, 2001) carrying out contracted projects in China on behalf of their Western customers – it is not so much FDI as FII – Foreign Indirect Investment.

The same is true of the major Commodity Manufacturing Enterprises (CMEs) which now play a pivotal role in the production of consumer electronics. Four CMEs of US origin (Solectron, Flextronics, SCI and Jabil

Circuits) and one from Canada (Celestica) have emerged as major players in the IT industry (Boy, 2002). These CMEs 'unlike the more traditional manufacturers and multinationals, do not make their own brand-name products, instead deploying global networks with fast-response capabilities to provide production and other (mainly logistics) services to brand marketers' (Chen Shin-Hong, 2002: 251). Such enterprises often operate in China through regional affiliates. Singapore Flextronics, for example, invests in China on behalf of Microsoft, Motorola, Dell, Palm and Sony Erickson. In all these cases, the 'Made in China' brand will appear on the good – a good which carries a non-Chinese brand name, but the investment and trade figures will show inter-Asian trade and investment.

For Chen Shin-Hong (2002: 249) this changing structure of international manufacturing has provided an opportunity for Taiwanese intermediary producers to 'go global', 're-deploying their production networks – and more recently their logistics networks – overseas so as to maintain their cost efficiency in order to better serve their [US] customers'. In the case of Taiwan, this process of going global takes two forms. On one level, Taiwan has developed its own CMEs such as BenQ and Hon Hai Precision Industry (Boy, 2002). On another level, Taiwanese investment in the computer industry in China is by companies that operate under Original Equipment Manufacturer (OEM) deals with either Japanese or US companies (Sasuga, 2002). Unlike the CMEs, OEM producers use their own brand names, but are dependent on core technology and operating platforms produced in Japan and the US. As such, the Taiwanese invested factories in China, which typically concentrate on low-value-added labour-intensive processes, represent the end stage of a production process that spans the most industrialized global economies such as the US and Japan, intermediate states such as Taiwan, and developing states like China.

China matters – but how and who for?

Economic security

For business elites, primarily in the more developed regional states (Japan, South Korea, Taiwan and Hong Kong), seeking to reduce production costs to maintain export competitiveness, and to gain new business as intermediaries in global production chains, China matters very much. But while investing in China has been profitable for individual regional companies, there is some concern in regional governments that the extent of investment in China has worrying long-term consequences that threaten economic security. In Hong Kong, there is concern that the transfer of manufacturing production has led to the domestic economy becoming 'hollowed out', contributing to growing unemployment (Hornik, 2002; Phar, 2002). There are similar worries in Japan that some industries –

notably textiles – are becoming hollowed out as production moves to China, where wages are just 4 per cent of comparable Japanese manufacturing wages (Hiranuma, 2002). Manufacturing labour costs in China in 2001 were a mere US$0.53 an hour. It makes little or no sense for Japanese producers to pay US$19.51 in Japan, or even US$0.91 in Thailand (Coutts, 2003: 2).

The biggest concerns are in Taiwan, where economic issues combine with political fears. In short, there is a real worry that economic dependence on the mainland will increase China's ability to force its will on Taiwan in political spheres. But, despite government attempts to encourage a diversification of investment away from China, the lure of cheaper production costs means that China remains the primary destination for Taiwanese FDI.

These three examples show that what is good for the investor might not be as beneficial for the 'national interest'. And while China matters in one respect for workers who are fearful of their jobs migrating to lower-cost production sites, it matters in a very different way for investors seeking to maximize profits.

Competitive development

One area which Gerry did not consider in his 1999 article is the extent to which China matters as a competitor to other regional states – particularly those which follow similar export-led strategies to China's. In re-engaging with the global economy, China learnt from the experiences of regional developing states, and emulated a number of their strategies. Of course there were many differences as well, but I contend that there was a clear intention to emulate, and thus compete with, other export oriented developmental states in the region. And to this end, a key challenge for other exporting states came with the above-mentioned 'restructuring' of China's foreign exchange-rate system in 1994. At first sight, China appeared to undertake a 50 per cent devaluation when it moved to a new exchange rate of RMB8.7 to the dollar. In reality, many currency transactions were already taking place at this level prior to devaluation, and the real value of devaluation was probably nearer to 20–30 per cent for most exporters. Indeed, Fernald *et al.* (1998: 2–3) put the figure at a mere 7 per cent.

For some observers, this devaluation was the starting point for regional financial chaos that resulted in the financial crises of 1997 (Bergsten, 1997; Huh and Kasa, 1997; Makin, 1997). This interpretation is too extreme, and ignores the many other contributory factors. Nevertheless, combined with the other incentives offered to exporters, by 1994 China was an increasingly important recipient of FDI and a source of exports. And while it is not the case that the investment–trade nexus in Asia represents a zero-sum game, it is true that China was increasingly competing with other export-oriented states for foreign investment, and competed with the same states for access to the key lucrative markets of the US, Japan and the EU. This process has led the *New York Times* (2002) to argue that China 'is grabbing' much of the investment that had previously gone to other regional states. In short, the suggestion is that there is only so much room in the 'market place' for countries searching for the same FDI to produce the same goods for export to the same markets. The potential problem for late-developing states emphasizing low costs as a means of attracting investment to spur export-led growth is that an even later developer with even lower costs might erode their comparative advantage.

This view is not shared by all. Fernald *et al.* (1998) argue that the data show that the growth of Chinese trade did not have an impact on exports from other regional states. Wu *et al.* (2002) from the Singapore Ministry of Trade look at investment rather than trade, and similarly argue that increased investment into China did not cause the Asian financial crises – rather the crises themselves were the cause of the decline in investment into other regional states. Nevertheless, they accept that some of the investment that has gone into China might well have gone to ASEAN under other circumstances, and accept the general premise that the increasing popularity of China as an investment site does create competition for the rest of the region. While all of the above analyses concentrate on national figures, the Japan External Trade Organization has disaggregated overall figures and analysed individual products. These figures suggest that there is indeed a correlation between the rise of Chinese exports to the US and Japan of specific goods, and the decline in exports of those same goods from Malaysia, Thailand, Indonesia and the Philippines.

In politics, perceptions are often more important than reality. And whatever the reality of this debated impact of China on regional states really has been, there remains a perception that China matters as a competitive threat. Neither is this simply a historical matter. Writing on the perceived importance of China's entry into the WTO, Braunstein and Epstein (2002: 2) argue that 'many competitors in Southeast Asia and elsewhere worry that the PRC's entry will lead to an acceleration of investment flows to the PRC and a corresponding reduction in flows to themselves.' This fear is supported by calculations by World Bank economists (Kawai and Bhattasali, 2001), which suggest that the closer a state's export profile to that of China, then the more that state is expected to lose. Indonesia alone is expected to lose US$73 million as a result of China's WTO accession, with the impact on certain sectors, most notably textiles, expected to be even more dramatic.

Throughout Asia, this conception of China as a super-competitor is informing not only media debates, but also official policy. Lee Kuan Yew has famously described the economic relationship between China and Singapore as an 'elephant on one side and a mouse on the other' (Eckholm and Kahn, 2002). Malaysia's Mahathir Mohamad has similarly aired his concern that 'There's not much capital going around. Whatever there is gets sucked in by China' (Chandler, 2003) with claims that 16,000 jobs were lost in Penang alone in 2002 as major high-tech producers moved capacity to China (Eckholm and Kahn, 2002).

Does China matter? A reality check

If Mahathir and Lee are right, then Gerry was wrong in his estimation of how China mattered for the regional economy. Nevertheless, Gerry was right in arguing that China's economic power is often exaggerated, and that growth figures in themselves do not always give an accurate reflection of China's real significance in the regional economy. In the spirit of the original 'Does China Matter?', it is time to take on a more sceptical tone.

It is quite easy to form a vision of an economically powerful China by relying simply on aggregate figures, and more importantly, on growth figures. When you have a population the size of China's then aggregate GDP can still be very high even with very low per capita income. And if you start from a very low base level, then it is relatively easy to achieve high growth figures.

For example, China's rapid economic growth is often juxtaposed against economic stagnation in Japan – and even if we are slightly sceptical about the veracity of official Chinese growth figures, the contrasting growth experiences of the two states cannot be denied. Growth figures suggest that China is doing much better than Japan – and in many ways it is. But China's share of world output is still only one-third of Japan's, and even the highest calculations of China's per capita national income come out at roughly one-sixth of the figure for Japan. Indeed, after 20 years of growth, China's per capita GDP still comes out at about half that of Russia's.

Of course, national figures for China hide the massive sectoral and regional differences. One of the key impacts of economic reform on China as a whole has been a growth in inequality. The Gini coefficient measurement of inequality for China in 1981 was a very low 0.288, rising to 0.388 in 1995 and on to 0.46 in 2002. Hsu (2002) argues that if you add in illegal and unofficial income that does not show up in the official data, then the figure is already more than 0.56. But even if we accept official figures, then China is fifth in the league table of the world's most

Table 8.3 Uneven integration into the global economy

Province	Share of FDI 1979–1991	Share of FDI 1992–1998	Share of foreign-invested exports
Guangdong	36.6	27.6	44
Shanghai	5.8	8.5	12
Jiangsu	2.7	12.6	11
Fujian	6.5	10.1	7
Shandong	2.4	6.4	7
Tianjin	1.7	4.1	5
Liaoning	4.2	4.5	5
Zhejiang	1.2	3.3	4
Coastal 8			95

Source: Information provided by the Institute of World Economics and Politics, Chinese Academy of Social Sciences, and Francoise Lemoine (2000) 'FDI and the Opening Up of China's Economy', CEPII Research Centre Working Papers 2000–2011: 30.

unequal states, and if Hsu is right, then only South Africa and Brazil have greater levels of inequality than China.

The biggest source of inequality comes from the urban–rural divide, with the gap between rural and urban incomes continuing to rise. But, for the purposes of this chapter, I will concentrate on the coastal–interior divide. Table 8.3 shows how China's coastal provinces have received the vast majority of FDI. Even these figures do not tell the true story. Investment in Liaoning is heavily concentrated on Dalian, while the Pearl River Delta has received the lion's share of investment in Guangdong Province. And, as Table 8.3 also shows, this uneven share of provincial FDI is also reflected in the uneven distribution of exports by foreign-funded enterprises.

So perhaps the question should not be: does China matter, but rather: which parts of China matter? Or perhaps we should go back to the Lasswellian definition of politics and ask who gets what? As we have seen, the growth in Chinese exports has relied very heavily on FDI to produce exports. While the Chinese authorities may have initially hoped that FDI would help reinvigorate the domestic Chinese economy by using domestically produced components, the majority of regional investors choose to import key components from existing plants overseas, with the Chinese sites typically only concentrating on labour-intensive component assembly.

This does not suggest that China has not benefited from the export of assembled goods. It has created jobs – although typically low-wage and low-skilled jobs – and generated income. But it does suggest that China has not gained as much as simply looking at bilateral figures for export growth initially suggests. Rather, we need to take a more holistic view of trade figures, and consider the value added, rather than the nominal value, of exports. As such, many of the gains that have been made through China's growth have accrued to economic actors across the region, rather than to 'China' itself. China matters, but it is perhaps not as important in its own right as the figures suggest.

One final factor warrants consideration here. In considering economic regionalization in East Asia, Bernard and Ravenhill (1995: 197) argued that 'foreign subsidiaries in Malaysia's EPZs were more integrated with Singapore's free-trade industrial sector than with the "local" industry'. Similar trends are evident in China. Lardy (1995: 1080), for example, has referred to the lack of linkages with the domestic economy as creating 'enclave' economies for foreign producers. In its extreme form, this can lead to what is termed 'technologyless growth', in that the technology base of the national economy is not advanced, as economic growth occurs through the assembly of external productive forces, rather than domestic productive forces. Of course, wholly technologyless growth is a pure type that is not reflected in reality. Participation in the global economy has seen technological upgrading in China. But what is significant here is that linkages between export-oriented areas and sectors and the rest of the domestic national economy remain relatively weak. The technological and developmental spill-overs of export-oriented growth remain, in many areas, to be attained.

Intra-regional relations

In the years since Gerry was writing, China's significance has increased not only as a bilateral economic partner for other regional states, but also in the evolution of regional forums. On a very simple level, there is a recognition within the rest of East Asia that any viable regional organization has to include China – even if this makes the inclusion of Taiwan politically difficult if not impossible. From the Chinese side, a former Chinese diplomat in the region argues that increasing willingness to promote region-wide bodies reflects China's transition to becoming a 'normal' state – a state that pursues its interests through dialogue and cooperation based on accepted norms, rather than through unilateral action based on a rejection of such norms.

It is also a result of the transition to a unipolar world order after the collapse of the Soviet Union. The US is perceived as seeking to impose its beliefs in a unipolar world, unrestrained by any counter-weight to its hegemony. The resulting 'new American hegemony' (Zhou, 2002) is pursued in all areas – including using both bilateral pressures on developing states, and US power in the international financial institutions, to promote US economic values. Far better, then, to fight this hegemony through the increased power of a regional organization which promotes alternative norms to those of the hegemon.

In many respects, the Asian financial crises marked a key watershed in both China's and ASEAN's understanding of the efficacy of wider regional cooperation. As China increasingly liberalizes its economy, not least in the wake of WTO entry, then it becomes increasingly enmeshed within the regional economy, and increasingly affected by how well the region fares. Working together to head off potential crises at a regional level is therefore increasingly seen as being in China's own self-interest – especially if such regional cooperation can mitigate the need to rely on the US-dominated global financial institutions in times of crisis.

On the ASEAN side, Webber (2001) argues that the financial crises of 1997 exposed the inability of both the 'small' version of regionalism in ASEAN and the 'large' version of regionalism in APEC to act in any meaningful manner. Frustration at this failure combined with a resentment towards the type of solutions imposed by Western-dominated financial institutions – particularly when US pressures stymied Japanese proposals to establish an Asian Monetary Fund in 1997.

This combination of Chinese and ASEAN approaches have come together in two of the three major regional economic initiatives that China has embraced. The first is the ASEAN Plus Three (APT) process where China joins with Japan and South Korea in formal dialogue and consultation with ASEAN. Although originally initiated as a means of finding a regional voice that could talk to Europe through the ASEM process in 1995, the APT has evolved into a major – and notwithstanding the persistence of APEC perhaps *the* major – forum for regional dialogue and consultation.

The second is the Chiang Mai Initiative (CMI), which was finally agreed by APT finance ministers in May 2000. The CMI allows signatory states to borrow US dollars from other members' reserves to buy their own currency, thus providing a bulwark against global financial flows and speculative attacks (Wang Seok-Dong, 2002). The CMI works through the creation of bilateral swap deals under a regional umbrella, with the full lattice of bilateral agreements now all but complete. Although a similar swap process existed within ASEAN prior to the CMI, the reason for its expansion, and another example of why China matters, is quite straightforward – when consensus was reached in 2000, China's foreign reserves were greater than the entire reserves of all ASEAN states combined (and Japan's reserves were even greater).

The third regional initiative that China has embraced moves beyond financial regionalism towards trade-based regionalism in the proposals to create an ASEAN–China Free Trade Area (ACFTA). First proposed at the Manila summit in 1999, the ACFTA initiative took on a new impetus with the signing of the Framework Agreement on ASEAN–China Comprehensive Economic Cooperation at the Eighth ASEAN Summit Meeting in Cambodia in 2002. ACFTA is conceived as a dual-speed process, with initial common tariff reduction to be completed by 2006, and a full free-trade area in place by 2013.

On the face of it, the ACFTA is an important symbol of China's importance for the regional economy, as well as an important practical step in fostering closer economic integration. It is intended to act as a spur to intra-regional investment, and to increase access to the Chinese market for ASEAN producers – although the other side of the same coin is a fear that it might also lead to a new influx of Chinese imports. But ACFTA is in many ways a means to other ends, rather than just an end in itself. Stubbs notes that Japan was originally reluctant to join the APT process for fear of antagonizing the United States:

> Although Japan was still reluctant to get involved, the Chinese government's agreement to take up ASEAN's invitation essentially forced Tokyo's hand. Beijing was interested in building on the economic ties that were developing with Southeast Asia and the Japanese government could not afford to let China gain an uncontested leadership position in the region.
>
> (Stubbs, 2002: 443)

In a similar vein, ACFTA can be seen as a means of trying to force the Japanese government's hand and promote a type of Asian regionalism first embodied in Mahathir Mohamad's proposals to establish an East Asia Economic Group in 1990. Indeed, Mahathir is explicit in his desire to see ACFTA as a stepping-stone to a pan-Asian Free Trade area and to 'go back to the original proposal for an East Asian Economic Group' (Hennock, 2001). China clearly matters for the architects of region building in East Asia, but in economic terms, and for the time being at least, Japan still matters even more.

Conclusion

What was to become 'Does China Matter?' first appeared in a special section of *New Political Economy* on the future of China that I put together in 1998 (Segal, 1998). In discussing his contribution, Gerry was willing to accept that he was painting a deliberately negative portrait of China. His aim was to provide an antidote to what he perceived to be the hyperbole, primarily emanating from the United States, that placed China as a 'near competitor' and vastly exaggerated China's importance in global affairs. In this respect, his analysis of China's regional economic role is very useful, in that it leads us to question whether, despite impressive growth figures, China is as significant as many automatically assume it to be.

But having said that, Gerry's approach went too far. This is primarily because of Gerry's emphasis on considering China's importance as a market for regional producers. By extending the analysis to consider China's importance as an export platform, then we reach different conclusions to Gerry that suggest that China is more important than he perceived. China matters very much for the regional economy, but matters in different ways for different actors in different countries. The extent to which China matters has come into sharper relief since the 1997 regional financial crises – and the concept of crisis is apposite here. 'Crisis' in Chinese is *weiji*. The first of these characters, *wei*, on its own means danger, while one of the meanings of the second, *ji*, on its own is opportunity. This combination of *wei* and *ji* is an apt summary of the two divergent ways that China matters. The danger for some lies in the potential of increased competition from China in domestic markets. More immediately, it also lies in loss of growth and jobs through the diversion of investment and the production of exports to China. And it is precisely this rise of China as 'the workshop of the world' (Chandler, 2003) that provides the opportunity for others to benefit from China's growth by exploiting the comparative advantage that China possesses as an export platform.

Ultimately, though, the question 'does China matter?' is fundamentally misconceived. Maintaining a focus on the nation-state as the basic unit of analysis obscures more than it clarifies in considering the dynamics of change in contemporary China. States and state actors are clearly still important – although the Chinese case suggests that even here we need to disaggregate the state and consider the role of state actors at the local level rather than simply focusing on the ideas and actions of national leaders.

Similarly, using simple bilateral statistics does not allow us to really understand who or what 'matters' in the regional or the global economy. Increasingly, it is companies that matter, and the networks of commodity-based relationships that are created – indeed are deemed necessary – for global sourcing and production. And these networks can mean that while US trade representatives are complaining about the trade deficit with China, and others complain about the China challenge to American jobs, it is often American companies that are reaping the rewards of China's growth through lower costs and increased profits. It may not be fashionable to cite Engels, but the argument that he made in 1880 that good political analysis should consider 'what is produced, how it is produced, and how the products are exchanged' (Engels, 1970) strikes me as having a lot to tell us about how China matters in the modern world.

9 China as a regional military power

Bates Gill

Introduction: global v. regional influence

In asking the question, 'does China matter?', Gerry Segal answered with an emphatic 'no' most of all when gauging the country's influence at a geostrategic and global level. However, when discussing China's import-ance at a regional level, he appeared more inclined towards a qualified 'yes' (Segal, 1999).

For example, in discussing whether China matters economically, he argued while 'China is at best a minor ... part of the global economy', he noted that it 'matters a bit more to Asian countries' (Segal, 1999: 28). Similarly, while judging China as a 'second-rate' military power because it cannot take on America, it is not 'third-rate' like its Asian neighbours: 'China poses a formidable threat to the likes of the Philippines', is 'clearly a serious menace to Taiwan', and is a 'problem to be circumvented or moved' with regard to progress on the Korean Peninsula (Segal, 1999: 29, 32). And, while he argued that China 'does not even matter in terms of global culture', he would probably agree that it does retain a strong historical and cultural influence over many of its near neighbours (Segal, 1999: 34; see also Goodman, this volume, Chapter 6).

Gerry did not make the point explicit, but he drew the right distinc-tion: China matters far more at a regional than at a strategic and global level. This is certainly true in regional military matters, and probably more so today than when Gerry penned his article in 1998–1999. While in comparison to such potential military rivals as the United States and Japan, the Chinese military may be a 'second rate' power regionally, it never-theless has devoted considerable investment over the past decade into developing a far greater regional presence and is poised to steadily expand its presence and potential even more. China has always 'mattered' as a regional military power, appears destined to matter even more in the years ahead, and is on a trajectory to become the foremost military power among the countries in East Asia. As such, China's growing regional military capabilities are worthy of greater concern and attention. Moreover, if China intends to use force to achieve certain political objectives – regarding Taiwan in particular – and draw other powers into the fray, such as the United States, Japan, and possibly other American regional allies, China's growing regional military capability and confidence should be a source of special concern for all with an interest in East Asian stability.

This chapter examines these points by first briefly reviewing China's military development as a regional power from the founding of the People's Republic through to the early 1990s. Noting a key turning point from the mid-1990s, the chapter goes on to describe a more serious and ongoing military modernization effort in China along three key axes – decisive doctrinal shifts, advanced hardware acquisition, and critical 'software' reforms – which further bolster China's credibility as a regional military power. A particular emphasis will be given to this latter, often unseen issue of 'software' reforms, examining important developments for China in terms of military organization, funding, education, training and logistics, and how they have begun to make a difference for Chinese military modernization. The chapter will briefly consider how China's growing regional military capability compares to military modernization programmes among China's neighbours, programmes which often have growing Chinese military capabilities in mind. The chapter wraps up with some important caveats and conclusions regarding China's growing significance as a regional military power.

Long-standing regional military influence

From 1949 and the establishment of the People's Republic of China ('PRC' or 'China'), the country steadily succeeded in expanding its military control and political influence over nearby regions, such as the forceful integration of Tibet (1959), while at the same time strengthening a basic ability to deter invasion of the mainland. Moreover, the Chinese military proved entirely capable, even in the early 1950s, of greatly complicating the plans of militaries seeking to extend their reach at or near Chinese border regions, as US-led forces painfully learned in the Korean and Vietnam wars. China succeeded in extending its line of control southward and acquiring additional territory in its border war with India in October and November 1962. China also stood firm in violent clashes with the Soviet Union over disputed territory along the Assuri/Wusuli and Amur/Heilong Rivers in early 1969. However, China was less successful in its short-lived incursion to 'teach Vietnam a lesson' in early 1979.

By the mid- to late 1960s, China succeeded in developing and testing an indigenous ballistic missile capability, becoming the first Asian power to detonate a fission weapon (1964) and a thermonuclear device (1967). China has steadily built up its nuclear forces to become the world's third-largest nuclear power, and, from the beginning of its nuclear weapons programme, has maintained forces with an eye to regional contingencies. For example, China's earliest strategic forces were developed with the intention of targeting American bases in Japan and Taiwan. As Chinese missiles scientists achieved greater ranges, other places in the Asia-Pacific region – such as the Philippines, Guam, and Hawaii – were targeted (Lewis and Hua, 1992: 17). Early this decade, China's medium-range nuclear missiles – with ranges of between 1,800 and 5,000 kilometres and capable of reaching regional targets such as India, the Philippines, Guam and Japan – outnumbered China's longer-range strategic nuclear weapons by a ratio of 5 to 1. This estimate would count approximately 40 DF-3As, 20 DF-4s, 48 DF-21As, and 12 JL-1s, versus about 20 to 24 DF-5As (range of 13,000 kilometres), (Gill *et al.*, 2001).

Even with the ongoing reduction of some 2 to 3 million troops since the 1980s, the Chinese People's Liberation Army (PLA) still boasts a formidable force in sheer numbers alone: some 2.27 million troops, over 8,000 tanks, some 17,000 artillery pieces and multiple rocket launchers, over 1,300 fighters and ground attack aircraft (including some 166 Su-27s and Su-30s from Russia), some 250 bombers, nearly 70 submarines, 63 surface combatants, and hundreds of smaller coastal patrol craft (International Institute for Strategic Studies, 2002: 145–148). These figures do not include the personnel and equipment of the People's Armed Police (PAP), China's domestic paramilitary force, numbering between 1 and 1.5 million strong (International Institute for Strategic Studies, 2002: 148; Tanner, 2002: 611). China also claims a citizen militia which in theory numbers in the tens of millions. Taken together, China's military forces are easily the largest in the world, and dwarf those of its regional neighbours.

Increasing potential from the mid-1990s

China's increased regional military capability involves critical developments along three important axes: decisive doctrinal shifts, advanced hardware acquisition, and critical 'software' reforms. From the early to mid-1990s, the Chinese military increasingly shifted its doctrinal mission from a 'People's War'-style approach concerned with deterring land-based threats emanating from its interior borders – such as from Russia, Central Asian neighbours, India or Vietnam – to addressing the greater challenges perceived from its east – such as from Japan, Taiwan and the United States. According to Chinese military thinking, these new missions demanded a PLA posture of 'active defence' in order to fight and win 'limited, local wars under high-tech conditions.' This security outlook envisions that China's most likely military confrontations will be relatively limited both in time and space, will be fought in narrowly defined regions along the mainland's periphery (such as within the Taiwan Strait), and will likely be against foes with more advanced military technologies. Such expected conditions demand that the PLA be prepared to engage in technologically sophisticated, fast-paced, and intensive combat, calling for massive and effective offensive operations early in the engagement as a way to inflict strategically decisive blows at the outset of hostilities. The new doctrine also requires the PLA to consider more seriously than ever how successfully to execute missions in the air and over water, involving the more technologically sophisticated air and naval forces, the introduction of improved command, control, communications and intelligence, and the conduct of joint inter-service operations, as opposed to the heavily land-based, army-centric, mechanized and/or guerrilla-oriented tactics and strategy of 'People's War'.

Most importantly for our discussions in this chapter, this new and evolving mission requirement foresees the PLA projecting its presence especially to China's east and southeast, so as to operate successfully in the Western Pacific region, particularly in the area between the mainland and out to a line running along what Chinese strategists call 'the first island chain': Japan, the Ryukyus, Taiwan, the Philippines, and the Greater Sunda islands encompassing parts of Malaysia and Indonesia. By and large, however, the situation across the Taiwan Strait is the primary driver behind this significant reshaping of the PLA's doctrinal and mission requirements. This has been particularly true since the mid- to late 1990s, as Beijing viewed the democratization process on Taiwan and the island's steady political drift away from the mainland with increasing concern, and provided the PLA with the political go-ahead and financial resources to meet this challenge.

Second, in order to meet this new and expanded mission as a more capable and expansive regional military power, China had to close the gap between operational aspirations on the one hand, and military capabilities on the other. However, China's woeful defence–industrial base was largely unable to develop and produce the high-technology weapons and systems that the PLA would need to meet these new requirements. As a result, one of the most crucial pathways China has chosen to bridge this gap is its heavy investment in the acquisition of more advanced military hardware over the course of the 1990s, with a particularly strong emphasis on procurement of foreign – especially Russian – systems and technologies (Frankenstein and Gill, 1997).

This massive procurement process clearly has a particular regional contingency in mind – Taiwan – but provides greater capability for China to operate as a more muscular regional military power broadly defined. The Chinese buying spree from Russia began in 1991–1992, and centred around the acquisition of 26 Su-27 fighters. This order was followed by additional off-the-shelf purchases of about 50 Su-27s, and the agreement with Moscow in 1996 to assemble up to 200 Su-27s (designated

J-11s in China) in Shenyang over the course of 1998–2007 (some 15 to 20 of these aircraft have been assembled and are in service as of 2003). In addition, based on an agreement reached with Russia in 1999, China imported 38 Su-30 fighter/ground-attack aircraft, and reportedly received an additional 38 more over 2002–2003. China also purchased its most advanced naval vessels from Russia in the 1990s, including two Sovremenny-class destroyers (with two more on order), and four Kilo-class submarines (Stockholm International Peace Research Institute, 2002: 420). In addition to these advanced weapons and systems from Russia, China has also been active in importing high-tech military platforms and dual-use technologies from other foreign sources as well, especially Israel. All of these advanced systems provide China with its most technologically sophisticated force yet, and allow the PLA to begin more militarily effective operations in its offshore periphery. More purchases from Russia, including additional aircraft and submarines, as well as from other foreign sources, can be expected in the years ahead, and will further bolster this capability.

In addition, China also poured considerable resources since the mid- to late 1990s into the development and deployment of indigenous weapons and technologies. Most impressive in this regard – with a clear emphasis on projecting a deterrent and area denial capability to China's east and southeast precisely for region-based contingencies within the 'first island chain' – have been advances in naval and missile systems. Since the mid-1990s, China has produced and launched two new classes of destroyers – two of the 4,800 ton Luhu class (Type 052) and one 6,600 ton Luhai class (Type 054) – and has begun construction on up to four even larger destroyers displacing approximately 8,000 tons, which will begin entering service around 2006. In this period, China also developed and launched a new and more advanced indigenous submarine programme, the Song-class (Type 039), and had three in operation as of 2003. Importantly, these new naval systems incorporate a range of systems and technologies either acquired or derived from foreign sources, including stealth technologies, propulsion systems, and anti-air defence systems, signalling significant advances in capabilities over previous major naval vessels produced in Chinese shipyards.

As noted above, China's indigenously developed ballistic missiles and nuclear weapons have been a critical element for China's regional power from the 1970s. However, since the 1990s in particular, China has developed and deployed a number of new systems which, given their basing and ranges, are clearly intended for regional targets as well. China's first road-mobile ballistic missiles, the DF-21 and DF-21A, have been operational since the early 1990s, and have a range of approximately 1,800 kilometres. The DF-21's basing and ranges suggest targets in Japan, Korea, Okinawa, the Philippines, or Vietnam, in addition to targets in the Russian

Far East and India. In addition, China has invested enormous resources in the development and deployment of conventionally armed ballistic missiles – such as the DF-11 and DF-15, with ranges of 300 and 600 kilometres, respectively – which are clearly intended for contingencies involving Taiwan, and which numbered about 450 missiles currently deployed opposite Taiwan in mid-2003; China is expected to have some 600 deployed by 2005 (Gertz and Scarborough, 2003). Moreover, China has also strengthened its development and deployment of various anti-ship and land-attack cruise missiles with ranges of up to 150 or 200 kilometres, again with an eye toward projecting power regionally, especially toward a potential Taiwan-related conflict (Stokes, 1999: 79 *et seq.*).

Receiving less fanfare and still in early operational stages, the deployment of the indigenously produced J-10 fighter and JH-7 fighter-bomber (also known by its export designator, the FBC-1), is also notable. Both of these projects were very long in gestation and development, and as of 2003 are deployed in small numbers. But they represent some important breakthroughs for China's military aviation development, which has been a weak link in the country's defence–industrial base. The J-10 is envisioned to contribute to air superiority missions, and the JH-7, deployed with the naval air force and armed with air-launched cruise missiles, serving in an air-to-surface, anti-ship role.

Third, an even more critical set of developments for China's increasing strength as a regional military power has to do with improved 'software'. In other words, China's increasing regional military capabilities from the mid-1990s to the present were not only evident in terms of hardware, but also in important non-hardware areas such as administrative and bureaucratic organization, budgets, personnel, training and education, and logistics. These developments do not usually make the headlines and are often more difficult to quantify. Nevertheless, improvements in these areas are the foundation for doctrinal advances and the effective operation of a more high-tech force, and form the basis for China's steadily greater capability as a regional military power.

Organizationally, in response to the new demands and challenges it faced, the PLA leadership hierarchy, the Chinese defence industrial base, and the PLA's non-military activities were extensively reorganized in 1998–1999. In April 1998, in the first major organizational reform of the PLA operational leadership structure since 1958, a new, fourth General Department was established: the General Armaments Department (GAD), which joined the General Staff Department, the General Logistics Department, and the General Political Department. Consistent with the PLA's heightened requirement for advanced hardware and technologies, the GAD was set up to serve as the procurement branch for the PLA (from both foreign and domestic weapon sources) and to act as a watchdog and 'quality control' mechanism over weapons production, while also conducting some of its own research, development, testing and evaluation (RDT&E) of the output from China's defence plants. In the reorganization, the GAD gained control of a diverse array of departments and bases from parts of the Chinese defence industrial base, such as weapons testing centres, satellite launch bases, intelligence and research facilities, and some schools and universities focusing on military–industrial training. In addition, the GAD drew from within the PLA, including arms-procurement and arms-export related bureaux from the General Logistics Department and the General Staff Department. Perhaps most importantly, the GAD took control of what its officers termed 'comprehensive equipment management', overseeing research, design, and testing, procurement bidding, procurement, deployment, maintenance and retirement (Interview, 1998). In short, this critical administrative reorganization aims to place far greater control of military hardware procurement decisions in the hands of uniformed and experienced soldiers and military personnel, and will likely have a serious effect on the direction and pace of the PLA's modernization as a regional power.

China's defence–industrial base also went through a major organizational overhaul in 1998–1999. At the first session of the 9th National People's Congress in March 1998, the Commission on Science, Technology and Industry for National Defence (COSTIND), which, since August 1982 had overseen the Chinese defence technology and weapons complex, was formally abolished. Then it was immediately reconstituted as a strictly 'civilian' entity with the same name, under the direction of the State Council (it had previously been jointly overseen by a government entity – the State Council – and a military one – the Central Military Commission). The new COSTIND was given an entirely civilian leadership and its military-related agencies were turned over to the GAD. The new COSTIND was given a largely administrative role to manage the production – both military and civilian products – of China's vast defence–industrial base, as well as oversee and implement its continued downsizing and reform. A year later, in July 1999, the Chinese government announced a further restructuring of the defence industry: each of the five giant state-owned, quasi-corporatized defence–industrial ministries would be broken into two, thereby forming ten new 'defence–industrial enterprise group companies'. The principal aim of this major bureaucratic and organizational restructuring was to streamline the management structure of the defence industries, introduce greater intra-sector competitiveness, and accelerate national defence modernization.

A third key reorganization in 1998–1999 began with the July 1998 order by China's Commander-In-Chief, Jiang Zemin, for the PLA to abandon the vast majority of its business activities. 'PLA, Inc.', as it had come to be known, had increasingly and often illegally become enmeshed in a range of commercial enterprises, ranging from airlines, transport companies, hotels, construction firms, and karaoke bars to illicit activities such as brothels and smuggling operations. However, what had begun in the early 1980s as a means for the PLA to help meet budget shortfalls had become a vast agglomeration of military-owned commerce, some of it shady, much of it lining personal pockets, and nearly all of it a growing distraction from military readiness. In issuing this order, Jiang had the support of the uppermost brass of the PLA which saw first-hand how PLA business activities undermined the army's military mission and spread a corrosive corruption throughout middle and lower ranks. By December 1998, some 2,900 firms belonging to the PLA and the People's Armed Police had been transferred to local governments, and an additional 3,900 companies were simply shut down (Mulvenon, 2001: 198). Some PLA business activities continue, but with some exceptions, these are mainly very small, subsistence-oriented activities such as farming, conducted at local unit levels. For China, pushing the PLA out of business should be considered a success in terms of refocusing the PLA's attention on military professionalism and modernization.

With regard to budgets, it is worth noting that as China has advanced along the three important axes of doctrinal development, hardware procurement and 'software' reform during the 1990s, it has done so in close parallel with growing fiscal resources, especially since the mid- to late 1990s. The officially announced Chinese defence budget more than doubled in real terms (adjusted for inflation) between 1989 and 2000. Importantly, coinciding closely with the stepped-up changes in doctrine, hardware and software development since the mid-1990s outlined above, the official Chinese defence budget grew by 58 per cent between 1995 and 2000 alone. It grew an additional 17.0 per cent in 2001, 17.7 per cent in 2002, and 9.6 per cent in 2003 (Bitzinger, 2003: 167; International Institute for Strategic Studies, 2002: 298). However, nearly all outside analysts recognize that the official budget does not account for all military expenditures. An important 'off-budget' category is foreign arms procurement, which, as noted above, was significant over the 1990s and into the early 2000s. According to figures compiled by the US Department of State, China spent an average of approximately US$750 million per year from 1989 to 1999 in purchasing foreign weapons. According to this data, average annual spending for arms imports was even greater in the latter half of the 1990s, reaching an average of $837.2 million per year for the period 1995–1999 (Department of State, 2001: table II). Chinese acquisition of foreign weapons continued apace in the early 2000s, with China spending twice as much in 2001 on arms imports as it did in 1999, propelling China to become the world's second largest arms importer for the period 1997–2001 (Stockholm International Peace Research Institute, 2002: 403).

Personnel reform, education and training form another key set of 'soft-ware' developments which have seen important advances since the mid- to late 1990s. To begin, the PLA has continued to shed soldiers from its bloated force structure. In 1997, the PLA announced it would reduce the armed forces by some 500,000 troops, which it accomplished by 2000, bringing the number of PLA soldiers to about 2.5 million. Further reduc-tions of nearly a quarter-of-a-million troops down to its current size of approximately 2.27 million means that, since 1997, the size of the PLA has decreased by almost 25 per cent. To improve recruitment and retention, the PLA introduced a two-year conscription system for all services (previously, the army required a three-year sign-up, with four years for the army and navy). At the same time, the Chinese military has stepped up its recruitment of officer candidates from universities, im-proved the level of education at officer training institutions and military universities, strengthened a more professional non-commissioned officer corps system within its ranks, and introduced a military scholarship programme to cover the college education costs of students who commit to enlisting as officers upon graduation; in 2003, the PLA announced it would recruit 4,000 students graduating from this national defence scholarship programme (*Zaobao Daily News*, 2003). According to offi-cial Chinese data, more than 80 per cent of the PLA's officers and senior civilian employees have an education of junior college or higher. New laws promulgated in 1999 and 2000 require officers to receive higher education degrees and established institutional links between the PLA and some 50 Chinese universities – including Peking University and Tsinghua University – to provide education and training for PLA officers (State Council, 2002).

The strengthening of the non-commissioned officer (NCO) corps may prove to be an especially critical reform. With the reduction in the terms of conscription came higher turnover among young recruits and the need for an 'institutional memory' and permanent training structure. To strengthen supervision and training of these recruits, the PLA promul-gated new regulations in the late 1990s to reform the NCO system. In January 2001, the PLA introduced extensive regulations to govern and reform the NCO system (Foreign Broadcast Information Service, 2001). NCOs are now recruited either from the general population, or from conscripts who have shown promise after their two-year term of service. Career NCOs can serve in the PLA for up to 30 years, creating an institu-tional continuity not provided by the national conscription system. NCOs are given pay and benefits equal to junior officers, with senior NCOs being paid as much as battalion-level officers. Technical-specialist NCOs receive training from military academies lasting at least two years, versus two to three months for non-technical NCOs. NCOs are even authorized to go overseas for training if their units deem it necessary. While morale and ideological training is still the responsibility of political officers, NCOs will take an active role in training the professional and technically proficient soldier. Over time, solidifying the foundation and function of the NCO corps will likely bring greater efficiency, consistency, proficiency and preparedness to the ongoing PLA modernization effort at its most basic unit – the individual Chinese soldier (Foreign Broadcast Information Service, 2002b).

Military training and exercises have also increased in the way of size, duration, inter-service and inter-regional officer exchanges and joint operations, tempo, and the introduction and expansion of computer simulation techniques. The Chinese military press is increasingly open in reporting advances in new forms of training and live-fire exercises by the army, navy and air force. In recent years, the PLA has staged increasingly large, sophisticated and sustained exercises, sometimes involving hundreds of thousands of troops. A large, tactical training centre was opened in 1999 in northern Inner Mongolia, with a resident 'Blue Army' made up of the 27th Group Army from the Beijing Military Command. Rotating units train against the Blue Army, which is reportedly structured to mimic the tactics of Taiwan's Armoured Brigade and the US Armoured Cavalry. As many as 200,000 Chinese troops have reportedly trained at this centre (*Kanwa Intelligence Review*, 2002). In exercises, the Blue Team is ordered to do everything possible to defeat the visiting 'Red Team' to generate valuable training lessons. In 2002, the director of the PLA General Logistics Department, General Wang Ke, emphasized the importance of more realistic training:

> Military science and technology training is an in-depth reform of military training. The essence of the reform is to link training more closely to actual combat. In the past, all tactical exercises followed the same pattern. Rehearsals were held before the exercises, and only outstanding units were selected to take part in the exercises. The purpose was to 'concentrate the best forces' to win honor and attain high ranks in the contest. This is what the new training program has to discard.
>
> (Foreign Broadcast Information Service, 2002a)

One of the largest exercises the PLA has ever held was in the summer 2001, along the Fujian coast near Dongshan Island, opposite Taiwan. The exercises, held over three months and known as Donghai 6, culminated with a massive amphibious landing and mock ballistic missile launches, considered as training for potential offensive operations against Taiwan. These exercises involved some 100,000 troops, drawn from army divisions based in Beijing, Chengdu, Guangzhou, Jinan and Nanjing, and included naval and air force units as well. Similarly large summer exercises were conducted in 2002, with a focus along the Fujian coast. In two smaller but illustrative breakthroughs for China's regional military aspirations since the late 1990s, the PLA Navy made its first crossing of the Pacific Ocean in March 1997, visiting ports in the United States, and completed its first circumnavigation of the globe, visiting 10 countries from May to September 2002.

A critical aim of the intensification in training and exercises is to improve the PLA's ability to conduct joint operations. As noted in a major article in the *Liberation Army Daily*:

> There is no denying the fact that our army's joint training is still in the preliminary stage and we urgently need to advance it to a higher stage. . . . At the beginning of this year, the General Staff Department issued an instruction saying: 'All military units must adapt to the changes in the pattern of modern warfare and popularize and advance training in joint operations to a new stage. Various armed services and arms must enhance the awareness of joint military operations. Battle and tactical drills and specialized exercises must be conducted against the backdrop of joint military operations without exception. Emphasis must be placed on confrontation and verification to comprehensively improve the organization and command ability of the commanders and headquarters over joint military operations as well as to improve the ability to fight in air, land, sea, aerospace, and special battles.' It is fair to say that 2002 is a year of training in joint military operations for the whole army and a year of crucial importance to command training in joint operations.
>
> (*Liberation Army Daily*, 2002)

Logistics have also become a focus of reform in recent years, with the introduction of new procurement guidelines and the concept of utilizing civilian contractors as a 'logistical multiplier'. Following the establishment of the GAD in 1998, the PLA has moved towards a more coordinated logistics and supply mechanism which it terms a 'tri-service, joint supply' system, with an initial emphasis on materiel commonly required across services, such as fuel, medical support and ground vehicle upkeep. In addition, the PLA has approved the 'socialization' (*shehuihua*) of logistical support, meaning reliance on contract bidding and civilian contractors to meet non-combat needs. For example, according to the 2002 Chinese defence white paper, the PLA has 1,500 messes, 1,000 postal exchanges, 1,800 barracks and 300 other support enterprises and farms turned over to civilian and local authorities for operation and maintenance on a contracted basis. Since 2002, the PLA requires a formal procurement bidding process for the purchase of materials and equipment valued at more than 500,000 yuan, and for building projects costing more than 2 million yuan (State Council, 2002).

More broadly, the PLA recognizes that effective and sustained logistics support for joint combat must be its overriding goals. This becomes an increasingly difficult challenge for the PLA, given its vast size and diverse mix of weapons systems – both foreign and domestic. Accordingly, the General Logistics Department in 1999 introduced sweeping logistics reforms to intensify training, expand linkages with China's burgeoning civilian/private sector, and accomplish five key goals: joint logistics of the armed forces, standardization of military supply; standardization of the officer welfare system; 'socialized' logistics supply system (greater use of civilian and commercial contractors); and scientific management of logistics (Puska, 2002: 264–270). As a specialist of the PLA's logistics system concludes, China's capabilities in this area cannot be dismissed: 'Based on its history of flexibility, adaptation, and continual improvement, PLA logistics has the potential to ruin someone's day in a regional crisis, and to effectively ensure deterrence during peace' (Puska, 2002: 270).

One final element of growing Chinese regional military influence is Beijing's stepped-up military diplomacy. Since the early to mid-1990s, the PLA has rapidly expanded its military-to-military relations, especially with its regional neighbours. In 2000–2002, the PLA had more than 130 major exchanges, dispatched senior military delegations to more than 60 countries and hosted senior military officers from some 60 countries. Among its regional neighbours, the PLA has regular, formalized military-to-military dialogue and exchanges with such countries as Australia, India, Japan, Kazakhstan, Kyrgyzstan, North Korea, Pakistan, Russia, South Korea, Thailand and the United States; in October 2002, China requested a regularized security dialogue with the North Atlantic Treaty Organization (NATO) which will involve PLA participation. China has also boosted the level and frequency of PLA participation in such regional security dialogues as the Shanghai Cooperation Organization, the Association of Southeast Asian Nations (ASEAN) Regional Forum, and in a range of non-official, 'second-track' exchanges (State Council, 2002). In a first for the PLA, in October 2002, China held joint military exercises with its western neighbour, Kyrgyzstan, conducting counterterrorism manoeuvres along their mountainous border. Similar exercises with other Central Asian neighbours can be expected in the future, under the auspices of the Shanghai Cooperation Organization.

Comparative regional power

It is important to recall that China's growing weight and capability as a regional power will not proceed in a vacuum. Obviously, China's neighbours will react in various ways that may have a constraining or countervailing effect. Overall, however, it appears that over time China will steadily gain militarily in relative terms in comparison to nearly all of its neighbours.

To begin with, a serious military conflict in the region, such as in the Taiwan Strait or on the Korean Peninsula, will have a dramatic effect on China's regional military aspirations, both positively and negatively, depending on the result. The critical variable will be the involvement of the United States in such crises, and whether US and Chinese forces come into conflict. Major conflicts on the Korean peninsula or in the Taiwan Strait, whether they involve direct military hostilities between the United States and China or not, would dramatically alter regional power relationships and shift regional perceptions about Chinese military capability. Depending on outcomes, the United States and its allies could be seen as diminished influences, with China rising in power, or Chinese military influence could be set back by American and allied assertiveness in the region.

Even in the absence of conflict, growing Chinese military power in the region will likely be encumbered by the continued forward-based presence of the United States. US and Chinese forces already find themselves in more frequent contact with one another around China's maritime periphery, sometimes with dangerous results, as the April 2001 EP-3 episode demonstrated. The United States is also likely to maintain its strong commitment to providing for the defence of Taiwan, both through arms sales and, if necessary, through military intervention in the Taiwan Strait in a time of crisis. The United States has also clearly signalled its concern towards China, and Washington's intention is to deter and prevent a serious challenge from any rival power. The language of the 2001 quadrennial defense review (QDR) was clear in its views about American power in the Asia-Pacific and in its not-so-subtle reference to China. Among 'enduring national interests' the document included 'precluding hostile domination of critical areas', including Northeast Asia and the East Asia littoral, the latter defined as 'the region stretching from south of Japan through Australia and into the Bay of Bengal' (Secretary of Defense, 2001: 2). The QDR continues:

> Maintaining a stable balance in Asia will be a complex task. The possibility exists that a military competitor with a formidable resource base will emerge in the region. The East Asian littoral – from the Bay of Bengal to the Sea of Japan – represents a particularly challenging area. ... This places a premium on securing additional access and infrastructure agreements and on developing systems capable of sustained operations at great distances with minimal theater support.
>
> (Secretary of Defense, 2001: 4)

China–Russia relations will also be critical: China continues to rely heavily on Russia for the provision of advanced weapons systems; Russia tightly controls the provision of the high value-added systems such as propulsion for aircraft and naval vessels – technologies where China is relatively weak. Russia also maintains control over provision of spares and maintenance for many of the more advanced systems that it has exported to China, meaning that in a time of war, Beijing will be even more dependent on Russian goodwill. Moreover, while Russia–China relations remain friendly and constructive, they rest more on a 'marriage of convenience' than on a firm, long-term foundation. Russian public and elite views of China vary widely, both positively and negatively, and, in a time of crisis, could shift Russian strong military–technical support away from China.

Other major players in the region, such as Japan, Taiwan, India and Southeast Asian states, will continue their military modernization processes, often with China in mind. For Taiwan, this process will be largely a defensive one, and singularly focused on repelling Chinese attacks – not a process of regional power projection. Nevertheless, some prominent voices in Taiwan call for a more offensive military capacity to counter the Chinese arms build-up, including the deployment of ballistic missiles. Moreover, even if Taiwan procurement can be deemed largely 'defensive' in nature, China's acquisitions in response are clearly offensive in character. In short, a low-level arms race dynamic is under way across the Taiwan Strait, but it is one that over time Taiwan by itself is unlikely to win.

Japan has increasingly bolstered its military capability and presence in East Asia in becoming a more 'normal' power, and is the one country in East Asia which could hinder China's trajectory to regional military predominance. In the post-Cold War era, Japanese politicians and strategists increasingly see threats emanating from China, and will plan accordingly, placing some check on China's regional military power. However, to rival Chinese military capability over the medium-term will require substantially increased investments in Japanese armed forces, to include longer-range offensive capabilities such as missiles and even nuclear weapons. Such moves would mean breaking the long-standing political, normative and legal constraints on offensive Japanese military development, including Article 9 of the Japanese Constitution. Moreover, given Japan's current and continuing economic woes, a significant and long-term investment in a major military build-up would meet with serious fiscal restraints from within the government and from the general public.

Of the major Asian military powers, India seems most openly determined to counterbalance growing Chinese military capabilities. This is most obvious in Delhi's successful pursuit of nuclear weapons and in developing increasingly sophisticated and long-range ballistic missiles. India possesses a formidable array of Soviet and Russian weaponry, including Su-30 and Su-27 fighters and Kilo class submarines. India also deploys a large standing army of more than 1 million troops, and is seeking to expand its naval reach to include seas to the east of the Bay of Bengal. However, the most intense competition in the near term between China and India will be in the strategic nuclear realm, where China already has a clear advantage. India will likely remain consumed by internal ethnic and religious strife and a constant concern with its more immediate military rival – Pakistan. Only over the medium to longer term could India expect to compete effectively with Chinese military, political and economic influence in the maritime regions east of the Malay peninsula and north of the Indonesian archipelago, and even then it would be questionable how welcome Indian projection of military power would be in Southeast Asia.

Southeast Asian states, with an eye to China's growing regional military strength, continue to hedge their bets through ongoing military modernization programmes of their own and through intensification of military-to-military relations with the United States. As Huxley and Willett documented, Southeast Asian military spending, arms procurement, and defence industrialization grew at a significant pace throughout most of the 1990s, in part in response to growing Chinese military power in the region. However, the 1997 financial crisis set back many of these plans in Southeast Asia, while leaving Chinese military modernization efforts unscathed (Huxley and Willett, 1999). Governments such as Singapore and Malaysia, and, to a lesser extent, the Philippines, can be expected to resume a more robust arms procurement effort over the medium term, but, as smaller powers, they cannot expect to match Chinese military capability over time. Others with more serious domestic economic and social concerns, such as Vietnam and Indonesia, will not be in a strong position to pursue significant military modernization efforts. Some in the region – such as US allies the Philippines and Thailand, as well as quasi-allies such as Singapore – are working out closer military-to-military relations with Washington, to include improved access and infrastructure support arrangements, as envisioned in the QDR noted above. Malaysia, Indonesia and even Vietnam are considering similar overtures from Washington.

Beijing is increasingly sensitive to regional concerns about the 'China threat', especially in Southeast Asia, and is likely to constrain overt military coerciveness in the region (Taiwan excepted) in the interests of winning over neighbours economically and diplomatically over the long term (see Breslin and Kim, this volume). This approach, manifested by a far more active acceptance of multilateral diplomacy in the Association of Southeast Asian Nations (ASEAN) Regional Forum (ARF), initiation of the ASEAN

Plus Three (APT) process, conducting annual China–ASEAN bilateral summitry, seeking a China–ASEAN Free Trade Area by 2012, and reaching a 'Declaration on the Conduct of Parties in the South China Sea' in November 2002 to govern the activities of claimants to various parts of the South China Sea, and reduce the potential for tension and conflict in the disputed area, are all indicators of Beijing's emphasis on diplomatic and economic channels in its dealings with Southeast Asian neighbours, even as it bolsters its military capability as a regional power.

Caveats and conclusions

Barring serious social, political and economic setbacks for China, China's weight and influence as a regional military player seem likely to continue growing in importance, in both objective and relative terms. Since the late 1990s, the convergence of doctrinal adjustments, continued high-tech weapons procurement, and improved organizational, budgetary, educational and logistical support, have significantly advanced China's aim to become the most powerful East Asian regional power, and helped China to gain in relative military terms in comparison to most of its regional neighbours. In the view of a prominent, bipartisan taskforce of experts convened by the Council on Foreign Relations to assess China's growing military power, while the military balance between the United States and China will likely remain in favour of the former well past 2020, 'China is a regional power . . . [and] will become the predominant military power among the nations of East Asia' (Council on Foreign Relations, 2003: 2).

With the likelihood of becoming the predominant military power among East Asian countries, China certainly 'does matter' militarily at a regional level. But the pace and scope of China's growing influence as a regional military power may be constrained and counterbalanced by a number of important factors. We have discussed how the reactions of other regional military powers will affect China's rise. But, in addition, three other important factors internal to China also deserve serious consideration.

First, the stepped-up and converging improvements regarding doctrine, hardware and software that we have observed since the mid- to late 1990s appear to be driven primarily with an eye to a very narrow and specific regional challenge that Beijing believes it faces: the need for military action to coerce and, if need be, attack Taiwan, in order to thwart Taiwan independence and ultimately bring about reunification on Beijing's terms. The short-range missile build-up opposite Taiwan is most obvious in this regard, but so too are other major doctrinal, hardware and software developments. For example, the Sovremenny-class destroyers were originally designed by the Soviet Union precisely to counter US Aegis destroyers and carrier battle groups. With their powerful 'Moskit' anti-ship missiles (also known as the 'Sunburn' or SS-N-22 in the West) with a range up to 130 kilometres, and the possibility that China will acquire the even longer-range follow-on anti-ship missile, the 'Yakhont', the Sovremenny warships operate close-in to shore under land-based air cover and keep enemy fleets at a distance. For China, this means trying to make US fleet commanders think twice about sailing around and into the Taiwan Strait during a crisis. However, given China's relative inexperience in at-sea and maritime air operations, these new elements of Chinese military power will not so readily extend in the near term to other regional scenarios from the South China Sea, to the Senkaku/Diaoyutai Islands, to the Korean Peninsula.

Second, while the critical doctrinal, hardware and software developments discussed here have been in train for a decade or so, the PLA continues to have difficulties putting all the pieces together in a fully effective way. Many factors explain this. For example, the new doctrines and missions faced by the PLA in the 1990s called for a fundamentally different and challenging approach for a military whose wartime tradition, strategic thinking and order of battle is dominated by the land-based army forces, as opposed to the naval and air forces which continue to rank as 'junior services'. Navy and air force officers rarely reach the senior-most leadership of the PLA. Even the official names of those service arms – the People's Liberation *Army* Navy (PLAN) and the People's Liberation *Army* Air Force (PLAAF) – point to the conceptual and practical obstacles to overcome in developing a doctrine consistent with new mission requirements.

With regard to hardware, the Chinese military continues to have trouble mastering and taking full advantage of its new and more advanced weapons and systems. While more advanced systems help make the PLA – and especially its air force and navy – more capable, the integration of these high-tech weapons has been fraught with problems. The PLA Navy has had extensive problems with at least two of the Kilos in their inventory, and reportedly sent them both back to Russia for repairs to the battery systems. Chinese pilots have crashed several Su-27s, and training regimens are careful not to push the pilot or the aircraft to their limits. A May 2002 article in the *Jiefangjun Bao* (*Liberation Army Daily*) newspaper sums up the issue:

> Some officers and men say: 'we expected to have new weapons when we did not have them; and now we have them, and we are afraid of them.' Some others observe: 'We were eager to have new weapons, but now they are here and we do not know what to do with them.'

The shortage of expert-type technicians has become the 'bottleneck' that restricts new weapons from becoming fighting strength. Thus the assignment of creating a contingent of expert type technicians has become a real and urgent task for us.

(Foreign Broadcast Information Service, 2002c)

Moreover, China's defence–industrial base continues to face problems, and is unlikely to be able to provide the PLA with the kinds of advanced weapons that it deems necessary, with the exception of missile systems, it appears. Chinese high-tech aircraft – including fighters and airborne early-warning and command-and-control aircraft – are a particular bottleneck, meaning that the PLA will have to turn to foreign suppliers in these and other areas of technology for the foreseeable future.

As to implementing 'software' reforms and achieving the PLA aim of 'joint operations', this may be the most difficult and lengthy task of all. The concept and successful execution of 'jointness' will take many years for the PLA to master, and demands changes not only in thinking, but also the introduction and effective absorption of new weapons, technologies and procedures in order to close the gap between the Chinese military's aspirations on the one hand, and its capabilities on the other. Nevertheless, the Chinese military leadership clearly recognizes these shortcomings, and is working hard to alleviate and overcome them. As a result, China's regional neighbours should expect its military capability to advance, but only steadily so, and with setbacks and problems along the way.

Third, China's ability to expand its role as a regional military power will also depend on Chinese internal developments. In many respects, what happens *inside* China over the next decade will be a more decisive factor in determining how Chinese power manifests itself *outside* China. The new Chinese leadership faces an ever-lengthening list of political, social and economic challenges at home: Party reform, political decentralization, widespread under- and unemployment in old-line smokestack industries and the agricultural sector, growing income disparities across regions and social strata, endemic corruption, localized political and economic unrest, a weakening banking sector, ailing social welfare and public health systems, and environmental degradation – to name a few. In short, Chinese leaders face a double-edged sword: they must retain Party legitimacy and authority through continued stable socioeconomic development and growth, but the very process of societal opening and economic expansion, if not properly managed, may undermine Party rule and bring deepening social and economic challenges. The outcomes of the ongoing political, social and economic transformation of China are of enormous strategic importance, not only to the Beijing leadership, but to China's neighbours and international partners as well. In the near to medium term, it appears that these internal concerns will consume much of China's energy, and will be another likely constraint on China's rising importance as a regional military power.

In conclusion, while Gerry did not explicitly say so in his 1999 *Foreign Affairs* piece, he appeared implicitly to recognize the point: China may not matter as a global military power, but does matter regionally to a limited degree. This chapter agrees, but argues that China's regional military influence and potential impact have grown in significant ways since the mid-1990s and particularly since Gerry wrote in 1998–1999, and in ways few persons, including Gerry, envisioned. Within a narrow regional security context, we can see that China is worthy of greater concern and attention. China is transforming itself from a land-based, heavily mechanized force to one with air and sea capabilities for operations within several hundred miles of its shores. This is a change of historic proportions for the PLA, and one that China's regional neighbours are watching warily. In particular, because war in the Taiwan Strait could draw other powers into the fray – the United States first and foremost, but also possibly Japan – China's growing regional military capability and confidence about dealing with Taiwan should be a cause of concern for all with an interest in East Asian stability. As one of Gerry's conclusions posited, 'China matters most for the West because it can make mischief, either by threatening its neighbors or assisting anti-Western forces further afield' (Segal, 1999: 35). It is unclear at the moment whether China has such military intentions in the near term, and many of the constraints noted above will weigh against their realization to the extent that they exist. Indeed, in an interesting paradox, as China has become increasingly capable in the military sphere since the late 1990s, it has tended to downplay overtly military coerciveness and increased its political and economic levers of power to project a greater regional presence. However, over the longer term, we cannot dismiss the possibility that China will choose to utilize its increased military capabilities, not only to 'make mischief' but to exert itself more forcefully around its periphery. In that sense China *does* matter militarily in the region.

10 Conclusions

How and to whom does China matter?

Barry Buzan

China, of course, matters to the Chinese, and the liberal side of Gerry Segal was keen to encourage the domestic reforms that he thought would improve the wealth, welfare and liberty of the people in China. But the main thrust of his article, and this book, is on the question of how China matters to those outside it, and what policies they should have towards it. These two concerns link inasmuch as how China organizes itself internally is a key factor in shaping how it relates to its neighbours and the rest of the world. As Michael Yahuda has noted, Gerry's aim was to send a wake-up call both to the Chinese and to those who have to deal with China. He felt that exaggerated perceptions of China's power and capability were distorting policy both within China and outside it. By playing on its potential, and seducing or bullying others into doing the same, China was both reducing its internal incentives for reform and weakening the demands that international society should be placing on it. Gerry concluded that whether looked at economically, militarily or politically, China was a middle-ranked power that mattered much less than many thought. It was therefore vulnerable to a robust policy of 'constrainment' in a way that it would not be if it really was a great power. He advocated such a policy on two grounds: that it was necessary to encourage and if need be pressure China into domestic reforms; and that China could 'make mischief' for the West 'either by threatening its neighbors or assisting anti-Western forces further afield'. Gerry was, in effect, trying to chart a middle path between the dangerous extremes of choosing either realist containment or liberal engagement. As a group of authors, our opinions on this question are inevitably less tightly focused than Gerry's, but that has not prevented us from re-examining Gerry's case with a sceptical eye and the advantage of several years more of observation.

In the preceding chapters we have used the luxury of having more space and time than were available to Gerry to reassess the main points of his argument. In doing so, we have extended the range of inquiry by introducing culture as a distinct concern, and we have made into a feature something that was mostly implicit in Gerry's article: the distinction between China's relationships with Asia and with the international system as a whole. So what do we conclude? At some risk of oversimplification, the argument in Chapters 3–9 could be summed up as being that China matters much more to its neighbours in Asia than it does to the world at large. In global economic terms, and despite some flaws in Gerry's argument, China is still trading more on potential than reality, although the reality of its global economic presence is rising steadily (Harris, this volume, Chapter 5). But in Asia it is looming large, affecting in a substantial way the patterns of trade, investment, industrial development and regional management for many of its neighbours (Breslin, this volume, Chapter 8). Similarly, in the military sector, China has not sought to develop large-scale intercontinental capabilities or commitments (Freedman, this volume, Chapter 3), but has developed capabilities and concerns that give it increasing clout in its immediate periphery (Gill, this volume, Chapter 9). Politically, China is perhaps better integrated into global international society, and therefore less of a problem, than Gerry thought (Kim, this volume, Chapter 4), while regionally, especially with the economic decline of Japan, it matters more and more (Lehmann, this volume, Chapter 7). Culturally, China's global influence is probably greater than Gerry thought, even though somewhat hobbled by the narrow concerns of the Chinese Communist Party (CCP). Regionally, and despite some over-playing of the 'Greater China' idea, its position is underpinned by its extensive and well-placed, although fragmented, diaspora (Goodman, this volume, Chapter 6).

To say that China matters more in Asia than in the world at large risks assuming that the Asian and global 'universes' are distinct and disconnected realms. This is clearly not the case, as hinted at in Gerry's point that one of the problems China posed for the West was the threat it could pose to its neighbours, several of which are important to the US as allies, and to the West generally as players in the global political economy. The question to be investigated in this chapter is thus how China's importance in Asia matters to its importance in the world. In order to pursue this question, I need for analytical purposes to draw a quite sharp distinction between the dynamics of China's relationships with its Asian neighbours on the one hand, and the dynamics of its relations with the non-Asian great powers, especially the US, on the other. I am fully aware that this distinction is much muddied by the strong and active US presence in Asia, which affects how China relates to its neighbours, and which is often interpreted as signifying that the US is part of the East Asian region (for example, Goldstein, 2003: 181; Lake and Morgan, 1997: 12, 21, 29–30; Ross, 1999). But I am firmly of the view (Alagappa, 2003: xii–xiii; Buzan and Wæver, 2003, chapter 2; Buzan, 2004) that there is much to be gained analytically by rejecting the view that the US is an

Asian (or European, or Middle Eastern) power, and following instead the idea that it is a superpower from outside of these regions. Part of the US's claim to superpower status is precisely that it has sustained substantial interventions in several regions, and its foreign policy seeks to legitimize these through super-regional constructions such as 'the North Atlantic community', 'Asia-Pacific', and 'the Western hemisphere'. But at the end of the day, the US can leave, or be thrown out of, Asia, Europe and the Middle East in a way that, respectively, China, Germany and Egypt cannot, and there are regular debates within both the US and the regions about these options. This difference matters. So although I will take account of the US impact in Asia in what follows, I will not think of it as an Asian power in the same sense as China and Japan. The chapter will focus on two main points: first, how China's general relationship with its region affects its global standing; and second, within that, how its specific relationship with Japan affects the status claims of the US as the world's sole superpower.

China, East Asia and the world

The underlying argument in this section is that there is a strong link between the global standing of a major power and the way that power relates to the other states in its home region. As a general rule, the status of great power, and more so superpower, requires not only that the state concerned be able and willing to project its political influence beyond its immediate region, but that it also be able in some sense to manage, and perhaps lead, its region (Buzan and Wæver, 2003). The US clearly does this in North America, and more arguably for the Western hemisphere as a whole, and the EU does it in Europe. The Soviet Union did it from 1945 to 1989, and the possible inability of Russia to do it (and its desperation to do so) explain the current question marks around its status. India's failure to do it is a big part of what denies it the great-power recognition it craves. During the Cold War, and up to a point still, Japan could exploit its political geography to detach itself from much of Asian politics, and float free as a kind of economic great power. China does not have that kind of geopolitical option. Like Russia and India, it cannot escape regional politics. China's global standing thus depends crucially on what kind of relationship it has with its neighbours. If China is able to reassert some form of hegemony over twenty-first century Asia – getting most or all of its neighbours to bandwagon with it – then its global standing will be hugely enhanced. But if China inspires fear in its neighbours – causing them to balance against it – then like India, and possibly Russia, it will be locked into its region, and its global standing will be diminished. Since the US is strongly present in Asia, its influence also plays into this equation.

Indeed, if China is at odds with its neighbours then its position will be worse than that of Russia and India. In their immediate regions, those two have only to deal with powers much smaller than themselves. In China's region there are several very substantial powers whose antagonism would be a real burden. The importance of regional relations for a major power's global standing is easily shown by two extreme scenarios for China's future. In the first, China's development provides it with the strength and the identity to become the central hub of Asia, in the process largely displacing the US. It projects an acceptable political and economic image, and its neighbours bandwagon with it out of some combination of fear, prudence, admiration and hope for economic advantage. Its economy becomes the regional locomotive, and in political and military terms it is acknowledged as *primus inter pares* by Japan, Korea and the ASEAN states. Japan takes up a similar subordinate relationship with China to that it now has with the US, and China is able to use the regional institutions created by ASEAN rather as the US uses the Organization of American States. If the other Asian states fear to antagonize China, and don't balance against it, then China is both free to play a larger global role, and is insulated against pressure from the West. And if China succeeds in positioning itself at the centre of an Asian economy, then it can claim 'locomotive' status along with the US and the EU in the global economy. In the second scenario, China inspires fear in its neighbours. Japan's alliance with the US deepens, and India, Southeast Asia, Japan and possibly Russia coordinate their defences against China, probably with US support. Under the first set of conditions, China acquires a stable regional base which gives it both the status and the capability to play seriously on the global political stage. Under the second set of conditions, China may still be the biggest power in East Asia, but its ability to play on the global stage would be seriously curtailed.

The task for this section is thus to examine the social and material forces in play and ask how they might support or block a move in either of these directions. Is it likely that China will acquire hegemony in East Asia, or is its rise to power more likely to produce US-backed regional balancing against it? I will examine the factors playing into this question on three levels: China's capabilities and the trajectory of its internal development; China's relations with its Asian neighbours; and its relationships with the US and the other great powers.

China's capabilities and the trajectory of its internal development

Debates about China's capability and prospects for development can be placed within a matrix formed by two variables:

- Does China get stronger (because its economic development continues successfully) or weaker (because its development runs into obstacles, or triggers socio-political instability)?
- Does China become a malign, aggressive, threatening force in international society (because it becomes hypernationalist or fascist), or does it become more benign and cooperative (because economic development brings internal democratization and liberalization)?

If China's development falters and it becomes weak, then it will neither dominate its region nor project itself on to the global stage. Whether it is then politically benign or malign will be a much less pressing issue in terms of how others respond to it in the traditional politico-military security domain. What could happen in this scenario is that a breakdown in the socio-political order, perhaps triggered by economic or environmental troubles, might well trigger large-scale migrations, political fragmentations, or wider economic crises that would pose serious threats to China's neighbours. A major political collapse in China could also pose threats at the global level, via the scenario of a failed nuclear weapon state. But, if China becomes strong, then the malign or benign question matters a great deal. The benign and malign options could be alternative paths, or could occur in sequence, with a malign phase giving way to a benign one, as happened with Germany and Japan during their comparable phases of industrialization. The likelihood of just such a sequence was what underpinned Gerry's concern to promote constrainment.

On the current evidence, the chances of China continuing to rise through the ranks of the great powers to the point where it might bid for superpower status look quite good, although the plethora of variables in play make it difficult to say how long this will take. China has a fast-growing and rapidly modernizing economy. Although still technologically backward in many respects, it has successfully mastered the technology for both nuclear weapons and space launchers, and presents a plausible image of itself as making sustained progress across the board in economic development. This image was further enhanced in October 2003 after the successful launch of a manned space flight. On the back of this expanding economy, it maintains strong conventional forces and a modest nuclear deterrent. China has behaved sensibly in not allowing its military development to outpace and compromise its economic one. There is a short-term price to be paid for this in a certain military technological backwardness, but the longer-term prospects of this policy look formidable.

Serious questions can nevertheless be raised about China's prospects for an inexorable rise to the top ranks of the great powers. Will China grow strong, or become more internally fragmented by uneven development, penetration of foreign capital and ideas and a weakening political centre? The combined impact of marketization (which stimulates mass internal migration, decentralization of power, challenge to authority, corruption, crime, environmental problems and dangers of structural instability and overheated economic growth), and political uncertainty (the succession struggles, the loss of ideological authority, the rise of nationalism), mean that the outcome of China's rapid development during the 1980s and 1990s is very hard to read. The profound internal contradictions of market communism, the tensions of uneven development between the coast and the interior, the uncertain state of the ruling CCP, and the widening gap between central and provincial political authority, all point towards a potentially much more erratic future. The government's somewhat hysterical securitization of the Falun Gong is suggestive of a deep insecurity about the political future. In this perspective, the chance of China fragmenting, or undergoing prolonged political and economic turbulence, seemed just as great as the chance of its emerging as an Asian or global great power (Roy, 1994; Segal, 1994; Shambaugh, 1994; Van Ness, 2002: 139–143).

Perhaps the most basic question is whether China can reconcile the mounting contradiction between its authoritarian government and its rapidly marketizing economy. It is ironic that a profoundly anti-liberal state such as China, should so firmly embrace the quintessentially liberal doctrine of separating economics from politics. Market socialism looks like an oxymoron whose historical run will be short. In addition to the pressures generated by capitalist development, there is some open resistance of a more traditional sort to Beijing's control in Tibet, Xinjiang and Inner Mongolia. The uncertainty about China's development is in part just about the pattern of boom and bust that attends all forms of capitalist development. There is no reason to expect that China will escape from the pains of adjusting its culture, social practices and internal distribution of power to the demands of market-based development, and at a minimum one might therefore expect periods of setback and turbulence. China could falter economically and politically, succumbing for a time to the many internal contradictions building up from its rapid development, and so fail to fulfil the material aspirations to international power as quickly as some predict. Just as plausibly, it could continue to gather strength with relatively minor ups and downs in the process.

Despite these uncertainties, China successfully plays on expectations about its future capability in order to enhance its status in the present. For at least the last half-century, China has been good at trading on the supposed strength of its future prospects (Segal, 1999). Expectations of China's rapid rise to great-power status, or at least regional challenger in Asia (Christensen, 2001) have remained strong (see Johnston and Ross, 1999; Brown *et al.*, 2001). Unless the country suffers a major internal crisis, the tendency of the rest of the world to believe in the inexorability of China's rise to power will help its status – perhaps even before its material capability is fully up to scratch. This means that as its capability rises, helped by its success in attracting foreign direct investment, it should find a receptive environment internationally to its status claims, regardless of whether those claims are welcomed or feared. Overall, China's material prospects look strong enough to give real force to concerns about whether its internal development will be politically malign or benign in relation to its neighbours and the rest of the world.

Those wanting to take a malign view of China's future draw on the following kinds of arguments. There is the general idea that rising powers seek to assert their influence (Segal, 1988; Roy, 1994; Shambaugh, 1994). Attached to this are two ideas that seemed to amplify it. First is that China is a revisionist power, not closely wedded to the existing international order, and with many territorial, cultural and status grievances. This argument was stronger during the Maoist period (Zhang, 1998), but elements of it remain plausible for an ascending power (Wu, 1998) still contesting unresolved territorial issues with several neighbours, and still confronting a major unresolved status issue with much of the international community over Taiwan. Second is the idea that China is a classic model of authoritarian modernization (Bracken, 1994: 103–109), unrestrained by democracy, and vulnerable to nationalism and militarism. Such views have been reinforced by China's lack of transparency, its willingness to resort to aggressive behaviour and threat or use of force against its neighbours, its continued cultivation of historical hatred of Japan, and its robust opposition to US hegemony (To, 1997: 252, 261; Soeya, 1998: 204–206). In support of these malign views were China's favouring of traditional *realpolitik* in much of its international thought and behaviour (Hughes, 1997: 116–119; Li, 1999: 6, 18). Additional evidence could be drawn from its attitude towards nuclear testing and the export of missile and nuclear technology to Pakistan and Iran, and the reaction against its practices of industrial piracy and prison labour. Its behaviour in the South China Sea, and towards Taiwan, offered a distinctly mixed prospect to those hoping that China could somehow be brought into the regional process of dialogue and diplomacy.

The more benign scenario depends on whether the process of development leads in time to a liberalization of China's society and politics, and therefore to a closing of the ideological gap between China and the West. This is the hope of those promoting economic engagement with China, and the implicit Asian models are Japan, South Korea and Taiwan – all of which have developed through a period of authoritarian capitalism and into democracy, if not yet deep-rooted liberalism. It also depends on the idea that China can be 'socialized' into responsible behaviour in its neighbourhood or will come to appreciate the benefits of interdependence. Some argue that China will be militarily incapable of serious aggression for some time (Dibb, 1995: 87–88; Kang, 1995: 12–13); and/or that it would be restrained from such adventures both by its interest in development (Kang, 1995: 12; Mahbubani, 1995) and its adaptation to international society (Zhang, 1998; Foot, 2001). China has already conceded much of the economic game to market capitalism, and unlike the former Soviet Union it does not any longer pretend to offer an alternative universal model for the future.

Some (Sutter, 2002; Johnston, 2003a; Kim and Gill, this volume, Chapters 4 and 9) argue that China cannot really be seen as revisionist, that in many ways it accepts substantial elements of the status quo both globally and regionally, and that it is already quite conscious of, and responsive to, the dangers of being seen as threatening by its neighbours, and indeed the US. Its so-called 'New Security Concept', first introduced in 1997 and emphasized again in July 2002, reflects this in its emphasis on cooperative security, peaceful resolution of territorial and border disputes through negotiations, and support for the ARF method of providing security through dialogue (Sutter, 2002: 4; http://www.fmprc.gov.cn, 31 July 2002). China has been especially active in promoting such ideas with Southeast Asian states, a strategy that complements these states' so-called 'Gulliver Strategy' designed to enmesh China in regional networks. To support its goal of reassurance, Beijing signed with ASEAN members in November 2002 a Declaration on the Conduct of Parties in the South China Sea as well as the Framework Free Trade Agreement (see Breslin and Gill, this volume, Chapters 8 and 9). Although this South China Sea Declaration is not a formal Code of Conduct, it is a restraining mechanism. While it does not commit the parties to stop building new structures on reefs and islets that have already been occupied, it does commit them to peaceful resolution of disputes, and requires them to refrain from occupation of presently uninhabited islands and reefs. These developments, plus active Chinese efforts to sign 'strategic partnership' agreements with many of its neighbouring states, to build and maintain productive ties with South Korea despite Beijing's continuing link with Pyongyang, and to give support to other multilateral institutions such as the Shanghai Cooperation Organization and the ASEAN Plus Three (APT) could be interpreted as actions designed to support Beijing's claim that its rising power represents no danger to its neighbours.

As of 2003, China's material development seemed relatively steady, and there was no decisive turn towards either the malign or benign scenario. Fear of China's disintegration and collapse was counterpointed by fear that its success would generate an overbearing and politically unpleasant power and economic costs for those elsewhere in the region. These twin fears posed sharp and ongoing dilemmas for those outside as to how to balance the risks and opportunities of pursuing engagement and containment at the same time (see Breslin, this volume, Chapter 8) only ameliorated by the hopes that China's attempts to reassure would be sustained and that its enmeshment in regional networks would lead to an appreciation of the benefits of interdependence. The worst outcome for both China's neighbours and the West would be a China strengthened by trade and investment, but still authoritarian, nationalistic and alienated from Western-led international society. The best would be a China successfully coaxed more into line with international society both globally and regionally, and without the containment element triggering nationalist reactions.

China's relations with its Asian neighbours

This section rests on the assumption that China continues to grow stronger, keeping open the issue of whether its development takes benign or malign paths. In that context, what evidence does recent history offer about whether China is more likely to dominate East Asia or divide it? In other words, will China be able to get its neighbours to bandwagon with it in some form of consensual hegemony, recreating a Sino-centric regional international society, or is it more likely to trigger balancing behaviour?

The demise of the Soviet Union contributed strongly to the relative empowerment of China in Asia. The withdrawal of Soviet power from the region meant that both India and Vietnam lost their main external balancer against China, and that China became the central focus of East Asian (and up to a point South Asian) regional security dynamics (Buzan and Wæver, 2003: Part II). But although China's hand was strengthened in East Asia, it does not yet dominate the region, and not only because the US remains heavily engaged there as an external balancer. In China's position within the region there is some historical parallel with Japan, in that China also inspires historical fears amongst its neighbours. Neither country is therefore well placed to take up a consensual leadership role in East Asia, and both could trigger balancing reactions if they tried to assert hegemony in a coercive way. China also has the additional complication of its unresolved dispute with Taiwan. China sees this as a domestic question, but much of the rest of the world, including the US, sees it additionally as an international one, and this contains potential for poisoning China's relations both with its neighbours and the US.

China's regional position also bears some resemblance to that of Germany between 1870 and 1945. Although it is a big and relatively powerful state within its region, many of its neighbours are formidable powers in their own right (see Gill, this volume, Chapter 9). Some (Japan, South Korea, Taiwan, Singapore) possess not just military capabilities more modern than China's but also very substantial financial and economic resources. Others (India, Pakistan, Vietnam) can put large conventional forces in the field. Several either have (North Korea, India, Pakistan) or could quite quickly acquire (Japan, South Korea, Taiwan) nuclear weapons capability. China is neither in the happy position of the US (having only weak powers as neighbours), nor in that of the EU (having institutional legitimacy as a basis for both keeping its region peaceful and, up to a point, for integrating it as a single actor). If one accepts the essentially (neo)realist, Westphalian, assumption that states will balance in the face of preponderant power, then China would seem to face serious obstacles within its region to any bid for regional hegemony. Given the historical fears that it attracts, its lack of soft power resources and leadership legitimacy in the region (Van Ness, 2002: 143), and the actual and potential military and economic strength of its neighbours, China might well expect to attract local balancing reactions as its power increases, and thus to remain trapped within its region.

Yet the contemporary record of behaviour in the region suggests that there is not much balancing against China, even though China's absolute and relative power in the region have increased. I will examine the possible reasons for this in the final part of this section, but first I want to review the material and social relations among China and its Asian neighbours.

Since Japan is the other Asian great power, the first thing to note is its failure to emerge as a contender for regional leadership after the Cold War. The juxtaposition of China's strong economic growth during the 1980s and 1990s, with the faltering of Japan's economy during the 1990s (Alvstam 2001; Lehmann, this volume, Chapter 7) and its continued political weakness, downgraded Japan as a possible regional rival. In addition, Japan's potential as a regional leader remained hobbled by its failure to resolve historical questions with its neighbours. An attempt by Japan in 1996 to bolster the security dimension of its relationship with ASEAN got a cool response, as ASEAN proved unwilling to provoke China with any hint of an anti-China alliance (*Strategic Survey 1996–7*: 180–182). If Japan could set itself up as an alternative regional leader, then the possibility for Chinese regional hegemony would be seriously compromised. Although Japan has not made much progress in building the foundations for political leadership, for quite some time during the 1980s and 1990s it seemed to be creating a strong claim for economic leadership. The Japan-centred East Asian economic interdependence took the form of a hierarchy of finance, production and technology spreading out from Japan in concentric circles of investment in its neighbours, with Korea and Taiwan in the first circle, and Southeast Asia and China further out (Helleiner, 1994). It rested on strong commitment to shared pursuit of economic development goals, and in many ways it was also based on shared adherence to the Japanese model of political economy. These arrangements delivered unprecedented rates of growth during the 1980s and first half of the 1990s, and this growth plus the shared commitment to development goals came to assume an important role in the region's self-understanding and self-presentation of its security (Cossa and Khanna, 1997). But signs of economic downturn in the region as a whole were appearing by 1996, and in 1997 this turned into a financial and then an economic catastrophe. Doubts about the Asian development model undermined confidence in the future, and these doubts were reinforced both by the prolonged failure of Japan to find its own way out, and by its ceding of leadership in the crisis to the US-dominated IMF.

The seeming failure of Japan's economic project undercut a possible challenger to China, and opened a gap for China to fill. Although China was far from being immediately strong enough economically simply to step into Japan's shoes, it could and did begin to build the foundations for an economic claim to regional leadership. China seemed to escape the economic turbulence in East Asia, and gained some credit for its stabilizing influence by not devaluing the renminbi during the economic crisis. China also had its own regional network to compete with Japan's, the so-called 'Greater China', in which Chinese communities in Hong Kong, Taiwan, Singapore and elsewhere played a leading role in promoting trade with, and investment in, China (Yu, 1996; Goodman, this volume, Chapter 6), so adding to the economic interdependence between Northeast and Southeast Asia. Even with Taiwan, where political difficulties were extreme, Beijing encouraged extensive manufacturing investment by Taiwan, as well as by Hong Kong and South Korea, and this meant that the Taiwanese and mainland economies were increasingly tied together in a shared boom (Tucker, 1998–1999: 159–161). It remains unclear whether China will be able to sustain its own economic stability, let alone become the regional hub. Among other things, because it is less developed than Japan, China is less able to create a division of economic labour with its neighbours, although in November 2002 it signed a Framework FTA with the ASEAN states. China's economic success as an exporter could come at the expense of its neighbours' export markets, although this loss might be balanced by the investment opportunities that the new China offers for its neighbours (Breslin, this volume, Chapter 8). The events of the late 1990s made it easier for China to move towards regional economic leadership, and greatly weakened the economic project of its most obvious rival. There seemed to be no end to Japan's economic and political weakness, and no will in Tokyo either to claim regional leadership or to develop a more independent line from the US. Japan continued to be active, and in some ways influential, in Asian diplomacy, and its economy remained a giant despite its deep troubles. But Japan's political reticence meant that China had no active great power rival within Asia.

The conspicuous absence of balancing behaviour includes Japan, but was much more widespread. Even when China's policies have been militarily provocative towards its neighbours, as in its missile and nuclear assistance to Pakistan, its use of intimidatory behaviour to consolidate its territorial claims in the South China Sea, and its military threats towards Taiwan, this behaviour has met with rather meek responses. The ASEAN states, India and Japan all go out of their way to avoid provoking China's ire. Even China's open and continued cultivation of historical hatred of Japan did not provoke much official response, with most Japanese either not seeing China as threatening (Drifte, 2000: 451–452; Twomey, 2000: 169), or not much (Soeya, 1998; Clermont, 2002: 25–28; Sansoucy, 2002: 11–14). Yahuda (2002) argues that attitudes towards China in Japan are in fact deteriorating, and that the failure of both states to cultivate sensitivity towards the other's security concerns makes both them and the whole of Asia dependent on the US to hold the ring. The other potential rival to China in Asia, India, also seemed disinclined to securitize China to any great extent, despite having compelling reasons for doing so (Buzan and Wæver, 2003: chapter 4). Although New Delhi does justify its nuclear weapons mainly in relation to China, it has been remarkably restrained about China's substantial role in the nuclear arming of Pakistan.

The lack of balancing against China is perhaps most interestingly observed through ASEAN. Like the rest of the world, only more intimately and immediately, ASEAN faces the choice of whether to engage with China or to try to contain it (or somehow do both at the same time). There is a longstanding tension within ASEAN between the preferred option of trying to engage China diplomatically by building a regional international society, maximizing the engagement of outside powers in the region, and trying to extend an ASEAN-style security regime to East Asia; and the fallback option of putting in place the means to resist China should engagement fail. One part of the story here (the other being these Southeast Asian countries' ties with the US) is the emergence and evolution of the ASEAN Regional Forum (ARF) which came into being in 1994. Japan played a significant role in this development, although eschewing leadership for itself (Foot, 1995: 242) or having its bids turned down (Okawara and Katzenstein, 2001: 176–182). ARF linked together the middle and small powers of ASEAN with 'dialogue partners', eventually including all of the East Asian states except Taiwan, and the US, Japan, China, Russia, India, Australia, New Zealand and the EU. On the basis of its membership, ARF had some standing as a loose Asia-Pacific security regime. As Leifer (1996: 55) put it 'The undeclared aim of the ARF is to defuse and control regional tensions by generating and sustaining a network of dialogues within the over-arching framework of its annual meetings, while the nexus of economic incentive works on governments irrevocably committed to market-based economic development.' One way of understanding the setting up of ARF is to see it as a post-Cold War response to ASEAN's inability to construct itself as a counterweight to China, and the need therefore to try to socialize China into being a good citizen (Foot, 1998).

After initially being uncomfortable with multilateralism, China quickly adjusted to the ARF, seeing advantage in using its soft procedures to fudge conflicts (Cossa and Khanna, 1997: 222) or, more charitably, because it recognized its value as a forum in which it could attempt to reassure some of its smaller neighbours. China upgraded its participation in the ARF in 1996 in response to deteriorating relations in Northeast Asia, with the US, and with ASEAN over the Mischief Reef Incident in 1995. ASEAN was always an unlikely candidate for regional security leadership, and it could only seize the initiative because of the constraints on both China and Japan (and in a different sense the US) in relation to that role. Increasingly, it had to struggle hard to maintain its leadership within an ARF containing several large powers. There was a tension between, on the one hand, the desire of many East Asian states (especially Japan) to keep the US engaged in the region to provide the balancer to China that they were unwilling to provide themselves, and, on the other hand, the tendency of ASEAN to appease China, or not resist its encroachments. But the ARF was effective in tying the northern powers, especially China and Japan, to Southeast Asia, and in enabling China to reassure its neighbours about its regional good citizenship. Since China insisted on the exclusion of Taiwan from the ARF, its most sensitive issue was kept off the ARF's agenda. The ARF made no response to the Taiwan Straits crisis in 1995–1996. Neither did ASEAN nor ARF put up much resistance when in 1995 the Chinese military extended their earlier expansions in the Spratly Islands by occupying the Mischief Reef, long claimed by the Philippines, although not occupied by it. China – like the other claimants – did not budge from advancing its sovereign rights, but after 1995 did put more emphasis on peaceful resolution of this many-sided dispute and did also agree to continue discussing the issue within the ASEAN/ARF framework (Foot, 1998: 430–431).

Given the post-1997 disarray in ASEAN, the dominance of Northeast Asia in the East Asian region was increasingly symbolized by the 'ASEAN Plus Three (APT)' (the three being China, Japan and South Korea) meetings, in which ASEAN was no longer in the leading role. These developments gave China an increasingly central position in the region's institutions, and steadily shifted them away from any balancing role and towards one in which China could use them to assert and consolidate its influence.

ARF might initially have been seen at least in part as a balancing move against China. But in the event it has not developed down that line. Neither ARF, nor the countries most directly affected by China's more bellicose behaviour (India, Taiwan, Vietnam, Philippines), have pursued balancing policies against China with other Asian states. Within East Asia Vietnam is the only country ever to have seriously tried balancing against China (late 1970s to late 1980s), but the effect of this was lost because of its simultaneous opposition to the US and ASEAN during those years. After the withdrawal of Soviet power from Southeast Asia, Vietnam no longer had the means to pursue balancing, and joined ASEAN. Chinese provocative behaviour towards India, ASEAN and Taiwan all failed to trigger balancing responses within the region. Taiwan can be allowed as a special case because many states in Asia give some weight to China's claim that its problem with Taiwan is a domestic issue rather than an international one. Nevertheless, the similarity of China's behaviour towards Taiwan, and its behaviour in South Asia and the South China Sea, is as striking as the lack of balancing response towards it.

Some saw China and Japan as 'natural rivals' (Roy, 1994: 163), but, aside from the maintenance, and marginal strengthening of, its alliance with the US, Japan hardly featured as a balancer against China. Japan did move towards collaboration with the US in developing theatre missile defences (TMD), and Goldstein (2003) observed that 'Japan is in the distinctive position of being able to piggyback its balancing efforts geared towards the anticipation of increased Chinese capabilities on its short-term effort to counter the dangerous capabilities North Korea may be deploying'. Without Japan being at the centre of it, there could be no realistic Asian counter-China coalition, and there were no signs at all that Japan was interested in such a role, except as junior partner to the US.

The contemporary record in Asia thus suggests that there is not much propensity to balance against China, even when its behaviour is provocative. If this behaviour persists, then it becomes difficult to avoid the conclusion that, if China can maintain its growth and modernization, the prospects for its being able to establish some form of hegemony in Asia look strong.

China's relationships with the US and the other great powers

At the global level, the question is about China's relationship with the US as the sole superpower, and with Russia and the EU as the remaining non-Asian great powers (for the argument about why these two should be understood as great powers, see Buzan and Wæver, 2003: chapter 2). There is almost no strategic component to China's relationship with the EU. Neither matters much to the other, except economically to a degree, and through their relationships with the US. Russia matters more to China, and vice versa, but again largely as mediated through their relationships with the US. The implosion of the Soviet Union left Russia as a mainly European power with only a weak presence in Asia. Although Russia and China have longstanding reasons for treating each other with suspicion, since the end of the Cold War they have cultivated a loose *entente* against the US. Russia is a significant supplier of advanced weapons to China, and in 2001 they signed a treaty of friendship and cooperation. They share dislike of US hegemony, and up to a point campaign jointly in favour of a multipolar vision of international society. As the poorest and least technologically developed great powers, China and Russia are not in a position to balance seriously against the US, and certainly not so long as the US is supported by its alliances with Europe and Japan.

For China, as for all the other great powers, its relationship with the US is the most important one. Perhaps the best that one can say about it since the ending of the Cold War is that it has been difficult. There have been some positive developments, most notably China's membership of the WTO, and many more high-level and regular meetings between Chinese and American officials, but mainly the relationship has been tense, and occasionally – as during the Taiwan Straits crisis of 1995–1996, and the spy plane incident of April 2001 – confrontational. China and the US no longer share a common concern about the Soviet Union, and there were tensions between them, *inter alia*, over trade; copyright violations; human rights; Chinese arms and nuclear and missile sales to Iran, Pakistan and others; US arms sales to, and political support for, Taiwan; US plans for missile defences; nuclear weapons testing in the run-up to the 1995 NPT renewal conference and the CTBT negotiations; and navigation rights. Before 11 September 2001, and after the fading of Japan during the mid-1990s, China became the chief object of Washington's apparent search for some sort of enemy or threat around which to organize its foreign policy. The attention of the US was drawn away from China as a possible peer competitor by September 11th and the wars against terrorism and Iraq. But the US commitment in the National Security Strategy statement of 2002 (Bush, 2002: 29–30) to maintaining its own dominance and preventing the rise of other powers made clear that the China question remained firmly on the long-term agenda. And the Bush administration's strengthening of its military ties with Taiwan kept warm the danger that the US and China could be drawn into a confrontation over an issue sensitive to both (Johnston, 2003a: 38, 47, 53). An American commitment to pressing for long-term regime change in China was also signalled in the 2002 Strategy statement: 'China is following an outdated path that, in the end, will hamper its own pursuit of national greatness. In time, China will find that social and political freedom is the only source of that greatness' (Bush, 2002: 27).

The key fact in the US–China relationship is that the pattern of US engagement in Northeast Asia was remarkably little disturbed by the ending of the Cold War. Indeed, after a period of uncertainty in the early 1990s, the US presence in the region got somewhat stronger. And after September 11th, stronger still, given Washington's subsequent closer ties with Pakistan, India, and the Central and Southeast Asian states that have all been drawn into the struggle against terrorism. The US role in Korea also became more central with the actions taken to stem North Korean nuclear proliferation. Its engagement with Taiwan deepened as a consequence of the major US military role in the Taiwan Straits crisis during 1995–1996 (Tucker, 1998–1999). Japan remained committed to keeping the US active in the East Asian security equation, and did not challenge US leadership. The removal of the Soviet factor stripped away any ambiguity about the reasons for continued US military engagements in Northeast Asia: with Soviet power gone, the ongoing US presence could only be to contain China (and to a lesser extent North Korea).

Why the absence of regional balancing?

In sum, what we have is a China with reasonably good prospects for increasing its absolute and relative power within Asia, a set of neighbours disinclined to balance against it, and a robust US presence in East Asia whose function of balancing China is no longer disguised by the Cold War. How do the regional and global levels play into each other, and what light does this interplay throw on the puzzle of the apparent underperformance of the regional balancing mechanism? There are five possible explanations for underbalancing.

First, is that the traditional sort of strategic analysis that sees threats emanating from China to its neighbours is simply wrong. Either China does not represent a serious threat to its neighbours, and they are therefore correct in keeping their securitizations of it at a rather low level; or it does, but its neighbours are somehow blind to the facts. This would require them to interpret somewhat differently what others have seen as sustained, and overtly military, Chinese pressure on India (by seizing disputed territory and nuclearizing Pakistan), on ASEAN (by occupations and claims in the dispute with Vietnam over the Paracels and in the many-sided dispute over the Spratly Islands), on Taiwan (by frequent threats and military demonstrations), and on Japan (cultivation of historical hatred, disputing of unresolved maritime claims).

Second, is that Chinese diplomacy has somehow been so effective that it has been able to intimidate its neighbours into a form of appeasement that restrains them from publicly responding to its provocations. The mechanism here is a combination of the more ameliorative and sensitive diplomacy discussed above, and the threat that any balancing responses will cause an immediate worsening of relations and escalation of threats. This mechanism could be a plausible explanation, given China's ability to deal with the separate regions of Asia more or less in isolation from each other, and the formidable costs and difficulties of constructing an anti-China coalition stretching from India through ASEAN to Japan. There is also the fact that China's behaviour towards Taiwan is (rightly) seen as a special case, and its similarity to China's behaviour in Southeast and South Asia therefore gets underplayed, making the whole pattern less visible.

Third is the possibility that the Asian region is dressed in Westphalian clothes, but is not performing according to a Westphalian script. This line of thinking (Fairbank, 1968; Huntington, 1996: 229–238; Kang, 1995, 2003) projects Asia's past into its future. It assumes that what Fairbank labelled the 'Chinese World Order', and Huntington 'Confucian civilization' – a Sino-centric and hierarchical form of international relations – has survived within the cultures of East Asia despite the superficial remaking of Asia into a Western-style set of sovereign states. Its principal effect is to subvert the expectation of balancing as the normal response to threat and power imbalance in a Westphalian system, and to replace it with a propensity among the weaker powers to bandwagon. The idea is that hierarchical behaviour remains so deeply ingrained in Asian cultures that it makes their international relations not conform to the realist model of IR. This intriguing, and potentially extremely important, proposition cannot really be tested unless the US pulls out of Asia, leaving the Asian states to sort out their relationships on their own terms. Its prediction does explain the observed underperformance of balancing, although it is hard put to explain India's conformity with it, given that India was never part of the Chinese world order. If this interpretation is true, then China has much better prospects for gaining some form of hegemony over East Asia if its relative power rises.

The fourth explanation goes in the opposite direction from the 'Confucian' one by arguing that the Westphalian-style state has successfully consolidated itself in East Asia, with the result that a society of states of the type highlighted by the English school has developed within the region (Alagappa, 2003: 471–487). This interstate society is mainly pluralist, but it has developed significant restraints on the use of force and intervention, quite strong expectation of multilateral diplomacy as the norm, and acceptance of substantial amounts of economic liberal practice. This combination reduces incentives to balance, as it has done within the West. Alagappa argues that the contribution of this regional interstate society to the security order in Asia is significant, but largely overshadowed by the prominence given to the influence of the US. China fits into this type of explanation, in that its desire to concentrate on domestic economic development and the maintenance of political stability undergirds its support for a rule-based regional interstate society. This would explain its search for 'partnership' agreements with many of its neighbours, higher levels of support for multilateral institutions, and frequent reference to ASEAN norms of non-use of force for settling disputes and non-interference in domestic affairs.

The fifth explanation is that the impact of the US engagement in Asia explains the underperformance of balancing: in other words, that there is a strong interplay between the regional security dynamics of Asia, and those at the global level concerning US–China relations. The argument is that the US presence as security ringholder in Asia allows Asian governments to see the job of balancing China as falling to the US. Interestingly, the US actively encourages such underperformance in several ways. It projects nuclear non-proliferation norms strongly on to the two Koreas, Japan, Taiwan, India and Pakistan; it cultivates Japan as a military dependent; and it has traditionally opposed Asian multilateral security initiatives. This behaviour is not simply a local application of US global policy, since the US has made little attempt to restrain Israel's nuclear deterrent, or earlier those of Britain and France. Since the US has to worry about China at the global level, and since China's global prospects are heavily conditioned by its position in Asia, this underperformance of balancing locks the US in. It potentially stimulates US–China rivalry by putting the US into the front line against China. This logic has unsettling links to both the interstate society and Chinese world order ones sketched above. The dominant position of the US weakens Asian interstate society both by retarding the development of Asian institutions (Alagappa, 2003: 594–595), and by allowing Japan and China to continue neglecting the central relationship between them (Yahuda, 2002). Westphalian logic suggests that if the US drew back from its ringholding position, then other Asian states would be forced to balance, thus doing the US's job for it at the global level. But while that interpretation creates incentives for the US to disengage, two other considerations keep it locked in. First, the unresolved China–Japan relationship introduces a radical and potentially very dangerous uncertainty into the scenario of US withdrawal. Second, the Chinese world order interpretation makes disengagement much more hazardous. If Asian international behaviour is to bandwagon with threateners – or even with a China that is perceived to be more benign – then US disengagement would hand China a regional hegemony in Asia which would greatly enhance its global position.

China benefits either way. So long as the US stays engaged in East Asia, China's neighbours will leave the balancing job to it, and China will have a relatively clear path to a slow extension of its regional hegemony. Only if China became so malign as to frighten its neighbours into a (probably US-backed) counter-coalition does this scenario look likely to be upset. If the US gives up the balancing job, China may well benefit from bandwagoning within its region. On the basis of this reasoning, China is in possession of a long-term strategy which could work either with or against the long-term hope of liberals that economic engagement with China will eventually generate a more benign domestic politics. China has but to wait, grow, and not be too aggressive, and regional hegemony should come steadily into its grasp whether it liberalizes or not. As it does so, China's ability to act on the world stage will improve.

China and the US–Japan alliance

Embedded in the general question of how China's standing in its region affects its place at the global level, is the more specific question about how China can affect the status of the US as the sole superpower. One aspect of this is simply that China might eventually qualify as a superpower in its own right, shifting unipolarity to bipolarity. Another, more subtle factor, is that the process by which China rises might undermine some aspects on which the US claim to superpowerdom rests. The current singular status of the US is no longer based on the kind of huge economic and industrial lead that it enjoyed during the early decades of the Cold War. Its military lead is very significant, but, as the Soviet Union demonstrated in its heyday, not beyond challenge in the medium term should others decide to devote comparable resources to strengthening themselves in that way. The fact that they have not done this so far rests in part on the relative acceptability and legitimacy of US leadership/hegemony – an asset that has been in decline as US policy under the Bush administration took a more ideologically unilateralist turn, and which seems likely to be further undermined by the exposure of near-imperial pretensions in policy towards Iraq. The real key to US superpower status is that the next two biggest centres of capital and technology in the international system – Europe and Japan – accept its leadership and subordinate themselves to it by their membership in US-dominated alliances (Nye, 2002).

Despite Gerry Segal's heroic labours in trying to strengthen the ties between Europe and Asia, China has little leverage on US–Europe relations. But, within Asia, it is a different question, which is why the interplay between Asian regional developments and global ones could be so significant. The focus here is not China but Japan. What Japan does is crucial both for the global status of the US and for the regional (and global) possibilities of China. Japan has four possibilities. It can continue remaining closely tied to the US. It can break that tie, and reinvent itself, as it has done in the past, as an independent 'normal' great power. It can combine these two by building a more equal alliance partnership with the US. Or it can bandwagon with China. Much favours a continuation of the tie to the US (Yahuda, 2002). The US and Japanese economies are deeply entangled, and, since the ending of the Cold War, Japan began reforming its defence guidelines towards allowing a wider role for the Japanese Self-Defense Force (JSDF) and closer coordination with US forces in the region. China's carefully maintained historical antagonism towards Japan also favours the status quo, as do the restraints on Japan's military capability (Gill, this volume, Chapter 9). Although there are some incremental signs of moves towards a more equal alliance, Japan's seeming unwillingness to take up a more robust military policy, or to challenge the US, or to develop a more independent foreign and military policy, suggest that this will be a long time in coming – if ever. If the existing lopsided US–Japan alliance remains robust, then a key prop of US global status is maintained, and China's possibilities for hegemony within Asia are reduced. Either of Japan's other two options would pull away that prop and diminish significantly US claims to superpower status (even more so if they were matched by a similar breakdown of the Atlantic alliance).

The question then is, what could cause such a breakdown? There are three obvious possibilities. First is a revival of the Japan-bashing attitudes within the US that occurred during the late 1980s and early 1990s. This was when some in the US grew to fear that Japan's economic prowess and (at the time) the US's economic troubles, would enable Japan to over-take the US as number one. The possibility of either renewed US economic slump or a revival of the Japanese economy cannot be discounted, but, even so, this scenario no longer looks likely to be able to disrupt US–Japan relations. It did not do so even when Japan-as-number-one looked a real possibility. Now, the possibility of Japan's becoming number one has vanished over the horizon (not least because of the rise of China), and the US has plenty of enemies and is no longer casting around for challengers to securitize.

The second possibility is the most discussed, and perhaps the most serious. It is that Japan and the US will encounter policy differences so serious that their alliance will become unsustainable. Some observers see potential for such radical change in the differences between Japan and US on policy goals in East Asia, particularly on China and Taiwan, but also Korean reunification (Stokes, 1996; Drifte, 2000; Twomey, 2000: 204–205), and speculate whether these will corrode the US–Japan alliance. The most widely mooted scenario that could quickly break the US–Japan alliance is a major military crisis over Taiwan in which Japan failed to support the US. Despite some formal revision of the US–Japan defence cooperation guidelines in the mid-1990s, doubts remain about whether, and to what extent, Japan would support the US in a crisis. China makes no secret of the fact that it is deeply opposed to this aspect of the US–Japan alliance, making the stakes for Japan very high no matter how it responded to a crisis over Taiwan (Johnston, 2003a: 43). The full and exact reper-cussions of such an event are hard to predict, and might include a general US disengagement from East Asia. The point is that it lies within China's power – and, according to its rhetoric, also within its will – to precipi-tate precisely such a crisis if it thinks that Taiwan is formally moving towards independence. There is still a constituency in the US for con-structing China as the likely challenger to US hegemony, and these two things have a significant potential to play into each other. For Japan, being the front line in a tense relationship between a more imperially minded US and a rising China is not an attractive position. Hypothesizing a split between the US and Japan leaves open the question of whether Japan would then strike out as an independent great power, as it did after the First World War, or seek an accommodation with China. Japan could certainly mount its own deterrent against China if need be (Twomey, 2000: 185–193), but it is no longer capable of dominating East Asia by itself. Because the US plays such a big role in relation to the two Asian great powers – balancing China, and keeping Japan so closely tied to itself that Japan does not really have to develop a security policy of its own – it is very difficult to assess what Sino-Japanese relations would look like if the US ceased to play ringholder for the East Asian powers.

Whether or not a crisis over Taiwan or Korea could push Japan towards China is a question with too many variables to answer with any clarity: it might or might not. But the third possibility is that Japan might be tempted to bandwagon with a rising China (Ross, 1999: 115) simply on the basis of power considerations. Huntington (1996: 234–238) notes Japan's historic tendency to align with the dominant power in the system, and if such a tendency exists, it may well have been reinforced by Japan's dismal experience of going it alone during the 1930s and 1940s. This line of thinking relates to the Confucian interpretation of East Asian international relations sketched above, in which preponderant power triggers bandwagoning rather than balancing behaviour. Japan's Cold War and post-Cold War behaviour is understandable according to either (neo)realist or Confucian logic, and therefore gives no insight into which was operating. The test for Japan would come if China's internal development produced rising relative power *vis à vis* the US. A Sino-Japanese condominium might be a possibility, but it would require very radical departures from existing arrangements. It is hard to see how Japan would avoid becoming the junior partner in any such arrangement, thereby reproducing its existing unbalanced partnership with the US. Given its economic ties to East Asia, Japan no longer really has the option of exploiting its offshore geography to play the old British game of pretending not to be a member of any region. In this sense, Japan is uniquely in a pivotal position. If it took an independent great power line, it would both reduce the US position in Asia and the world, and complicate China's prospects for hegemony in Asia. If it shifted alignment to China it would, in one move, both greatly weaken the global position of the US, and greatly strengthen China's position not only in Asia, but in the world.

Conclusions

Gerry was not wildly wrong in his general argument that too many people inside and outside China were overplaying its real capabilities and standing in the world, and that the consequence of this was negative both for getting reform in China and for managing its place in international society. That said, the evidence supporting his argument can be questioned and widened, and doing so nuances the policy implications in several ways. Gerry was aware that China's capabilities had different implications for its neighbours in Asia than for the international system as a whole, but he did not look closely enough at the regional level, either in itself, or for the way in which developments and events there could have major impacts on world politics. How China ends up relating to Asia will have major implications for what sort of global power ambitions it can entertain.

Gerry was right to draw attention to the material and social capabilities that China possesses in the here and now, and to point out the consequences of misreading these. But he perhaps underplayed the real significance of potentiality in world politics. All politics is about the future, and there is no doubt that China matters for the future. Gerry thought that China was both taking and being given too much credit in the present for what it might become in the future. Most of the authors in this book would part company with him on his argument that 'China's influence and authority are clearly puny' (Segal, 1999: 34), feeling that China is already a major influence within its region, and increasingly, although still unevenly, in the world. China is still some distance from qualifying as a superpower, but its potential to do so is nevertheless a serious and valid consideration in how it gets treated in the present, and so is its capacity to undermine the whole framework of US unipolarity by bringing into question the US–Japan relationship. How much credit one should give in the present to assumed capabilities in the future depends on how long it will take to realize the potential, and how stable and reliable the structures are on which that realization depends. Gerry's legacy to us on this is that we must keep asking that question, and, while doing so, keep a sceptical eye on those both within and outside China who insist that the answers are 'soon', and 'very stable and reliable'.

Gerald Segal – biographical highlights

Born 3 February 1953 in Montreal. BA Hebrew University 1975. Ph.D. London School of Economics 1979: 'From Bipolarity to the Great Power Triangle: Moscow, Peking, Washington, 1961–68'. Lectured at the University of Wales (Aberystwyth) 1979–1981, the University of Leicester (1981–1984) and the University of Bristol (1984–1991) where he became Reader in International Relations. Married Edwina Moreton in 1984, daughter Rachel born 1988. On leave at the Royal Institute of International Affairs 1988–1991 running a project on comparative reform in communist party states. Founded the quarterly journal *The Pacific Review* in 1988, and edited it until 1995. Joined the International Institute for Strategic Studies in 1991 as Senior Fellow in Asian Studies, in 1994 raised £2.3m and became Director of the Pacific Asia Programme for the UK's Economic and Social Research Council, and appointed IISS Director of Studies in 1997. During the mid-1990s co-founded the Secretariats of both the European Council for Security Cooperation in Asia-Pacific (ECSCAP), and the European Secretariat of the Council for Asia–Europe Co-operation (CAEC). Made a 'fellow' of the World Economic Forum (Davos) in 1995. Died 1999 at the age of 46.

Principal publications (in chronological order 1976–1999)

Gerald Segal, 'Chinese Politics and the Soviet Connection', *The Jerusalem Journal of International Relations*, 2(1): Autumn 1976.

Gerald Segal, 'The Chinese Army and Professionalism' (with Ellis Joffe), *Problems of Communism*, November–December 1978.

Gerald Segal, 'Card Playing in International Relations: the United States and the Great Power Triangle', *Millennium*, 8(3): Winter 1979–1980.

Gerald Segal, 'China and the Great Power Triangle', *The China Quarterly*, 83: September 1980.

Gerald Segal, 'China's Strategic Posture and the Great Power Triangle', *Pacific Affairs*, 53(4): Winter 1980–1981.

John Baylis and Gerald Segal (eds), *Soviet Strategy*, London: Croom Helm, 1981.

Gerald Segal (ed.), *The China Factor*, London: Croom Helm, 1982.

Gerald Segal, *The Great Power Triangle*, London: Macmillan, 1982.

Gerald Segal, *The Soviet Threat at China's Gates*, Institute for the Study of Conflict, Conflict Papers, No. 143, January 1983.

Gerald Segal (ed.), *The Soviet Union and East Asia*, London: Heinemann/Royal Institute of International Affairs, 1983.

John Baylis, Lawrence Freedman, Edwina Moreton and Gerald Segal, *Nuclear War and Nuclear Peace*, London: Macmillan, 1983 (second edn, 1988).

Edwina Moreton and Gerald Segal (eds), *Soviet Strategy Towards Western Europe*, London: George Allen and Unwin, 1984.

Gerald Segal and William T. Tow (eds), *Chinese Defence Policy*, London: Macmillan, 1984.

Gerald Segal, *Defending China*, London: Oxford University Press, 1985.

Anne Gilks and Gerald Segal, *China and the Arms Trade*, London: Croom Helm, 1985.

Gerald Segal, *Sino-Soviet Relations after Mao*, International Institute for Strategic Studies, Adelphi Papers, No. 202, London: IISS, 1985.

Gerald Segal, *Modernising Foreign Policy*, The China Challenge, Chatham House Papers, No. 32, 1986.

Gerald Segal (ed.), *Arms Control in Asia*, London: Macmillan, 1987.

Gerald Segal, *The Guide to the World Today*, London: Simon & Schuster, 1987, second edition, 1988.

Gerald Segal (ed.), *The Political and Economic Encyclopaedia of the Pacific*, London: Longman, 1989.

Gerald Segal (ed.), *China's Reforms in Crisis*, London: Royal Institute of International Affairs, 1989.

David S. Goodman and Gerald Segal (eds), *China at Forty*, Oxford: Oxford University Press, 1989.

Gerald Segal, *Rethinking the Pacific*, Oxford: Oxford University Press, 1990.

Gerald Segal, *The Soviet Union and the Pacific*, London: Unwin Hyman, 1990.

Gerald Segal (ed.), *Chinese Politics and Foreign Policy Reform*, London: Kegan Paul International for the RIIA, 1990.

Gerald Segal, *The World Affairs Companion*, London: Simon & Schuster, 1991, 1993, 1996.

David S. Goodman and Gerald Segal (eds), *China in the Nineties*, Oxford: Oxford University Press, 1991.

Gerald Segal (ed.), *Openness and Foreign Policy Reform in Communist States*, London: Routledge for the RIIA, 1992.

Gerald Segal, *The Fate of Hong Kong*, London: Simon & Schuster, 1993. Translated into Japanese and published by Dobunshoin International, Tokyo.

Gerald Segal, 'The Coming Confrontation Between China and Japan?', *World Policy Journal*, 2: Summer 1993.

Gerald Segal, *China Changes Shape*, Adelphi Papers, No. 287, London: IISS, 1994.

Gerald Segal, *China Changes Shape*, Foreign Affairs, May 1994.

Barry Buzan and Gerald Segal, 'Rethinking East Asian Security', *Survival*, Summer 1994.

David S. Goodman and Gerald Segal (eds), *China Deconstructs*, London: Routledge, 1994.

Gerald Segal, 'Tying China into the International System', *Survival*, Summer 1995.

Gerald Segal, 'What is Asian About Asian Security', *The National Interest*, Winter 1995.

David S. Goodman and Gerald Segal, *China Without Deng Xiaoping*, Melbourne and New York: ETT, 1995.

Gerald Segal, 'East Asia and the "Constrainment" of China', *International Security*, Spring 1996.

Barry Buzan and Gerald Segal, 'The Rise of "Lite" Powers', *World Policy Journal*, 13(3): Fall 1996.

Richard H. Yang and Gerald Segal (eds), *China's Economic Reform: The Impact on Security*, London: Routledge, 1996.

David S. Goodman and Gerald Segal (eds), *China Rising: Nationalism and Interdependence*, London: Routledge, 1997.

Gerald Segal, 'Thinking Strategically About ASEM', *The Pacific Review*, 1: 1997.

Gerald Segal, 'How Insecure is Pacific Asia?', *International Affairs*, (73)2: April 1997.

Barry Buzan and Gerald Segal, *Anticipating the Future*, London: Simon & Schuster, 1998.

James Manor and Gerald Segal, 'Taking India Seriously', *Survival*, 40(2): Summer 1998.

Gerald Segal, 'The Asia-Pacific: What Kind of Challenge?' in Anthony McGrew and Christopher Brook, *Asia-Pacific in the New World Order*, London: Routledge, 1998.

Hanns Maull, Gerald Segal and Jusuf Wanandi (eds), *Europe and the Asia Pacific*, London: Routledge, 1998.

Gerald Segal, 'Does China Matter?', *Foreign Affairs*, 78(5): September/October 1999.

References

Alagappa, Muthiah (2003) 'Preface' and 'Managing Asian Security: Competition, Cooperation and Evolutionary Change', in Muthiah Alagappa (ed.), *Asian Security Order: Instrumental and Normative Features*, Stanford, CA: Stanford University Press, pp. ix–xv, 571–606.

Alvstam, Claes G. (2001) 'East Asia: Regionalization Still Waiting to Happen?', in Michael Schulz, Frederik Söderbaum and Joakim Öjendal (eds), *Regionalization in a Globalizing World. A Comparative Perspective on Forms, Actors and Processes*, London and New York: Zed Books, pp. 173–197.

Arima, Tatsuo (1969) *The Failure of Freedom: A Portrait of Modern Japanese Intellectuals*, Cambridge, MA: Harvard University Press.

Asia Research Centre (1992) *Southern China in Transition: China's New Regionalism and the Prospects for Australia*, Canberra: AGPS.

Baldinger, P. (1992) 'The Birth of Greater China', *The China Business Review*, May/June.

Baldwin, David (1979) 'Power Analysis and World Politics: New Trends versus Old Tendencies', *World Politics*, 31(2): 161–194.

Barshefsky, Charlene (1999) 'Statement of Ambassador Charlene Barshefsky Regarding Broad Market Access Gains Resulting from China WTO Negotiations', Office of the United States Trade Representative: Washington DC, 8 April.

Baylis, John, Freedman, Lawrence, Moreton, Edwina and Segal, Gerald (1983) *Nuclear War and Nuclear Peace*, London: Macmillan.

BBC News Online (2000) 'China in Denial over Nobel Laureate', 12 October 2000.

Beasley, William (1973) *The Meiji Restoration*, London: Oxford University Press.

Becker, Jasper (2002) *The Chinese*, London: Oxford University Press.

Bergsten, C. Fred (1997) 'The Asian Monetary Crisis: Proposed Remedies', presented to the US House of Representatives Committee on Banking and Financial Services, 13 November.

Bernard, Mitchell and Ravenhill, John (1995) 'Beyond Product Cycles and Flying Geese: Regionalization, Hierarchy, and the Industrialization of East Asia', *World Politics*, 47(2): 171–209.

Bernstein, Richard and Munro, Ross H. (1997) 'The Coming Conflict with America', *Foreign Affairs*, 76(2) (March/April): 18–32.

Bernstein, Richard and Munro, Ross H. (1998) *The Coming Conflict with America*, New York: Vintage Books.

Bhaskaran, Manu (2003) *China as Potential Superpower: Regional Responses*, Berlin: Deutsche Bank Research Report, 15 January.

Bitzinger, Richard A. (2003) 'Just the Facts Ma'am: the Challenge of Analysing and Assessing Chinese Military Expenditures', *China Quarterly*, 173: 164–175.

Bix, Herbert (2001) *Hirohito and the Making of Modern Japan*, New York: HarperCollins.

Bobbitt, Philip (2002) *The Shield of Achilles: War, Peace and the Course of History*, New York: Alfred Knopf.

Boy, Luthje (2002) 'Electronics Contract Manufacturing: Global Production and the International Division of Labor in the Age of the Internet', *Industry and Innovation*, 9(3): 227–247.

Bracken, Paul (1994) 'The Military Crisis of the Nation State: Will Asia be Different from Europe?', *Political Studies*, 42 (special issue): 97–114.

Braunstein, Elissa and Epstein, Gerald (2002) 'Bargaining Power and Foreign Direct Investment in China: Can 1.3 Billion Consumers Tame the Multinationals?', CEPA Working Papers 2002–13, Center for Economic Policy Analysis (CEPA), New School University.

Broad, Robin and Cavanagh, John (1988) 'No More Nics', *Foreign Policy*, 72: 81–103.

Brown, Michael E., Cote Jr, Owen R., Lynn-Jones, Sean M. and Miller, Steven E. (eds), (2001) *The Rise of China*, Boston, MA: MIT Press.

Bunnin, Nicholas and Cheng, Chung-ying (2002) *Contemporary Chinese Philosophy*, Oxford: Blackwell.

Buruma, Ian (1995) *The Wages of Guilt: Memories of War in Germany and Japan*, New York: Farrar, Strauss & Giroux.

Buruma, Ian (2001) *Bad Elements: Chinese Rebels from Los Angeles to Beijing*, New York: Random House.

Bush, George W. (2002) *The National Security Strategy of the United States of America*, Washington DC: White House, September.

Business Times Online (2003) 'US Must Force China to Drop Yuan Peg: Economist', 31 January.

Buzan, Barry (2004) *The United States and the Great Powers: World Politics in the 21st Century*, Cambridge: Polity Press.

Buzan, Barry and Segal, Gerald (1996) 'The Rise of "Lite" Powers', *World Policy Journal*, 13(3): 1–10.

Buzan, Barry and Segal, Gerald (1998) *Anticipating the Future*, London: Simon & Schuster.

Buzan, Barry and Wæver, Ole (2003) *Regions and Powers: the Structure of International Security*, Cambridge: Cambridge University Press.

Cha, Victor (2000) 'Globalization and the Study of International Security', *Journal of Peace Research*, 37(3): 391–403.

Chan, Anita (1996) 'Boot Camp at the Show Factory: Regimented Workers in China's Free Labour Market', *The Washington Post*, 3 November.

Chandler, Clay (2003) 'Coping With China: As China Becomes the Workshop of the World, Where Does That Leave the Rest of Asia?', *Fortune*, 16 January.

Chang, Gordon G. (2001a) Evidence to the House US–China Commission, 2 August (http://www.uscc.gov/tescha.htm).

Chang, Gordon G. (2001b) *The Coming Collapse of China*, New York: Random House.

Chen Chunlai (2002) 'Foreign Direct Investment in China: A Case Study', *Austrian Foreign Trade Yearbook 2001–2002*, Vienna: Federal Ministry for Economic Affairs and Labour.

Chen Shin-Hong (2002) 'Global Production Networks and Information Technology: The Case of Taiwan', *Industry and Innovation*, 9(3): 249–265.

Chia Siow Yue and Lee Tsao Yuan (1993) 'Subregional Economic Zones: a New Motive Force in Asia-Pacific Development', in Fred Bergstein and Marcus Noland (eds), *Pacific Dynamism and the International Economic System*, Washington: Institute for International Economics, pp. 225–269.

China Daily (1992) 'Common Heritage Binds Overseas Chinese Closely', 22 October, p. 4.

China Economic Quarterly (2003) 'Special Report: Truth or Consequences: China's GDP Numbers', 7(1): 32.

China Security Review Commission (2002) *Report to Congress: the National Security Implications of the Economic Relationship Between the United States and China*, Washington: US Congress, Chapter 6.

Chow Tse-tung (1960) *The May Fourth Movement: Intellectual Revolution in Modern China*, Cambridge, MA: Harvard University Press.

Christensen, Thomas J. (1996) 'Chinese Realpolitik', *Foreign Affairs*, 75(5): 37–52.

Christensen, Thomas J. (2001) 'Posing Problems Without Catching Up: China's Rise and Challenges for US Security Policy', *International Security*, 25(4): 5–40.

Chua Chin Hon (2003) 'Half of New Graduates in China Cannot Find Jobs', *The Straits Times*, 19 July.

Clermont, Jean (2002) 'Regional Rivalries in Northeast Asia', Paper presented to ISA Conference, 24–27 March, New Orleans.

Cossa, Ralph A. and Khanna, Jane (1997) 'East Asia: Economic Interdependence and Regional Security', *International Affairs*, 73(2): 219–234.

Council on Foreign Relations (2003) *Council on Foreign Relations Task Force on Chinese Military Power*, New York: Council on Foreign Relations.

Coutts (2003) *Investment Perspective, May/June 2003*, London: Coutts.

Cragg, Craig (1996) *The New Taipans: A Vital Source Book on the People and Business of the Pacific Rim*, London: Arrow Books.

Das, Gurcharan (2001) *India Unbound*, New York: Alfred A. Knopf.

de Bary, W. T. (1991) *The Trouble with Confucianism*, Cambridge, MA: Harvard University Press.

Department of State (2001) *World Military Expenditures and Arms Transfers 1999–2000*, Washington, DC: Government Printing Office.

Dibb, Paul (1995) *Towards a New Balance of Power in Asia*, Adelphi Paper, No. 295, London: IISS.

Dikotter, Frank (1992) *The Discourse of Race in Modern China*, Stanford, CA: Stanford University Press.

Dirlik, Arif (1996) 'Reversals, Ironies, Hegemonies: Notes on the Contemporary Historiography of Modern China', *Modern China*, 22(3): 256.

Dore, Ronald (1964) *Education in Tokugawa Japan*, Princeton, NJ: Princeton University Press.

Dower, John (1999) *Embracing Defeat: Japan in the Wake of World War II*, New York: Norton & Co.

Dowrick, Steve (2002) 'C20 Comparisons of Incomes and Prices', in Reserve Bank of Australia, *Globalisation, Living Standards and Inequality: Recent Progress and Continuing Challenges. What Can We Learn from the International Comparisons Program* (http://www.rba.gov.au/PublicationsAndResearch/Conferences).

Drifte, Reinhard (2000) 'US Impact on Japanese–Chinese Security Relations', *Security Dialogue*, 31(4): 449–462.

Eckholm, Erik and Kahn, Joseph (2002) 'Asia Worries About Growth of China's Economic Power', *New York Times*, 24 November.

The Economist (1992) 'The Overseas Chinese: a Driving Force', 18 July, p. 21.

The Economist (2002) 'Money Worries: The Banking System is in a Mess', 15 June, p. 8.

The Economist (2003) 'The Tortoise and the Dragon: Why is India So Far Behind China?', 25 January.

Economy, Elizabeth and Oksenberg, Michel (eds) (1999) *China Joins the World: Progress and Prospects*, New York: Council on Foreign Relations Press.

Einhorn, Bruce and Himelstein, Linda (2002) 'High Tech in China: Is It a Threat to Silicon Valley?', *Business Week*, 28 October.

Engels, Friedrich (1970) 'Socialism: Utopian and Scientific', in Karl Marx and Friedrich Engels, *Selected Works, Volume 3*, London: Progress Publishers, pp. 95–151.

Fairbank, John K. (1968) *The Chinese World Order: Traditional China's Foreign Relations*, Cambridge, MA: Harvard University Press.

Fairbank, John K., Reischauer, Edwin O. and Craig, Albert (1960) *East Asia: the Great Tradition*, Cambridge, MA: Harvard University Press.

Fallows, James (1994) *Looking at the Sun: the Rise of the New East Asian Economic and Political System*, New York: Pantheon.

Fan Gang (2002) 'China's Economic Growth and Structural Reforms after WTO membership', *The Evian Group Policy Briefs Compendium* (http://www.eviangroup.org/publications/publications).

Fernald, John, Edison, Hali and Loungani, Prakash (1998) 'Was China the First Domino? Assessing Links between China and the Rest of Emerging Asia', Board of Governors of the Federal Reserve System International Finance Discussion Paper, No. 604, 2–3.

Fewsmith, Joseph (2000) 'The Politics of China's Accession to the WTO', *Current History*, 99(638) (September): 268–273.

Fitzgerald, John (1994) ' "Reports of My Death Have Been Greatly Exaggerated": the History of the Death of China', in David S. G. Goodman and Gerald Segal (eds), *China Deconstructs: Politics, Trade and Regionalism*, London: Routledge, p. 21.

Fitzgerald, John (1998) *Awakening China: Politics, Culture and Class in the Nationalist Revolution*, Stanford, CA: Stanford University Press.

Foot, Rosemary (1995) 'Pacific Asia: the Development of Regional Dialogue', in Louise Fawcett and Andrew Hurrell (eds), *Regionalism in World Politics*, Oxford: Oxford University Press, 228–249.

Foot, Rosemary (1998) 'China in the ASEAN Regional Forum: Organizational Processes and Domestic Modes of Thought', *Asian Survey*, 38(5): 425–440.

Foot, Rosemary (2001) 'Chinese Power and the Idea of a Responsible State', *The China Journal*, 45: 1–19.

Foot, Rosemary (2003) 'Bush, China and Human Rights', *Survival*, 45(2): 167–186.

Foreign Broadcast Information Service (2001) 'PLA Regulations for Managing Noncommissioned Officers', *Daily Report: China*, 23 May.

Foreign Broadcast Information Service (2002a) 'Director of Logistics Department Wang Ke on Promoting Logistics Reform', *Daily Report: China*, 8 March.

Foreign Broadcast Information Service (2002b) 'PLA Noncommissioned Officer Structure', in *Daily Report: China*, 7 April.

Foreign Broadcast Information Service (2002c) 'JFJB Article Discusses Need to Train Specialists to Operate Modern Weaponry', *Daily Report: China*, 10 May.

Fox, William T. R. (1944) *The Superpowers: the United States, Britain and the Soviet Union – Their Responsibility for Peace*, New York: Harcourt Brace.

Frankenstein, John and Gill, Bates (1997) 'Current and Future Challenges Facing Chinese Defense Industries', in David Shambaugh and Richard H. Yang (eds), *China's Military in Transition*, Oxford: Clarendon Press, pp. 130–163.

Freedman, Lawrence (1982) 'The Triangle in Western Europe', in Gerry Segal (ed.), *The China Factor*, London: Croom Helm.

Froot, Kenneth and Rogoff, Kenneth (1995) 'Perspectives on PPP and Long Run Real Exchanges Rates', in Gene Grossman and Kenneth Rogoff (eds), *Handbook on International Economics*, Vol. 3, Amsterdam: Elsevier, pp. 1648–1684.

Fukuyama, Francis (1993) *The End of History and the Last Man*, New York: Avon Books.

Garnaut, Ross (2002) 'Catching up with America', in Ross Garnaut and Ligang Song (eds), *China 2002: WTO Entry and World Recession*, Canberra: Asia Pacific Press, pp. 1–16.

Garnaut, Ross, Song Ligang, Yao Yang and Wang Xiaolu (2001) *Private Enterprise in China*, Canberra and Beijing: Asia Pacific Press and China Centre for Economic Research.

Gasster, Michael (1969) *Chinese Intellectuals and the Revolution of 1911: The Birth of Modern Chinese Radicalism*, Seattle: University of Washington Press.

Gereffi, Gary, Korzeniewicz, Miguel and Korzeniewicz, R. P. (1984) 'Introduction: Global Commodity Chains', in Gary Gereffi and Miguel Korzeniewicz (eds), *Commodity Chains and Global Capitalism*, London: Praeger, pp. 1–14.

Gertz, Bill and Scarborough, Rowan (2003) 'Inside the Ring', *Washington Times*, 16 May.

Gill, Bates and Reilly, James (2000) 'Sovereignty, Intervention and Peacekeeping: the View from Beijing', *Survival* 42(2): 41–59.

Gill, Bates, Mulvenon, James and Stokes, Mark (2001) 'The Chinese Second Artillery Corps: Transition to Credible Deterrence', in James C. Mulvenon and Andrew N. D. Yang, *The People's Liberation Army as Organization*, Santa Monica, CA: RAND.

Gillin, Donald G. (1967) *Warlord Yen Hsi-shan in Shansi Province, 1911–1949*, Princeton, NJ: Princeton University Press.

Godement, Francois (1999) *The Downsizing of Asia*, London: Routledge.

Goldstein, Avery (2003) 'Balance of Power Politics: Consequences for Asian Security Order', in Muthiah Alagappa (ed.), *Asian Security Order: Instrumental and Normative Features*, Stanford, CA: Stanford University Press, pp. 171–209.

Goodman, David S. G. (1998) 'Are Asia's "Ethnic Chinese" A Regional Security Threat?', *Survival*, 39(4): 140–155.

Goodman, David S. G. (2001) 'Contending the Popular: The Party State and Culture', *Positions: East Asia Cultures Critique*, 9(1): 245–252.

Goodman, David S. G. (2002) 'Structuring Local Identity: Nation, Province and County', *The China Quarterly*, 172: 837–862.

Goodman, David S. G. and Gerald Segal (ed.) (1994) *China Deconstructs: Politics, Trade and Regionalism*, London: Routledge.

Greider, William (1997) *One World, Ready or Not: The Manic Logic of Global Capitalism*, New York: Simon and Schuster.

Guo Yingjie (2003) *Cultural Nationalism in Contemporary China: The Search for National Identity under Reform*, London: Routledge.

Haass, Ambassador Richard N. (Director, Policy Planning Staff US Department of State) (2002) December, 'China and the Future of U.S.–China Relations' to the National Committee on US–China Relations, New York, NY (http://www.ncuscr.org/articlesandspeeches/haass_speech.htm).

Hall, Ivan P. (1997) *Cartels of the Mind – Japan's Intellectual Closed Shop*, New York: Norton & Co.

Hamrin, Carol (1990) *China and the Challenge of the Future*, Boulder, CO: Westview.

Hanson, Gordon and Feenstra, Robert (2001) 'Intermediaries in Entrepôt Trade: Hong Kong Re-exports of Chinese Goods', NBER Working Paper, No. 8088.

Harrold, Peter and Lall, Rajiv (1993) 'China Reform and Development in 1992–93', World Bank Discussion Papers, No. 215, Washington DC: World Bank.

Helleiner, Eric (1994) 'Regionalization in the International Political Economy: A Comparative Perspective', Eastern Asia Policy Papers, No. 3, Toronto: University of Toronto and York University Joint Centre for Asia–Pacific Studies.

Hendrischke, Hans (1988) *Populäre Lesestoffe: Propaganda und Agitation im Buchwesen der Volksrepublik China* (*Popular Reading: Propaganda and Mobilisation in PRC Publishing*), Bochum, Germany: Brockmeyer.

Hendry, Joy (1987) *Becoming Japanese*, Honolulu: University of Hawaii Press.

Hennock, Mary (2001) 'East Asian Pact Trades Up', BBC News Online, 7 November (http://news.bbc.co.uk/1/hi/business/1641613.stm).

Hevia, James L. (1995) *Cherishing Men From Afar: Qing Guest Ritual and the Macartney Embassy of 1793*, Durham, NC: Duke University Press.

Hiranuma, Takeo (2002) 'Sugu Soko ni Aru Kiki, Shitsugyo Maneku Kudoka wa Koshite Kaihi Suru' ('How to Avoid a Hollowed Out Industry That Will Lead to Unemployment'). *Toyo Keizai*, 5 January, (with thanks to Chris Hughes for the information and translation).

Hornik, Richard (2002) 'Who Needs Hong Kong?', *Fortune*, 2 May.

Hourani, Albert (1970) *Arabic Thought in the Liberal Age – 1798 to 1939*, London: Oxford University Press.

Howell, Jude (1993) *China Opens Its Doors – The Politics of Economic Transition*, Boulder, CO: Harvester Wheatsheaf.

Howell, M. (1992) 'The New Chinese Superstate', *Global Finance*, 6(2): 52–73.

Hsu Chih-Chia (2002) 'The Increasingly Uneven Distribution of Wealth in Mainland China', *Division of Strategic and International Studies Peace Forum* (China Studies), Essay No. 08/21/2002.

Hu Sheng (1991) *Zhongguo Gongchandang Qishinian* (*Seventy Years of the Chinese Communist Party*), Beijing: Zhongguo Gongchandang Lishi Chubanshe.

Hu Zulia and Khan, Mohsin (1997) 'Why is China Growing So Fast?', *Economic Issues* No. 8. IMF, Washington, June.

Huang Yashing (2003) 'Foreign Direct Investment in China: Why Surging Levels of FDI May Indicate Serious Economic Problems', Presentation to Carnegie Endowment for International Peace, 16 January (http://www.ceip.org/files/events/events.asp?EventID+566).

Hughes, Christopher (1997) 'Globalisation and Nationalism Squaring the Circle in Chinese International Relations Theory', *Millennium*, 26(1): 103–124.

Huh Chan and Kasa, Kenneth (1997) 'A Dynamic Model of Export Competition, Policy Coordination, and Simultaneous Currency Collapse', Center for Pacific Basin Monetary and Economic Studies, Economic Research Department, Federal Reserve Bank of San Francisco WP PB97–08.

Huntington, Samuel P. (1996) *The Clash of Civilizations and the Remaking of World Order*, New York: Simon and Schuster.

Huntington, Samuel (1999) 'The Lonely Superpower', *Foreign Affairs* 78(2): 35–49.

Huxley, Timothy and Willett, Susan (1999) *Arming East Asia*, Adelphi Paper, No. 329, Oxford: Oxford University Press.

International Energy Agency (IEA) (2000) *China's Worldwide Quest for Energy Security*, Paris: IEA.

International Energy Agency (IEA) (2001) *World Energy Outlook 2000*, Paris: IEA.

International Energy Agency (IEA) (2002) Press Release, Beijing, 26 September.

International Institute for Strategic Studies (2002) *The Military Balance 2002–2003*, Oxford: Oxford University Press.

International Monetary Fund (2003) *Direction of Trade Statistics Yearbook*, Washington, DC: IMF.

Interview (1998) Headquarters, General Armaments Department, Beijing, December.

Jenner, W. J. F. (1992) *The History of Tyranny: the Roots of China's Crisis*, London: Penguin Books.

Joffe, Ellis and Gerald Segal (1978) 'The Chinese Army and Professionalism', *Problems of Communism*, November–/December, 1–19.

Johnson, Chalmers (1982) *MITI and the Japanese Miracle*, Stanford, CA: Stanford University Press.

Johnson, Chalmers (1984) 'East Asia: Another Year of Living Dangerously', *Foreign Affairs*, 62(3): 721–745.

Johnston, Alastair Iain (1995/1996) 'China's New "Old Thinking": The Concept of Limited Deterrence', *International Security*, 20(3): 5–42.

Johnston, Alastair Iain (2003a) 'Is China a Status Quo Power?', *International Security*, 27(4): 5–56.

Johnston, Alastair Iain (2003b) 'China's International Relations in Northeast Asia: the Security Dimension', in Samuel S. Kim (ed.), *The International Relations of Northeast Asia*, Lanham, MD: Rowman & Littlefield.

Johnston, Alastair Iain and Ross, Robert S. (eds) (1999) *Engaging China: the Management of an Emerging Power*, New York: Routledge.

Kang, Dave (1995) 'The Middle Road: Security and Cooperation in Northeast Asia', Hanover, NH: Dartmouth College, Unpublished Manuscript, 6 July.

Kang, Dave (2003) 'Getting Asia Wrong: The Need for New Analytical Frameworks', *International Security*, 27(4): 57–85.

Kanwa Intelligence Review (2002) 'Military base training prevails in the Chinese military' (30 June, accessed at http://www.kanwa.com/free/2002/08/e0801b.htm).

Kao, John (1993) 'The Worldwide Web of Chinese Business', *Harvard Business Review*, 71.

Kapp, Robert A. (1973) *Szechwan and the Chinese Republic: Provincial Militarism and Central Power, 1911–1938*, New Haven, CT: Yale University Press.

Kawai, Masahiro and Bhattasali, Deepak (2001) 'The Implications of China's Accession to the World Trade Organisation', Paper presented at *Japan and China: Economic Relations in Transition*, January 2001, Tokyo (cited with authors' permission).

Kennedy, Paul (1987) *The Rise and Fall of Great Powers*, New York: Random House.

Khilnani, Sunil (1997) *The Idea of India*, London: Penguin Books.

Kim, Samuel S. (1979) *China, the United Nations and World Order*, Princeton, NJ: Princeton University Press.

Kim, Samuel S. (1999) 'China and the United Nations', in Elizabeth Economy and Michel Oksenberg (eds), *China Joins the World: Progress and Prospects*. New York: Council on Foreign Relations Press, pp. 42–89.

Kim, Samuel S. (ed.) (2000) *East Asia and Globalization*, Lanham, MD: Rowman & Littlefield Publishers.

Kim, Samuel S. (2003) 'China's Path to Great Power Status in the Globalization Era', *Asian Perspective*, 27(1): 35–75.

Kissinger, Henry J. (1979) *The White House Years*, London: Weidenfeld & Nicholson.

Krugman, Paul (1994) 'Does Third World Growth Hurt First World Prosperity', *Harvard Business Review*, July/August, 113–121.

Lake, David A. and Morgan, Patrick M. (eds) (1997) *Regional Orders: Building Security in a New World*, University Park: Pennsylvania State University Press.

Laperrouza, Marc (2002) 'China's Information and Communications Technologies Policy Making', *The Evian Group Policy Briefs Compendium* (http://www.eviangroup.org/publications/publications).

Lardy, Nicholas (1995) 'The Role of Foreign Trade and Investment in China's Economic Transformation', *The China Quarterly*, 144: 1065–1082.

Lardy, Nicholas (1998) *China's Unfinished Economic Revolution*, Washington DC: Brookings Institution.

Lardy, Nicholas (2002a) 'The Economic Future of China', address at Rice University, 29 April (http://www.ruf.rice.edu/~tnchina/commentary//lardy/o42902.html).

Lardy, Nicholas R. (2002b) *Integrating China into the Global Economy*, Washington, DC: Brookings Institution Press.

Lee Kuan Yew (2000) *From Third World to First: the Singapore Story, 1965–2000*, New York: HarperCollins.

Legrain, Philippe (2001) *Open World: the Truth About Globalisation*, London: Abacus.

Lehmann, Jean-Pierre (1982) *The Roots of Modern Japan*, London: Macmillan.

Lehmann, Jean-Pierre (1985) 'Dictatorship and Development in Pacific Asia: Wider Implications', *International Affairs*, 61(4): 591–606.

Lehmann, Jean-Pierre (2000) 'Dynamics of Paralysis: Japan in the Global Era', in T. C. Lawton, J. N. Rosenau and A. C. Verdun (eds), *Strange Power: Shaping the Parameters of International Relations and International Political Economy*, Aldershot: Ashgate.

Lehmann, Jean-Pierre (2001) 'Interesting Times, the Stakes are Very High in China's Latest Gamble', *OpenDemocracy*, October.

Lehmann, Jean-Pierre (2002) 'Bleaker Times May Await the Grandkids', *Japan Times*, 23 December.

Leifer, Michael (1996) *The ASEAN Regional Forum*, Adelphi Paper, No. 302, London: International Institute for Strategic Studies.

Lemoine, Francoise (2000) 'FDI and the Opening Up of China's Economy', CEPII Research Centre Working Papers 2000–2011.

Levenson, Joseph R. (1958) *Confucian China and its Modern Fate: the Problem of Intellectual Continuity*, Berkeley, CA: University of California Press.

Levenson, Joseph R. (1967a) 'The Province, the Nation, and the World: the Problem of Chinese Identity', in Albert Feuerwerker, Rhoads Murphey and Mary C. Wright (ed.), *Approaches to Modern Chinese History*, Berkeley, CA: University of California Press.

Levenson, Joseph R. (1967b) *Liang Ch'I-Ch'ao and the Mind of Modern China*, Los Angeles, CA: University of California Press.

Lever-Tracy, Constance, Ip, David and Tracy, Noel (1996) *The Chinese Diaspora and Mainland China: an Emerging Economic Synergy*, London: Macmillan.

Levy Jr, Marion (1992) 'Confucianism and Modernization', *Society*, 29(4): 15–24.

Lewis, John Wilson and Hua Di (1992) 'China's Ballistic Missile Programs', *International Security*, 17(2): 5–40.

Li Rex (1999) 'Partners or Rivals? Chinese Perceptions of Japan's Security Strategy in the Asia-Pacific Region', *The Journal of Strategic Studies*, 22(4): 1–25.

Liaw Fann Bey (2003) *Taiwan's Economic Diplomacy*, University of Warwick, Ph.D. Thesis.

Liberation Army Daily (2002) 'Strengthen Command Training in Joint Operations', translated in Foreign Broadcast Information Service, *Daily Report: China*, 9 April.

Lin Shuanglin (2003) 'China's Government Debt: How Serious?', *China: An International Journal*, 1(1): 73–98.

Lincoln, Edward J. (2001) *Arthritic Japan: The Slow Pace of Economic Reform*, Washington, DC: Brookings Institution Press.

Liu Enzhao (1989) 'Lianheguo weichi heping xingdong' ('UN Peacekeeping Forces'), *Guoji wenti yanjiu (Journal of International Studies)*, 2: 53–61.

Louie, Kam (1980) *Critiques of Confucius in Contemporary China*, New York: St Martin's Press.

Mackie, J. A. C. (1988) 'Changing Economic Roles and Ethnic Identities of the Southeast Asian Chinese', in J. W. Cushman and Wang Gungwu (eds), *Changing Identities of the Southeast Asian Chinese Since World War II*, Hong Kong: Hong Kong University Press.

Maddison, Angus (1998) *China's Economic Performance in the Long Run*, Paris: OECD.

Mahbubani, Kishore (1995) 'The Pacific Impulse', *Survival*, 37(1): 105–120.

Makin, John (1997) 'Two New Paradigms', *American Enterprise Institute*, October.

Mandelbaum, Michael (2002) *The Ideas that Conquered the World: Peace, Democracy and Free Markets in the Twenty-First Century*, New York: Public Affairs.

Martin, Will and Ianchovichina, Elena (2002) 'Implications of China's Accession to the World Trade Organisation for China and the WTO', *The World Economy*, 24(9): 1205–1219.

Maruyama, Masao (1963) *Thought and Behaviour in Modern Japanese Politics*, Oxford: Oxford University Press.

Mearsheimer, John (2001) *The Tragedy of Great Power Politics*, New York: W. W. Norton.

Miyoshi, Masao (1991) *Off Center: Power and Culture Relations between Japan and the United States*, Cambridge, MA: Harvard University Press.

Morphet, Sally (2000) 'China as a Permanent Member of the Security Council, October 1971–December 1999', *Security Dialogue*, 31(2): 151–166.

Mulvenon, James (2001) ' "Eating Imperial Grain": The Ongoing Divestiture of the Chinese Military–Business Complex, 1998–2000', in Andrew Scobell (ed.), *The Costs of Conflict: The Impact on China of a Future War*, Carlisle Barracks: US Army War College.

Nakane, Chie (1986) *Japanese Society*, Berkeley, CA: University of California Press.

Naughton, Barry (1996) 'China's Dual Trading Regimes: Implications for Growth and Reform', Seminar Paper 96–20, Centre for International Economic Studies, University of Adelaide.

New York Times (2002) 'Economic Juggernaut: China is passing US as Asian Power', 29 June.

Nye Jr, Joseph S. (1990) *Bound to Lead: the Changing Nature of American Power*, New York: Basic Books.

Nye Jr, Joseph S. (2002) *The Paradox of American Power: Why the World's Only Superpower Can't Go It Alone*, Oxford: Oxford University Press.

Okawara, Nobuo and Katzenstein, Peter J. (2001) 'Japan and Asia-Pacific Security: Regionalization, entrenched bilateralism and incipient multilateralism', *The Pacific Review*, 14(2): 165–194.

Oksenberg, Michel and Economy, Elizabeth (1999) 'Introduction: China Joins the World', in Elizabeth Economy and Michel Oksenberg (eds), *China Joins the World: Progress and Prospects*, New York: Council on Foreign Relations Press, pp. 1–41.

O'Neill, Barry (1997) 'Power and Satisfaction in the Security Council', in Bruce Russett (ed.), *The Once and Future Security Council*, New York: St Martin's Press, pp. 59–82.

Ong, Aihwa and Nonini, Donald (eds) (1997) *Ungrounded Empires: the Cultural Politics of Modern Chinese Transnationalism*, London: Routledge.

Overholt, William (2002) 'China vs Japan: The Race to Create a Market Economy', *Knowledge@Wharton*, March.

Palan, Ronen (2002) 'Tax Havens and the Commercialisation of State Sovereignty' *International Organization*, 56(1): 153–178.

Pang Zhongying (2002) 'China's International Status and Foreign Strategy After the Cold War', in *Beijing Renmin Wang* (2 May) as translated in FBIS-CHI-2002–0506 (5 May).

Pangestu, Mari (2003) 'ASEAN and China: Challenges and Opportunities', *The Evian Group Policy Briefs Compendium* (http://www.eviangroup.org/publications/publications).

Panitchpakdi, Supachai and Clifford, Mark (2002) *China and the WTO – Changing China, Changing World Trade*, London: John Wiley & Sons.

Pearson, Margaret (2002) 'China's Multiple Personalities in Geneva: Constructing a Template for Future Research on Chinese Behavior in WTO', Paper presented at Conference in Honor of Allen Whiting at Fairbank Center for East Asian Research, Harvard University, 8–9 November 2002.

People's Daily (2002) 'China to Draw US$50bn FDI, to be World's No. 1 Recipient', *People's Daily*, 5 December.

People's Daily (2003) 'Annual FDI to China Expected to Reach US$100 Billion', *People's Daily*, 2 January.

People's Daily Online (in English) (2000) 'Nobel Literature Prize Politically Used: Official', 13 October.

Pfeffermann, Guy (2003) 'The Global Balance Sheet – 1913 to 1998', *The Globalist*, June (http://www.theglobalist.com).

Phar Kim Beng (2002) 'Is Hong Kong Irrelevant?', *Asia Times*, 28 November.

Pilling, David (2002) 'The Korean Renaissance: Lessons for a Humbled Japan', *Financial Times*, 25 October.

Pillsbury, Michael (2000) *China Debates the Future Security Environment*, Washington DC: National Defense University Press.

Pomeranz, Kenneth (2001) *The Great Divergence: China, Europe, and the Making of the Modern World Economy*, Princeton, NJ: Princeton University Press.

Puska, Susan (2002) 'The People's Liberation Army (PLA) General Logistics Department (GLD): Toward Joint Logistics Support', in James C. Mulvenon and Andrew N. D. Yang, *The People's Liberation Army as Organization*, Santa Monica, CA: RAND.

Putnam, Robert (1988) 'Diplomacy and Domestic Politics: The Logic of Two-Level Games' *International Organization*, 42(3) (Summer): 427–460.

Rankin, Mary Backus (1986) *Elite Activism and Political Transformation in China*, Stanford, CA: Stanford University Press.

Rawski, Thomas (2002a) 'Where's the Growth?', *Asian Wall Street Journal*, 19 April.

Rawski, Thomas, (2002b) 'Measuring China's Recent GDP Growth: Where Do We Stand?', *China Economic Quarterly*, 2(1) (http://www.pitt.edu/~tgrawski/papers2002/measuring.pdf).

RMRB (2003) *Renmin ribao* (*People's Daily*), 11 February.

Ross, Robert S. (ed.) (1993) *China, the United States, and the Soviet Union: Tripolarity and Policymaking in the Cold War*, Armonk, NY: M. E. Sharpe.

Ross, Robert S. (1999) 'The Geography of the Peace: East Asia in the Twenty-first Century', *International Security*, 23(4): 81–118.

Rowen, Henry, S. (ed.) (1998) *Behind East Asian Growth: the Political and Social Foundations of Prosperity*, London: Routledge.

Roy, Denny (1994) 'Hegemon on the Horizon? China's Threat to East Asian Security', *International Security*, 19(1): 149–168.

Sansoucy, Lisa J. (2002) 'Japan's Regional Security Policy in Post-Cold War Asia', Paper presented to ISA Conference, New Orleans, 24–27 March, 16 pp.

Sasuga, Katsuhira (2002) *The Dynamics of Cross-Border Micro-Regionalisation Between Guangdong, Taiwan and Japan: Sub-national Governments, Multinational Corporations and the Emergence of Multi-Level Governance*, University of Warwick, Ph.D. Thesis.

Schiffrin, Harold Z. (1968) *Sun Yat-sen and the Origins of the Chinese Revolution*, Los Angeles, CA: California University Press.

Schwarz, Adam (1999) *A Nation in Waiting: Indonesia in the 1990s and Beyond*, Boulder, CO: Westview Press.

Schwarz, Benjamin (1964) *In Search of Wealth and Power – Western Thought in Chinese Perspective*, Cambridge, MA: Harvard University Press.

Secretary of Defense (2001) *Quadrennial Defense Review Report*, Washington, DC: Department of Defense, 30 September.

Segal, Gerald (1982a) 'An Introduction to the Great Power Triangle', in Gerald Segal (ed.), *The China Factor*, London: Croom Helm.

Segal, Gerald (1982b) *The Great Power Triangle*, London: Macmillan.

Segal, Gerald (ed.) (1983) *The Soviet Union and East Asia*, London: Heinemann/Royal Institute of International Affairs.

Segal, Gerald (1985a) *Sino-Soviet Relations After Mao*, Adelphi Paper, No. 202, London: IISS.

Segal, Gerald (1985b) *Defending China*, Oxford: Oxford University Press.

Segal, Gerald (1988) 'As China Grows Strong', *International Affairs*, 64(2): 218–231.

Segal, Gerald (ed.) (1990a) *Chinese Politics and Foreign Policy Reform*, London: Kegan Paul/Royal Institute of International Affairs.

Segal, Gerald (1990b) *Rethinking the Pacific*, Oxford: Oxford University Press.

Segal, Gerald (ed.) (1992) *Openness and Foreign Policy in Communist States*, London: Routledge/Royal Institute of International Affairs.

Segal, Gerald (1994) *China Changes Shape: Regionalism and Foreign Policy*, Adelphi Paper, No. 287, London: IISS.

Segal, Gerald (1996) 'East Asia and the "Constrainment" of China', *International Security*, 20(4): 107–136.

Segal, Gerald (1997) '"Enlitening" China?' in Gerald Segal and David S. G. Goodman (eds), *China Rising*, London: Routledge.

Segal, Gerald (1998) 'Still a Fragile Power', *New Political Economy*, 3(3): 442–444.

Segal, Gerald (1999) 'Does China Matter?', *Foreign Affairs*, 78(5): 24–36.

Sen, Amartya (1999) *Development as Freedom*, London: Oxford University Press.

Shackleton, Robert (1965) 'Asia as Seen By the French Enlightenment', in Raghavan Iyer (ed.), *The Glass Curtain Between Asia and Europe*, London: Oxford University Press.

Shambaugh, David (1994) 'Growing Strong: China's Challenge to Asian Security', *Survival*, 36(2): 43–59.

Shambaugh, David (2003) *Modernizing China's Military: Progress, Problems, and Prospects*, Berkeley, CA: University of California Press.

Shih Chih-yu (2002) *Negotiating Ethnicity in China*, London: Routledge.

Smith, Heather (1997) '"Western" versus "Asian Capitalism"', in Stuart Harris and Andrew Mack (eds), *Asia-Pacific Security: the Economics–Politics Nexus*, Sydney and Boston: Allen and Unwin and Holt, pp. 260–266.

Soeya, Yoshihide (1998) 'Japan: Normative Constraints Versus Structural Imperatives', in Muthiah Alagappa (ed.), *Asian Security Practice*, Stanford, CA: Stanford
University Press.

Spence, Jonathan (1996) *God's Chinese Son: the Taiping Heavenly Kingdom of
Hong Xiuquan*, New York: Norton & Co.

State Council (2002) *China's National Defense in 2002*, Beijing: State Council
Information Office.

Stockholm International Peace Research Institute (2002) *SIPRI Yearbook 2002:
Armaments, Disarmament and International Security*, Oxford: Oxford University
Press.

Stokes, Bruce (1996) 'Divergent Paths: US–Japan Relations Towards the Twenty-
first Century', *International Affairs*, 72(2): 281–291.

Stokes, Mark (1999) *China's Strategic Modernization: Implications for the United
States*, Carlisle, PA: Strategic Studies Institute, US Army War College.

Strategic Survey 1996-7, London: International Institute for Strategic Studies.

Stubbs, Richard (2002) 'ASEAN Plus Three: Emerging East Asian Regionalism?',
Asian Survey, 42(3): 440–455.

Sutter, Robert (2002) 'China's Recent Approach to Asia: Seeking Long-term Gains',
PacNet Newsletter, 23 (7 June) (http://www.csis.org/pacfor/pac0223.htm).

Swaine, Michael D. and Johnston, Alastair Iain (1999) 'China and Arms Control
Institutions,' in Elizabeth Economy and Michel Oksenberg, (eds), *China Joins
the World: Progress and Prospects*, New York: Council on Foreign Relations
Press, pp. 90–135.

Tang Jiaxuan (2002) 'Foreign Minister on China's Diplomacy in 2002: Exclusive
Interview', *People's Daily* Online, 20 December.

Tang Yongsheng (2002) 'Zhongguo yu Lianheguo weihe xingdong', *Shijie Jingji
yu Zhengzhi* (*World Economics and Politics*), 9: 39–44.

Tanner, Murray Scott (2002) 'The Institutional Lessons of Disaster: Reorganizing
the People's Armed Police After Tiananmen', in James C. Mulvenon and Andrew
N. D. Yang, *The People's Liberation Army as Organization*, Santa Monica,
CA: RAND.

Thalakada, Nigel (1997) 'China's Voting Pattern in the Security Council,
1990–1995', in Bruce Russett (ed.), *The Once and Future Security Council*,
New York: St Martin's Press, pp. 83–118.

Thornhill, John (2002) 'Changing China', *Financial Times*, 14 June.

To Lee Lai (1997) 'East Asian Assesments of China's Security Policy', *International
Affairs*, 73(2): 251–263.

Tow, William (1994) 'China and the International Strategic System', in Thomas
W. Robinson and David Shambaugh (eds), *Chinese Foreign Policy: Theory and
Practice*, Oxford: Oxford University Press.

Tsuru, Shigeto (1992) *Japan's Capitalism – Creative Defeat and Beyond*, Cambridge: Cambridge University Press.

Tucker, Nancy Bernkopf (1998–1999) 'China–Taiwan: US Debates and Policy
Choices', *Survival*, 40(4): 150–167.

Twomey, Christopher P. (2000) 'Japan: a Circumscribed Balancer', *Security Studies*,
9(4): 167–205.

Ullman, Richard (1999) 'The US and the World: An Interview with George
Kennan', *The New York Review of Books* (12 August) 46(13).

UN (United Nations) (1971) S/PV.1599, 23 November 1971.

UN (United Nations) (2002) S/PV.4681, 20 December 2002.

UN (United Nations) (2003) *World Economic Situation and Prospects 2003*, New York: UN Department of Economic and Social Affairs.

Van Ness, Peter (2002) 'Hegemony not Anarchy: Why China and Japan are not Balancing US Unipolar Power', *International Relations of the Asia-Pacific*, 2(1): 131–150.

Védrine, Hubert, Moïsi, Dominique and Gordon, Philip (2001) *France in an Age of Globalization*, Washington DC: Brookings Institution Press.

Wade, Robert (1990) *Governing the Market: Economic Theory and the Role of Government in East Asian Industrialization*, Princeton, NJ: Princeton University Press.

Waltz, Kenneth N. (1979) *Theory of International Politics*, New York: McGraw-Hill.

Wang Seok-Dong (2002) 'Regional Financial Cooperation in East Asia: the Chiang Mai Initiative and Beyond', *UNESCAP Bulletin on Asia-Pacific Perspectives 2002/03: Asia-Pacific Economies: Sustaining Growth Amidst Uncertainties*, New York: United Nations, pp. 93–100.

Wang Shaoguang, Hu Angang and Ding YuanZhu (2002) 'Behind the China Wealth Gap', *South China Morning Post*, 31 October.

Wang Xiaolu (2002) 'State-owned Enterprise Reform: Has It Been Effective?', in Ross Garnaut and Ligang Song (eds), *Private Enterprise in China*, Canberra and Beijing: Asia Pacific Press and China Centre for Economic Research, pp. 29–44.

Wang Xingfang (ed.) (1995) *Zhongguo yu Lianheguo: jinian Lianheguo chengli wushi zhounian (China and the United Nations: Commemorating the 50th Anniversary of the Founding of the United Nations)*, Beijing: Shijie zhishi chubanshe.

Wang Yizhou (1999) 'Mianxiang ershi shiji de Zhongguo waijiao: sanzhong xuqiu de xunqiuu jiqi pingheng', ('China's Diplomacy for the 21st Century: Seeking and Balancing Three Demands'), *Zhanlue yu guanli (Strategy and Management)*, 6: 18–27.

Webber, Douglas (2001) 'Two Funerals and a Wedding? The Ups and Downs of Regionalism in East Asia and Asia-Pacific after the Asian Crisis', *The Pacific Review*, 14(3): 339–372.

Weidenbaum, M. (1993) *Greater China: The Next Superpower*, Washington, DC: Georgetown University Press.

Williams, David (1994) *Japan: Beyond the End of History*, London: Routledge.

Wohlforth, William C. (1999) 'The Stability of a Unipolar World', *International Security*, 24(1): 5–41.

Wong Young-tsu (1989) *The Search for Modern Nationalism: Zhang Binglin and Revolutionary China 1869–1936*, Hong Kong: Oxford University Press.

World Bank (1993) *The East Asian Miracle*, New York: Oxford University Press for the World Bank.

World Bank (1997) *China 2020*, Washington, DC: World Bank, p. 75.

World Bank (2003) *World Development Report 2003*, New York: World Bank and Oxford University Press.

World Trade Organization (WTO) (2002) *International Trade Statistics 2002* (available on http://www.wto.org/english/res_e/statis_e/its2002_e/its02_toc_e.htm).

Wu, Friedrich, Poa Tiong Siaw, Yeo Han Sia and Puah Kok Keong (2002) 'Foreign Direct Investments to China and Southeast Asia: Has Asean Been Losing Out?', *Economic Survey of Singapore* (Third Quarter): 96–115.

Wu Xinbo (1998) 'China: Security Practice for a Modernizing and Ascending Power', in Muthiah Alagappa (ed.), *Asian Security Practice: Material and Ideational Influences*, Stanford, CA: Stanford University Press, 115–156.

Yahuda, Michael B. (2002) 'The Limits of Economic Interdependence: Sino-Japanese Relations', Unpublished Manuscript, London School of Economics, 13 pp.

Yamaguchi, M. (1993) 'The Emerging Chinese Business Sphere', *Nomura Asian Perspective*, 11(2): 3–23.

Yu Chung-hsun (1996) 'Unification of the Asian Economics [*sic.*] and Japan: With a Special Look at the Role by the Ethnic Chinese Economies', *Dokkyo International Review*, 9: 217–237.

Yu Yongding, Zheng Bingwen and Song Hong (eds) (2001) *Zhongguo 'RuShi' Yanjiu Baogu: Jinru WTO de Zhongguo Chanye (Research Report on China's Entry into WTO: The Analysis of China's Industries)*, Beijing: Social Sciences Documentation Publishers.

Zaobao Daily News (2003) '4,000 National Defense Scholarship Students to Be Recruited in 2003', translated in Foreign Broadcast Information Service, *Daily Report: China*, 17 April.

Zhang Ye and Jae Ho Chung (2002/2003) 'Chinese State, Chinese Society: Facing a New Century', *Brookings Northeast Asia Survey*, Washington DC: Brookings Institute.

Zhang Yongjin (1998) *China in International Society Since 1949: Alienation and Beyond*, Basingstoke: Macmillan.

Zhang Yongjin and Austin, Greg (eds) (2001) *Power and Responsibility in Chinese Foreign Policy*, Canberra: Asia Pacific Press.

Zhou Pailin (ed.) (2002) *Meiguo Xin Baquan Zhuyi (The New American Hegemonism)*, Tianjin, China: Tianjin Renmin Chubanshe.

Zittrain, Jonathan and Edelman, Benjamin (2003) 'Empirical Analysis of Internet Filtering in China', 20 March (http://cyber.law.harvard.edu/filtering/china/).

Index

Terms that occur in the text in both UK and US spelling are listed here under their UK spelling, unless they form part of a proper name.